Policy Networks

Max-Planck-Institut
für Gesellschaftsforschung
Köln

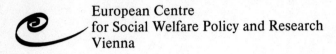

European Centre
for Social Welfare Policy and Research
Vienna

Bernd Marin, Renate Mayntz (Editors)

⟨Policy Networks⟩

Empirical Evidence and Theoretical Considerations

Campus Verlag · Frankfurt am Main
Westview Press · Boulder, Colorado

Copyright © 1991 in Frankfurt am Main
by Campus Verlag

Published in 1991 in the United States by
WESTVIEW PRESS
5500 Central Avenue
Boulder, Colorado 80301

ISBN 3-593-34471-8 Campus Verlag
ISBN 0-8133-1458-5 Westview Press

Library of Congress Cataloging-in-Publi-
cation Data available upon request

Die Deutsche Bibliothek – CIP-Einheitsaufnahme

Policy Networks : empirical evidence and theoretical
considerations / Max-Planck-Institut für
Gesellschaftsforschung, Köln ; European Centre for Social
Welfare Policy and Research, Vienna. Bernd Marin ; Renate
Mayntz (ed.). – Frankfurt am Main : Campus Verlag ; Boulder,
Colorado : Westview Pr., 1991
    ISBN 3-593-34471-8 (Campus Verlag)
    ISBN 0-8133-1458-5 (Westview Press)
NE: Marin, Bernd [Hrsg.]; Max-Planck-Institut für
    Gesellschaftsforschung <Köln>

Contents

Part Three · Cross-National Variations in Policy Networks

Part One

Theoretical Considerations

Chapter 1
Introduction: Studying Policy Networks

Bernd Marin and Renate Mayntz

Social scientists who, in a curiously self-referential process, attentively observe the changing conceptual "fashions" in their own discipline have lately pointed to the ascendance of a new key term: policy networks. By definition of what makes a theoretical "fashion", this term is attributed great analytical promise by its proponents, whereas critical commentators argue that its meaning is still vague and that the perspective it implies has not yet matured into anything like a coherent (middle range) theory. What they agree on is their subject of concern, discourse and dispute, and that is sufficient to establish "policy networks" on the theoretical agenda of contemporary social science, without necessarily guaranteeing the declared value. On the contrary, a speculative oversupply of networking terminology may inflate its explanatory power so that some form of intellectual control over the conceptual currency in circulation, both its precise designations and its amount of diffusion, become inevitably a clearance process within the profession.

This situation obviously entails a welcome challenge which we have taken up in organizing, with the help of Patrick Kenis and Volker Schneider, in December 1989 a conference under the heading "Policy Networks: Structural Analysis of Public Policy Making". The present volume grew out of this conference, though it is not simply a collection of conference papers. For one thing we have included only such conference contributions as would fit together in terms of topic and approach. Even so, several of the original papers had to be substantially revised to meet this goal. On the other hand we decided to include two papers not presented at the conference, but which appeared to fit well with the selection of conference contributions as chapters of the book.

In spite of the editorial efforts to put together a coherent volume rather than simply publishing yet another set of conference proceedings, we have not achieved, nor tried to achieve, anything like homogeneity - and even less so anything like an authoritative conceptual clarification. On the contrary, the book reflects the rather imperfect state of the art as to its colorful taxonomic and methodological pluralism, and at the same time provides the opportunity to learn from a great diversity of empirical studies.

As can be seen from the overview table, the chapters in this book cover a broad range of policy networks and governance foci, a wide variety of sectors analyzed, and many different, occasionally even multiple types of comparisons.

The table also indicates an axis for structuring the volume, by combining a substantial (policy sector and governance focus) and a methodological (type of comparison) dimension. What it does not indicate is the terminological as well as the methodological variety which may be found. What Laumann et al., for instance, call a policy domain is a policy sector in the parlance of most of the other authors. Again, what Coleman designates as a policy community is quite distinct from the meaning this term is given e.g. by Campbell et al. (1989). But there is no confusion resulting from such terminological diversity since in most cases the key terms are either explicitly or implicitly defined, so that the reader knows what the authors are talking about; this, of course, holds especially for empirical case studies such as we have assembled in this volume.

The chapters in the book also differ in their methodological approach. Some are qualitative analyses in the political science tradition (e.g. the chapters by Coleman and by Döhler), some use sophisticated quantitative methods of sociological network analysis (e.g. the chapters by Laumann et al. and by Pappi & Knoke); finally there is a third group of contributions which draw on both of these traditions - most clearly the chapter by Schneider & Werle. This diversity of approaches reflects the current "state of the art" in policy network research. In itself, "policy network" is a concept that appears to signal the confluence of two research traditions, (sociological) network analysis, and studies of policy making. In fact, however, as Kenis and Schneider note in chapter 2, most policy network studies to date have remained qualitative and "soft". As it is hoped that this volume will contribute to an intensified intellectual exchange between those working in a more qualitative approach and those working with quantitative data, we have quite intentionally selected examples from both research traditions for this book. This should also afford the opportunity to evaluate their respective potentials as well as

Table 1: Policy Network Studies

GOVERNANCE FOCUS	POLICY FIELD DOMAIN SECTOR	COMPARISONS		
		Between Countries Cross-National	Between Policy Fields Cross-Sectoral	Over Time Diachronic
ECONOMY	Agricultural Policy	———	*Laumann*	———
	Industrial Restructuring Policy	*Kenis*	———	*Kenis*
	Monetary Policy	*Coleman*	———	———
	Labor Policy	*Pappi*	*Laumann*	———
	Energy Policy	———	*Laumann*	———
SCIENCE & TECHNOLOGY	Telecommunications Policy	———	———	*Schneider/Werle*
	Superconductivity Policy	———	———	*Jansen*
HEALTH	Health Policy	*Döhler*	*Laumann*	*Döhler*

the chances of actually achieving that integration which the key term "policy network" only hints at now.

In spite of these differences between them, the chapters of this book also have a number of things in common. First, with the exception of the overview chapter by Kenis & Schneider, all contributions report on results from *primary research* and *empirical studies*. Whereas methodologies, techniques used and empirical evidence vary widely, all studies interpret findings based on genuine and primary research work and data generation.

Secondly, all of these studies are *comparative cross-sectoral,* or *cross-national,* or *diachronic* in design, comparing policy networks in different policy sectors, in different countries, or at different points in time; Döhler and Kenis even combine two comparative dimensions by studying a given policy field (health and industrial restructuring) cross-nationally and also diachronically, over different periods of time. Coleman and Pappi compare countries (Canada/US and Germany/US) in monetary and labor policy, Jansen and Schneider & Werle compare network developments within one high-tech sector such as superconductivity and telecommunications in one country (Germany) over time. And Laumann et al. compare networking in one country across a broad range of sectors - agriculture, energy, labor, and health in the United States.

Thirdly, with the exception of Laumann et al. who study networking processes without structured and organized policy networks, all other empirical studies focus on structured sets of corporate or collective actors (and on individuals only as representatives of formal organizations or agencies). This is a distinguishing characteristic of most recent policy network research: Policy networks do not refer any longer to "networking" of individual personalities, to group collusions, to the interlocking of cliques, elites, party or class factions, as in older traditions, but to the *collective action of organized, corporate actors,* and consequently to *interorganizational relations in public policy making.*

Fourthly, all studies analyze policy networks in their proper domain frame and that is on the *meso (sectoral) level* of specific policy fields. While the eight policy sectors analyzed in detail refer to three main contemporary macropolitical challenges one could call governance foci - governing the economy, promoting science and technology, and reforming health - the comparisons between policy fields, countries and over time always take place at the level where policy networks actually operate - in more or less well-defined sectors.

Finally, all chapters address questions about the nature, determinants, and consequences of policy networks as the social infrastructure of policy formulation and implementation. Taken together, they highlight the most salient theoretical issues in this new field of research.

In this introduction, we shall briefly indicate some of the more general conclusions that can be drawn from the various contributions to this volume. But before turning to substantive issues we must come back for a moment to the problems, briefly indicated, of terminology.

This book is *not* about conceptual issues. They are specifically addressed only in the overview chapter by Kenis & Schneider, and tangentially in some others (e.g. Jansen), but by and large the authors simply choose and use a specific terminology. In principle, conceptual issues can be easily resolved if one adopts a nominalist position. The properties of phenomena named "policy networks" cannot be derived from the concept (except in a tautological manner); we must choose what we want them to designate. This is good nominalist practice. That it seems so difficult to establish an accepted terminological convention in this case reflects the inevitable ambiguity which surrounds all concepts referring to phenomena of a highly abstracted, intangible character. In such cases there are normally many related and yet distinct ways of circumscribing the object of cognition, depending on the particular aspect of a complex reality singled out for closer inspection. Such differences in conceptual practice are even useful because they call attention to the various dimensions needed to describe empirical phenomena of the class one is interested in, to help in the construction of a multi-dimensional property space in which different policy making structures can be located.

Kenis's and Schneider's initial definition of policy networks as policy making arrangements characterized by the predominance of informal, decentralized and horizontal relations reflects what might be called *one* emerging mainstream view. Defined in this way, the concept emphasizes that the policy process is not completely and exclusively structured by formal institutional arrangements. It also emphasizes that the relationship among those who de facto participate in the process is not hierarchical. The actors making up a policy network are interdependent, but - by and large - formally autonomous. This is not to say that policy is never developed within hierarchical structures; the policy network concept simply calls attention to the fact that the participants in a collective decision process are often linked laterally (or horizontally) rather than vertically. This particular definitional characteristic of *policy* networks differs from the tradition of network analysis, as Kenis and Schneider point out; there, the relational structures investigated include hierarchies as one possible configuration. In this tradition of policy analysis, networks are *contrasted* to hierarchies. Yet power can be more or less concentrated: policy networks are characterized by a patterned distribution of decision making powers.

A somewhat contrasting view with regard to both traditional network analysis and the Kenis & Schneider counterposition is held by one of the editors (Marin 1990a: 19-20, 56-58). While policy networks *are* predominantly informal, decentralized and horizontal, they never operate completely outside power-dependence relations, i.e. outside asymmetric interdependencies and unequal mutual adjustments between autonomous actors, imbalanced transactions-chains, and vertically directed flows of influence. Hierarchies neither are one possible structural configuration among others nor the ideal typical counterpart to horizontal structures such as policy networks, but in the sense of Nobel Laureate H. A. Simon (1962) almost omnipresent asymmetric interdependencies between system elements and, therefore, continua or matters of degree: formal organizations are more or less hierarchically structured, and so are policy networks. What distinguishes bureaucracies and complex organizations in general from policy networks are not so much hierarchical vs. horizontal relations, but single organizational vs. interorganizational relations and the nature of power relations permeating *both*, but in *different* ways: the control over strategic rigidities in tight or loosely coupled systems, the conditions of entry/exit, inclusion/exclusion/expulsion, membership or other adherences, etc.

Policy networks are explicitly defined not only by their structure as *interorganizational* arrangements, but also by their function - the *formulation and implementation of policy*. This provides a useful criterion for boundary specification, the inclusion or exclusion of players of a specific game: actors who do not in one way or another participate in the collective decision process generating a policy are not included in the network. If policy is simply taken to mean a consistent strategy, policy networks need not refer to *public* policy (but may, for instance, refer to a collective market strategy of business firms, as in the study by Kenis), but this is how the term is understood by all other contributions to the volume.

If "policy" usually means public policy in policy network studies, this does not imply that state agents must be the focal or dominant participants. There are studies of networks composed mainly or even exclusively of public actors, as in the analysis of intergovernmental relations. In this book, Coleman presents a case where public actors and their interrelations predominate. In largely self-regulated sectors, on the other hand, *public* policy may well be formulated by private actors (to be initiated or subsequently endorsed by the proper political authorities). Most policy networks studied, however, are characterized by a mixture of public and private actors; in fact, the joint participation of public *and* private (corporative) actors is for many as much the hallmark of policy networks as is the decentering of the central state, the emergence of what is sometimes called a *"centerless society"*. As the relative weight - numerical and in terms of power - of each category becomes a descriptive dimension of focal importance, and that is a purely empirical question, there is and can no longer be any a priori assumption of a crucial, central, hegemonic actor, which is ultimately determinant or only significant or even simply present in all kinds of policy networks.

If the actors in a policy network are interdependent and interact in a collective decision process, this does not necessarily spell harmonious collaboration - or even only what game-theoretical language describes as coordination games. Instead, the extent - and exact structure - of consensus and opposition, symbiotic collusion or competition, cooperation or antagonism or antagonistic cooperation constitute another important dimension in the description of a given policy network. Marin (1990a) argues that the divergent, competitive or even antagonistic interests structurally prevailing in most policy networks make *antagonistic cooperation* the prevalent, if not defining, feature of such interorganizational arrangements.

There are other descriptive dimensions which could be used in a minimal definition of policy networks, and also to distinguish different types of policy networks. The *number of actors,* for instance, can vary greatly - but not indefinitely. While the classical "iron triangle" is composed of only three major actors, Laumann et al. identified around 80 participants each in the four policy networks they analyze. But could we reasonably think of policy networks with several hundreds of participants, with a sheer co-presence of many actors within the same political arena? Even the Laumann et al. case may be a kind of outlier due to their focus on networking rather than on policy networks proper: only a *few* or *not too many* actors can actually *inter-act* with each other - instead of either simply re-acting more or less uniformly to the same (political or price) market signals or of being organized into more or less uniform action within the same bureaucratic hierarchy. Policy networks are composed of autonomous, but interdependent actors, with divergent and mutually contingent interests - and the corresponding complexities put an obvious, even if not precisely and once and for all quantifiable limit to the number of collective actors able to operate a policy network and to interact strategically within it.

So far, we have a number both of defining components as well as of dimensions along which policy networks may vary, but within a certain range only in order not to lose their character as policy networks: being anchored in policy sectors; requiring collective action; composed of corporate actors; structured as interorganizational relations; predominantly informal and horizontal, but not without asymmetric interdependencies which means power relations; functionally defined by the formulation and implementation of policy; without stable central or hegemonic actors; involving not too many participants; and characterized by strategic interaction and a predominance of antagonistic cooperation or mixed-motive games.

There are other aspects with respect to which policy networks can vary. Policy networks, for instance, can exist on *different territorial levels*: there are international (e.g. European), nationwide, regional and even local networks; empirical research has so far concentrated on national policy networks, a fact that is fully reflected in this book. The *stability* of policy networks over time and across decision events, or issues, is another variable of great interest, to which several of the chapters devote attention. Finally, what one might call the *action focus* of policy networks can vary: some are of macro-political importance, as in corporatist networks dealing with a stream of different economic policy issues, some have a narrower focus (sectoral or subsectoral networks), and some are formed around a single issue.

In listing these dimensions along which policy networks may vary, it is important to keep apart matters of conceptual clarification which must be settled by definition (i.e. the choice of properties included in a minimal definition of policy networks) from empirical issues, i.e. the question what structures meeting the criteria which define policy networks actually look like. Major questions of this kind refer to variations across nations, sectors, and time - and to their causes and consequences. It is to such substantive issues that we now turn.

Empirical research on policy networks serves generally to test assumptions about policy making, particularly the structures which underlie - and shape - the process and its outcome. Behind this kind of cognitive interest stands the general premise that structured social relationships have more explanatory power than personal attributes of actors (Wellman 1988: 31). The specific question raised by the notion of policy networks - do those who are formally responsible for it actually monopolize policy making - is not new; it stands in a long tradition of comparing political reality with normative expectations. Thus the discovery of the "subgovernments" active in US policy making, an early version of policy networks (Jordan 1990), meant the destruction of an illusion, rather than indicating a change in reality. In contrast it is a major tenet of the policy networks approach, forcefully argued by Kenis & Schneider in chapter 2, that policy networks are indeed (relatively) new phenomena that have emerged in response to a growing dispersion of the resources and the capacities for action among public and private actors. In this perspective, structural changes in society and in the polity are ultimately responsible for the emergence of policy networks - as a new structure in, and mode of, policy making. This does not exclude that state agents have at times actively assisted in the process of network construction ("networking" as a political strategy).

If policy networks emerge in response to the exigencies of policy making under changing conditions, it should be possible to observe that policy networks change structurally over time. One such change, the expansion of small and stable "iron triangles" into large and fluidly bounded issue networks has been suggested, though not empirically proven, by Heclo (1978). In this volume, Schneider and Werle demonstrate a significant expansion of the German telecommunications policy network in the course of roughly 100 years. Jansen, looking at a subsectoral network in German R&D policy, shows how a breakthrough in superconductivity research in the 80s altered the opportunity structure for research laboratories and federal policy makers alike and resulted in significant changes in the superconductivity policy network.

Where policy networks are empirically identified by observing which actors participate de facto in the controversy, consultation, and bargaining which precede a given policy decision, the focus is normally on sectoral or even issue-specific networks rather than on macro-political constellations such as the literature on neo-corporatism has focused on (Lehmbruch 1984). It is an interesting question, not addressed in this volume, whether aside from the *analytical* distinction between comprehensive and sectoral policy networks there might be a *real* tendency toward sectoral disaggregation. Irrespective of such a trend we should, however, expect that network types differ between policy sectors - if indeed the structure of the target population (or regulatory field) affects the structure of sectoral policy networks. In this volume, it is especially the chapter by Laumann et al. which provides empirical evidence for such an expectation, as the authors compare size, composition, and cleavage structure of four policy sectors in the US.

Policy processes which crystallize about a single issue, or decision event, tend not to mobilize the full set of actors composing a sectoral policy network. It is again the research of Laumann et al. which provides convincing evidence for this. While roughly 80 different corporate actors make up each of the four sectoral policy networks studied, individual decision events activate only between 25 and 53 of them. Active participation is thus discontinuous rather than continuous. Moreover, the composition of the pro- and contra-coalitions is not stable over time, i.e. individual actors do not find themselves in one camp together with the same coalition partners each time they do participate. In spite of the existence of a more enduring *sectoral* pattern of relationships, issue-specific networks thus differ significantly from each other; the authors conclude that "... casual observers greatly exaggerate the degree of stability of participation, consensus and cleavage in policy making" (cf. Laumann et al. in this volume). The conclusion that issue networks in the same policy sector can differ substantially is confirmed by the contribution of Werle & Schneider. Looking more in detail at two policy networks within the German telecommunications domain which crystallized about two different issues, i.e. the introduction of a new service, and postal reform, they show how it is the (more technical and economic, or more political) nature of the issue which shapes the emerging networks.

Policy networks also differ between nations, if the sector is held constant. This is one of the results in the contribution by Pappi & Knoke, who compare labor policy networks in the US and Germany. While in this case, the reasons for the observed structural differences are not discussed at length, the causal question is at the core of Coleman's chapter. He shows how macropolitical institutions of the Westminster parliamentary vs. the US congressional type shape both the formal relationships and informal networks in the field of monetary policy.

The contributions in this volume do not only serve to show how policy networks differ in important respects. They also have accumulated evidence about the factors shaping the structure of policy networks, from the macropolitical institutional framework to the substantive content of issues. Evidence of the difference such structural differences make for policy is less rich and direct. Pappi & Knoke in their chapter do aim to explain labor policy decisions taken on specific issues, expecting them to be determined by the distribution of power and preferences, *mediated* by an exchange of control over policy sub-domains among the actors involved in the sectoral policy network; their research, however, is not yet sufficiently advanced to test this expectation. The chapter by Döhler, on the other hand, does offer a tentative empirical generalization. Comparing health policy networks in the US, Britain and Germany over time and looking at the extent to which neo-conservative reform policies have been successful in these countries he suggests that highly fragmented as well as highly centralized network structures have facilitated the formulation and implementation of neo-conservative programs. If, on the other hand, a sector is characterized by pronounced and legitimate self-government, it tends to resist a policy that would change its basic *modus operandi*. Important as these results are, and even considering the less explicit suggestions which several of the chapters contain by describing both specific substantive policies and the networks which generate them, it seems clear that there is much need here for future empirical testing.

This leads up to the final question to be raised by way of introduction, i.e. whether the contributions in this volume lend support to the expectation that a deliberate combination of (quantitative) network analysis and (qualitative) policy analysis offers the chance of cognitive advances in a difficult field. The reader will undoubtedly form his or her own judgment about this on the basis of the text, asking for instance such questions as: Could the structural differences between two issue networks which Schneider and Werle analyze quantitatively have been presented as convincingly and with as much detail if they had been content with a discursive description? Or: What would a quantitative analysis along the lines of Laumann et al. have added to Döhler's comparative study? The general answer we would give is that a *combined* qualitative and quantitative approach is obviously much more demanding in terms of research time and resources, but that it offers the chance of greater precision, and of discovering both details and comprehensive patterns that would otherwise have remained invisible.

Quantification always promises formal accuracy. The transformation of qualitative structural notions to operational constructs forces us to spell out clearly the relevant variables, so clearly that measurement becomes possible. In the course of doing so, and through the application of the formal procedures developed to establish the values of the variables in a given empirical case, we come to recognize facets of reality which otherwise might have gone unnoticed, or at least would have remained implicit. Examples of this are the surprisingly *large size* of policy networks and the *fluidity of their boundary*; both became visible when formal procedures were employed to identify the actors belonging to, or making up a given policy network. Another insight favored by formal measurement concerns the *variability of issue networks* emerging within a given policy sector. True, this could have been, and in fact has been recognized in purely qualitative studies (e.g. Mayntz 1990: 298-301); but compared to a narrative account there is simply more proof in empirical evidence expressed in figures, i.e. the results acquire a higher reliability and are more convincing than other forms of reasoning.

On the other hand there is always the danger that the price of higher reliability has to be paid in terms of a lower validity when only quantitative methods are used. The very procedure of operationalizing concepts to make them amenable to measurement usually requires simplification by reduction. An example is the reduction of substantive policy preferences to a simple pro/contra dichotomy as Laumann et al. are using. Formal network analysis in general reduces the properties of actors to a few categories (in the extreme case: public/private) and their relations to a few types, such as information and resource exchange, or power differentials (normally: reputational power as aggregate measure). But these measurable structural properties may not be the most salient ones; the fine-grained details of the distribution of jurisdictions and of the procedural rules defining the nature of the interdependencies between given actors easily escape quantification. To what extent, for instance, would it have been possible to include in a formal, quantitative analysis the fine distinctions between the American and the Canadian monetary authorities and the pattern of relations between central bank, top executive, and competent ministries which Coleman describes?

If such are the advantages and the drawbacks of the utilization of formal network analysis in the study of policy networks, much seems indeed to speak for the maxim already formulated, i.e. for the explicit attempt to *combine* both approaches.

References

Campbell, John C. et al., 1989: Afterword on Policy Communities: A Framework for Comparative Research. In: *Governance* 2, 86-94.

Heclo, Hugh, 1978: Issue Networks and the Executive Establishment. In: A. King (ed.), *The New American Executive Establishment.* Washington D.C.: American Enterprise Institute, 87-124.

Jordan, Grant, 1990: Sub-Governments, Policy Communities and Networks: Refilling Old Bottles? In: *Journal of Theoretical Politics* 2, 319-338.

Marin, B. (ed.), 1990a: *Generalized Political Exchange: Antagonistic Cooperation and Integrated Policy Circuits.* Frankfurt a.M./ Boulder, CO.: Campus/ Westview Press.

Marin, B. (ed.), 1990b: *Governance and Generalized Exchange: Self-Organizing Policy Networks in Action.* Frankfurt a.M./ Boulder, CO.: Campus/ Westview Press.

Mayntz, Renate, 1990: Politische Steuerbarkeit und Reformblockaden: Überlegungen am Beispiel des Gesundheitswesens. In: *Staatswissenschaften und Staatspraxis* 1, 283-307.

Simon, Herbert A., 1962: The Architecture of Complexity. In: *Proceedings of the American Philosophical Society* 106, 467-482.

Wellman, Barry, 1988: Structural Analysis: From Method and Metaphor to Theory and Substance. In: B. Wellman/ S. D. Berkowitz (eds.), *Social Structures: A Network Approach.* Cambridge: Cambridge University Press, 19-61.

Chapter 2
Policy Networks and Policy Analysis: Scrutinizing a New Analytical Toolbox

Patrick Kenis and Volker Schneider

1   The Network Perspective in Social Theory

A new catch word diffuses over the landscape of science and is more and more frequently encountered in a number of disciplines. The term "network" seems to match a growing need for the de-mystification of complexity in nature and society. Microbiologists are describing cells as information networks, ecologists conceptualize the living environment as network systems, and the newest fashion in computer science is neuronal networks with self-organizing and learning capacities. The term network is on the way to becoming the new paradigm for the "architecture of complexity" (compared to hierarchy as the old architectural paradigm of complexity: see Simon 1973).

However, at least in the social sciences, network thinking is not completely new. An antecedent was certainly provided by the German sociologist Georg Simmel, who presented an original theoretical stimulus for the network idea drawing upon formal sociology (for this interpretation see Rogers 1989: 167-168). Other precedents came from French structuralism. In his famous *Structural Anthropology,* Claude Lévi-Strauss conceived society "as a network of different types of orders"; and he suggested that these orders themselves could be classified according to different organizing principles, "by showing the kind of relationships which exist among them, how they interact with one another on both the synchronic and diachronic level" (Lévi-Strauss 1969: 312). It would

For comments during the conference and for suggestions and critics to the revised version of the paper, we thank Helmut Anheier, Gerhard Lehmbruch, Giandomenico Majone, Bernd Marin, Renate Mayntz, Fritz W. Scharpf, Frans Stokman, and Raymund Werle, Adrienne Windhoff-Héritier. For linguistic assistance, we are grateful to Susan Wylegala-Häusler.

not be difficult to find further dispersed roots of the network idea. The abundance and variety in which network concepts occur in contemporary social sciences, however, indicates a new quality. Networks as new forms of social organization are currently studied in the sociology of science and technology (see, for instance, the concept of actor networks in Callon 1986), in the economics of network industries and network technologies (for the concept of market interdependencies see Katz/ Shapiro 1985), and in different approaches of business administration (cf. Thorelli 1986 and Powell 1990).

Network thinking conveys its own picture of the world, its particular epistemological background. In contrast to the mechanical view of the world emerging in the 17th century and the bio-organic view originating in the 19th century, the network perspective implies a new perception of causal relations in social processes. The mechanical view of the world established the idea of linear causality explaining social states and events as determined by external forces. The bio-organic perspective shaped the notion of functional causality in which societal subsystems contribute to prerequisites and needs of a global social organism. Both the mechanical and biological world pictures conceived systemness and societal control as something beyond individual actors. Essentially, this perspective is changed in the network view of society. The core of this perspective is a *decentralized concept of social organization and governance:* society is no longer exclusively controlled by a central intelligence (e.g. the State); rather, controlling devices are dispersed and intelligence is distributed among a multiplicity of action (or "processing") units. The coordination of these action units is no longer the result of "central steering" or some kind of "prestabilized harmony" but emerges through the purposeful interactions of individual actors, who themselves are enabled for parallel action by exchanging information and other relevant resources. This perspective - like the older perspectives, too - is shaped by time and by the information age, and thus is more or less influenced by information and communication theory.[1]

---

1   According to Krippendorff (1989: 443), the science of control and communication (i.e., cybernetics) "is fundamentally concerned with organization, how organization emerges and becomes constituted by networks of communication processes, and how wholes behave as a consequence of the interaction among the parts". In such an approach, purpose and intelligence would be seen as "distributed (not centralized) and imminent in the way people interact or communicate with one another regardless of whether parti-

Although network thinking will have considerable impact on future social theory building in general, this chapter is certainly not the place for a general "philosophical" discussion. Based on the assumption that the network perspective will be, indeed, also fruitful for political analysis, we will focus our discussion on the specific use of network concepts in policy analysis. We will try to show that an important advantage of the network concept in this discipline is that it helps us to understand not only formal institutional arrangements but also highly complex informal relationships in the policy process. From a network point of view, modern political decision making cannot adequately be understood by the exclusive focus on formal politico-institutional arrangements. Policies are formulated to an increasing degree in informal political infrastructures outside conventional channels such as legislative, executive and administrative organizations. Contemporary policy processes emerge from complex actor constellations and resource interdependencies, and decisions are often made in a highly decentralized and informal manner.

2   The Discovery of Networks in Policy Making

In the literature of public policy making, the observation of network configurations can be traced back to the late 60s and early 70s, although the real take-off of network studies occurred only in the decade following. Since this time, an increasing number of authors have considered this term as a reasonable descriptor for a cluster of new facets in modern policy making. To be fair, some facets like informality and decentralization were clearly not new to political scientists. Many aspects were even core elements in pluralist theories of policy making (for such an interpretation see Jordan 1990). There is no doubt that one of the major criticisms of hierarchical, instrumentalist and formalist conceptions of politics came from pluralist theory. Bentley (1967) and Truman (1971), two of the most well-known thinkers of this current of theory, for instance, place great emphasis on a somewhat "fluid perspective" of the political process. They frequently pointed to the existence of horizontal relations between government, administration and organized interests. One should

cipants are fully aware of them". Cybernetics would shift attention from control *of* to control *within*.

not forget that it was Bentley (1967: 261) who coined the notion of government as a "network of activities".

A serious shortcoming of pluralist thinking, however, was its rather mystified image of world complexity: political life seemed to be fluid, amorphous and in constant change.[2] It was neo-corporatist theory and neo-institutional approaches which confronted pluralist visions with the pre-dominance of hierarchy, restricted access, selectivity and compulsory group structures in the political organization of modern societies.[3] The interest of neo-corporatism, however, focused more on the "general architecture" of nations and sectors with respect to group structures and relationships with the state. Networks between policy actors like government, administrative agencies and organized interests, gained the attention of neo-corporatist scholars only in the early and mid-1980s.[4]

One of the first authors who explicitly used the term network from a "post-pluralist" and neo-institutionalist perspective, was Rokkan (1969). Rokkan can be credited with emphasizing the importance of policy making structures besides conventional electoral-parliamentarian channels. For Rokkan, bargaining networks between corporate bodies and the government were not adverse or antagonistic elements of political decision making structures but complementary channels to conventional structures which created stability by integrating potential veto powers into the policy process.[5]

Another area where policy networks have been observed are studies of policy making in some restricted sectors or policy studies at the subgovernmental level. An influential study in this direction was Heclo and

---

2   Cf. Bentley's view of social life where "... activities are all knit together in a system .... they brace each other up, hold each other together, move forward by their interactions, and in general are in a state of continuous pressure upon another" (1967: 218). A similar picture is painted by Latham (1964: 48f.) on "public policy" making which he sees as an expression of equilibrium reached in group struggles, in a universe of "groups which combine, break, federate and form constellations and coalitions of power in a flux of restless alterations."

3   For the main texts of neo-corporatist theory see Schmitter/ Lehmbruch (1979) and Lehmbruch/ Schmitter (1982).

4   Kriesi (1982), Lehmbruch (1985), Atkinson/ Coleman (1985) and Traxler/ Unger (1990).

5   "At least in matters of internal policy it can rarely if ever force through decisions solely on the basis of its electoral power but has to temper its policies in complex consultations and bargains with the major interest organizations. To guard against difficulties and reversals in these processes of bargaining the government has over the years built up a large network of consultative boards and councils for the representation of all the relevant interests" (Rokkan 1969: 107-108).

Wildavsky's (1974) analysis of the British Treasury Department. In this book, the notion of the "policy community" was introduced to describe a phenomenon which was closely related to policy networks. Heclo and Wildavsky defined the policy community as a cluster of personal relationships between major political and administrative actors in a policy area. Among these relations, they especially emphasized the role of mutual trust, and governmental sectors were portrayed as closed village communities knitted together by confidence, common calculations and specific "climates". Interestingly, in this context the authors used the network notion for the "criss-crossing" relations within the executive community together (Heclo/ Wildavsky 1974: 389).

A network study focusing more on local governments was published by Friend, Power and Yewlett (1974). In contrast to the former use of the network idea, in this book the network concept was applied in a rather formalized context with some explicit references to social network approaches. One of the basic categories of the theoretical approach applied in this study was a multiple actor system operating in the formulation and implementation of a public policy. Networks in this context were seen as sub-elements of the "policy system" which was defined as a set of organizational and inter-personal arrangements dealing with decision problems related to a given policy (Friend et al. 1974: 26). Such relations between policy actors included not only linkages based on hierarchical authority patterns but also informal relationships such as interpersonal communication. The communication structure among people acting in policy systems was called a "decision network".

A further study on sectoral policy making can be found in Heclo (1978), a widely cited and influential article. The innovative aspect here was the focus on *issue specific* policy networks. This perspective was seen in contrast to elitist approaches in American policy making which explained governmental strategies by the interaction and exchange between a rather small and exclusive set of actors (i.e., the famous "iron triangle" between congress, administrative agencies and lobbying groups). To extend this restricted picture, Heclo introduced the concept of "issue networks" designating large and intricate webs comprising numerous policy making actors.[6] In these networks, governmental and administrative responsibility was seen to be increasingly dispersed among large numbers of policy intermediaries - very similar to Bentley and Truman's vision. It is important to note that Heclo also pointed to an observation similar to Rokkan's with respect to the parallel emergence of new, informal political decision and coordination structures beside party systems and parliamentary channels.[7]

A version of the policy network concept that focuses more on individual actors in concrete policy processes has been introduced by Hanf and Scharpf (1977) in a reader on horizontal coordination in policy making. This book explicitly draws some links between the formal network concept, interorganizational analysis in organizational sociology, and the use of these approaches in policy research. In the introduction Hanf writes:

> In its most basic sense, the term 'network' merely denotes, in a suggestive manner, the fact that policy making involves a large number and wide variety of public and private actors from the different levels and functional areas of government and society. By stressing the 'interrelations' and 'interdependence' of these individual actors, the term also draws attention to the patterns of linkages and interactions among these elements and the way in which these structure the behavior of the individual organizations. As far as the individual organizations are concerned, they are embedded in a particular set of relationships, the structure of which constrains the action options open to them and the kinds of behavior they can engage in as they go about their particular business (Hanf/ Scharpf 1977: 12).

A common theme in this book is how specific network configurations operate more successfully than others in policy making. Different network structures are seen as supportive or critical for coordinated efforts to reach a common policy objective within a collectivity of actors. Interestingly, already in this book Scharpf expressed the conviction that networks of interorganizational dependence could be identified by network analytical tools more precisely. This would eventually lead to an equally precise identification of prescriptive patterns of required coordination structures

---

6   Heclo (1978: 102): "Issue networks ... comprise a large number of participants with quite variable degrees of mutual commitment of dependence on others in their environment; in fact it its almost impossible to say where a network leaves off and its environment begins."

7   Heclo (1978: 117) insists that "... the growth of specialized policy networks tends to perform the same useful service that it was once hoped a disciplined national party system would perform."

between organizational units in interorganizational policy formation and implementation (Scharpf 1977: 363).

A policy network referring not to interrelations between concrete actors but more to linkages between broad social categories - such as the state, whole societal sectors and social coalitions - has been advanced by Katzenstein (1978). His "policy network" is a kind of political meta-structure integrating different forms of interest intermediation and governance, forming a symbiotic relationship between state and society in policy making. In the context of a study of foreign economic policy Katzenstein writes:

> The governing coalitions of social forces in each of the advanced states find their institutional expression in distinct policy networks which link the public and the private sector in the implementation of foreign economic policy. The notion that coalitions and policy networks are central to the domestic structures defining and implementing policy rests on the assumption that social life is structured not exclusively of course, but structural nonetheless by just those formal institutional mechanism (Katzenstein 1978: 19).[8]

Within this general idea of policy networks as a kind of broad societal governance structure, we will locate and develop our definition of the concept in section four of this chapter.

In the last decade, a few studies also emerged which applied quantitative network methods in policy network studies. Laumann and Pappi's (1976) community power book clearly was one of the first applications of advanced structural methods. Their interest, however, primarily focused on elite structures rather than on policy analysis. Empirical application of network analysis and structural methods with a focus on policy processes and domains emerged only within the 80s. Some of the rare examples are Laumann and Knoke's (1987) analysis of structural properties and exchange relations in the US health and energy policy domains, Schneider's (1988) analysis of the West-German policy process of the Chemicals Control Law, and Pappi and Knoke's USA-Germany comparison of exchange relations in the labor policy domain (Pappi 1990; Pappi and Knoke in this volume). A further example, finally, is Mandell's (1984) application of network analytical methods to the interorganizational implementation of a policy program. Apart from these few studies, the repercussions of formal structural models and methods on the "qualitative stream".of policy analysis have been marginal.

---

8   For an empirical application of Katzenstein's policy network concept for cross-national comparison see Katzenstein (1987).

Therefore, the quantitative studies certainly do not point to a general trend of methodological thoroughness in the analysis of policy networks. The majority of policy network studies, instead, focused more on conceptual variation and qualitative description. Examples of particularly well-known British applications in local government and government-industry relations are Rhodes (1981, 1986),[9] Sharpe (1985), Wilks/ Wright (1987) and Wright (1988); and for neo-corporatist theoretical reasoning certainly Lehmbruch (1985) and Atkinson/ Coleman (1985, 1989) have to be mentioned.[10] Most of these studies have their own perspective, and the meanings and connotations that were given to the term network, are still ambiguous. But despite such fuzziness, the idea of the policy network clearly has gravitated to a position of central importance. It became an accepted descriptor for policy making arrangements characterized by a predominance of *informal, decentralized* and *horizontal* relations in the policy process.

Moreover, parallel to the development of the policy network idea a number of other concepts were proposed which sometimes described very similar or even overlapping phenomena. Such concepts are, for example, the policy sector (Benson 1982), the policy domain (Laumann/ Knoke 1987), the policy topic's organization set (see for this concept Olsen 1982), the policy (actor) system (see, for instance, Sabatier 1987), the policy community (Jordan/ Richardson 1983, Mény 1989), the policy game, the policy arena and also the policy regime. The network concept and all these other policy concepts are variations of a basic theme: the idea of public policies which are not explained by the intentions of one or two central actors, but which are generated within multiple actor-sets in which the individual actors are interrelated in a more or less systematic way. However, each of the different policy concepts emphasizes a special aspect: for example, the institutional structures in decision making processes are highlighted by the arena and regime perspective; the conflictual nature of policy processes, again, is emphasized by the game perspective. The arena concept, in contrast, concentrates on conflict *and* institutional integration, and the community, system and sector perspec-

---

9   For a more detailed overview of British works with the network concept see also the recent article of Rhodes (1990).

10 Other examples in the application of the network concept in policy making are Zijlstra (1978/79: 359-389); Rainey/ Milward (1983: 133-146); Trasher/ Dunkerley (1982: 349-382); Trasher (1983: 375-391). For an overview see also Windhoff-Héritier (1985: 85-212).

tives emphasize a kind of structural closure within actor configurations, the presence of boundaries and certain integrating forces which give identity to the structural whole - even if this is only some form of inter-relatedness or interdependence of network actors.

What we have seen in this part is an entire range of different but, for the most part, complementary views which use the network concept for a description of structural and institutional arrangements in policy making, in which ongoing cooperation of autonomous but interdependent actors is emphasized. To arrive at a more explicit definition of policy networks in the next part, we allow ourselves to *reculer pour mieux sauter* in order to reveal the underlying trends of this upcoming concept.

3　Conjunctures and Transformations: The Emergence of Network Thinking in Policy Analysis

Despite some success in diffusing the policy network notion, it has not yet gained a clear, analytically distinctive meaning. In the main, it is used metaphorically to shed light on some specific empirical observations. This coining of a new metaphor during the 70s did not come about by coincidence but is related to at least three more general transformations:

1. transformations in the *political reality*, or in other words, in the reality of policy making as recognized by competent observers;
2. transformations in *conceptual and theoretical developments* in the political sciences in general and in policy analysis in particular;
3. the development of a *methodological apparatus* for structural analysis which in turn was the result of a more "structural approach" in the social sciences in general.

In the following, we will look at each of the three phenomena in more detail.

3.1   Transformations in Political Reality

At the end of the 70s, the *policy network* became an appropriate metaphor for responding to a number of empirical observations with respect to critical changes in the political governance of modern democracies. This was in some way a reaction to simplified and reductionist versions of modern political organization which lacked, for instance, concepts for institutional differentiation and fragmentation as well as the notions for complex interdependencies between state and society. These changes could be summarized as follows:

-   The emergence of the *organized society*: the increase in the importance of organized collectivities in social and political life is paralleled by a general rise in the number, importance and interdependency of collective actors and organizations; more and more resources are produced by or come under the control of organized collectivities; more and more social affairs are shaped by decisions and actions of collective and corporate actors.[11]
-   A further important change can be observed in the trend towards *sectoralization* (Wildavsky 1974; Kenis 1991: chap. 2) which is often also more generally discussed as increased *functional differentiation* (Mayntz et al. 1988). Policies, programs, and agencies have increasingly to be defined in limited, functionally differentiated terms. Increased societal complexity and a growing interdependence between many actors is closely related to growing sectoralization and functional differentiation.
-   Sectoralization and the emergence of more and more organized interests and corporate actors means both increasing intervention and participation by more and more social and political actors in policy making. Jordan and Richardson labeled this trend "overcrowded policy making" (Richardson/ Jordan 1983: 247-268).
-   Increased *scope of state policy making* and the proliferation of state intervention targets (so-called "policy domains") are other important facets of modern society.[12] In this context, Heclo (1978) speaks of "policy growth" and emphasizes that despite growing state involve-

---

11   For this general trend see Presthus (1962); Coleman (1974, 1982); Perrow (1989: 3-19). For an increased dominance of institutions in policy making see Salisbury (1984: 64-76).
12   For an empirical long-term perspective of the growth of state functions see Taylor (1983).

ment, the pool of state resources did not expand extensively enough. Effects and tensions resulting from this gap have been discussed as political overload or "governance under pressure".[13]

- With policy growth, many political scientists observed the *decentralization* and the *fragmentation of the state*. In the last decade, it has been frequently said that the state is not a monolithic whole but a set of relatively discrete institutional apparatuses that vary across industries, sectors, societies, and over time (Evans/ Rueschemeyer/ Skocpol 1985; Kenis 1991). These phenomena may have existed for a long time but tended to be overlooked because many of these institutional units (such as committees and boards) work rather through informal frameworks than through national councils and legislatures.

- Closely related to this decentralization of the state is the observation of a *blurring of boundaries between the public and the private*. Key words for these tendencies are "informal administrative action" (Hucke 1982: 130-140; Hanf 1982: 159-172), informal influence processes in policy formation, "quasi-legislation"; "soft-law"; or "state-sponsored self-regulation".

- A similar or closely related trend is pointed to in some recent studies on *private governments* (Nadel 1975: 2-34; Ronge 1980; Streeck/ Schmitter 1985) which take as an explicit starting point the fact that in many policy fields public tasks no longer can be fulfilled without the cooperation of private collectivities. A cooperative state evolves which delegates or supports organized self-regulation instead of a state traditionally viewed as the guiding, planning and regulating apex taking total responsibility for society.

- *Transnationalization of domestic politics* is another facet of contemporary politics. Today, national policy processes are deeply embedded in international policy environments and policy interdependencies. The membership of nation-states in supranational organizations and the international concertation of summits, places not only constraints but often directly influences national policy choices.[14]

---

13 For a discussion of the overload phenomena in policy analysis see Brodkin (1987: 571-587).
14 Jacobson (1979). For the relationship of nation-states as corporate actors to supranational organizations as international actors see Kenis/ Schneider (1987) and Schneider/ Werle (1990). With regard to regime configurations see Keohane (1984).

- Increased *interdependency and complexity* of social and political affairs leads to the growing *importance of* access to *information* for the coordination and control of political and social affairs, a trend which could be compiled under the label *informatization.* Closely related to this is obviously the growing need for scientific expertise in the policy making process, a trend that has sometimes been described as the *scientification of politics.*[15]

Societal differentiation, sectoralization and policy growth lead to political overload and "governance under pressure" (see Jordan/ Richardson 1983). Increasingly unable to mobilize all necessary policy resources within their own realm, governments consequently become dependent upon the cooperation and joint resource mobilization of policy actors outside their hierarchical control. Policy networks should therefore be understood as those webs of relatively stable and ongoing relationships which mobilize dispersed resources so that collective (or parallel) action can be orchestrated toward the solution of a common policy problem.

3.2 Conceptual Adjustments and Innovations

In view of these manifest changes in the political structures of contemporary society, political scientists were challenged to adjust their conceptual apparatus. Consequently, many of the observations discussed have been reflected in the development of new research programs or research *problematiques* in policy analysis. The major shift at this level can be summarized by a transformation in societal governance from *hierarchical control* to *horizontal coordination* (Hanf/ Scharpf 1977); Franz 1986: 479-494; Ostrom 1983: 135-147). Enlightened policy analysts have observed a change from a "state-centrist" or "government-focused" view of political and social processes to an image which has often been called the centerless or polycentered society (Mayntz 1987: 89-110; Willke 1983; Schuppert 1989). A shift in focus from formal organizational or constitutional structures to informal arrangements in the policy literature is related to this conceptual transformation. A detailed description of the historical transformation in political governance would go beyond the

---

15 For the trend of increased scientific policy advice see Plowden (1987) and Smith (1987: 61-76).

scope of this chapter. However, a short illustration of the major shifts within policy literature may provide some hints about the major turning points of this adjustment.

In the first phase, policy analysis was heavily influenced by the technological and methodological optimism produced by the dominant behavioralist paradigm[16] in political science during the 50s and 60s: it was generally believed that the application of newly developed "scientific methodologies" (e.g. operations research, statistical decision theory, communications theory, computer simulation, cost-benefit-analysis, cybernetics, econometrical models) would increase instrumental, informational and organizational capacities to control societal processes.[17] This produced long shelves of political planning literature and led, especially in countries which were governed by social-democratic parties, to a veritable "planning euphoria".

In the second phase, the planning ideology was hurt by the so-called "real world". It became increasingly questioned whether societal development could be purposefully guided by political instruments. Many experiences showed that good intentions and sophisticated plans during the reformist years were confronted by difficulties that emerged in the implementation and realization of policy programs (Mayntz 1979: 55-81). Such disillusion with the planning approach led to the emphasis on extra-governmental conditions of success and failure of governmental programs. These were specific context structures in implementation target fields, such as actor or interest constellations which supported or hampered the successful implementation of given policy programs. In the context of this literature, it was observed that program implementation often operates through horizontal and non-hierarchical forms of coordination and

---

16 For an excellent analysis of this relationship see Somit/ Tanenhaus (1967). One of the key behavioralist articles of faith was that data or findings should be quantified and, finally, stated as mathematical models or propositions. In contrast to old-fashioned institutionalism, it was believed that this would enable the modelling and prediction of *real* social and political processes. The authors take opinion polls and survey techniques as an example: "These provided instruments for developing vast new bodies of data. Research in this area was greatly facilitated by advances in mathematical statistics and the increased availability of electronic computers to perform what had previously been impossibly tedious computations" (Somit/ Tanenhaus 1967: 51).

17 Symptomatic for this believe is Lasswell/ Lerner's (1951) collection in which new methodologies such as probability methods, mathematical modelling and sociometrics techniques are presented as "research procedures" for "policy sciences". Instructive for the German case is Scharpf (1973) who presents cluster analysis and MDS as techniques for policy analysis and planning.

that even within the public sector, implementation structures are not
always hierarchically structured (cf. Mayntz 1983).[18]

Now, we seem to have entered the third phase which responds to
the problems and difficulties that manifested themselves during the implementation debate. It became apparent that the formal distinction between
policy formulation (planning) and policy implementation is often fairly
artificial. This is especially the case when central target actors cooperate
in the implementation process in exchange for participation in program
formulation. Especially in such cases, it makes no sense to study policy
phases separately. A similar problem here is the exclusive focus on state
intervention and public policy programs in the solution of societal problems. Problems which in some countries are solved or "processed" by
state policies may be solved in other countries by self-regulation through
para-state organizations or privately organized collectivities. In addition,
there may be societal problems which have not yet been perceived as
being relevant by private and public organized actors and consequently
do not arrive on any policy agenda.

In order to fully understand the conditions under which societal problems are processed by governmental and non-governmental activities,
policy research thus had to expand its narrow focus from "public policies" to "societal governance" in general (Anderson 1976: 191-221;
Marin 1990). Due to this widened perspective, policy research has to
include not only the analysis of general social structures and societal
institutions that condition and regulate this governance process but also
the specific dynamics and "auto-dynamics" (see Mayntz 1985 and
Mayntz/ Nedelmann 1987) of societal development in general as the
object of governance. Policy analysis thus needed to broaden its analytical focus to include whole societal domains and the dynamic dimension
of policy making (learning, positive and negative feedback, etc.) as well.
In sum, policy analysis could restrict its research object not only to
processes *within* a given and established institutional order, but they also
had to integrate the *problematique* of how an institutional order emerges
in a highly decentralized *and* interdependent world.

---

18 See also, for instance, Mayntz (1979a: 634): "As for central control, the public sector
    is never a fully integrated hierarchy but must rather be seen as a highly differentiated
    macro-system of organizations, a network which is more or less hierarchized by virtue
    of existing vertical lines of communication, but which is basically made up of relatively
    autonomous elements."

3.3   The Development of Methodological Tools

The third transformation with some influence on "structural thinking" in policy analysis is the development of new methodological tools. Today these concepts, methods and techniques enable empirical studies of complex structures in the policy making processes which would not have been possible twenty years ago. Such concepts and methods for structural analysis emerged at the end of the 60s and spread widely during the 70s:

- In the *sociology of organizations* and in administrative science, this was the development of the early "organization set" concept, "resource and power dependency" approach and the "interorganizational relations" approach.[19] In contrast to previous approaches where categorical variables played the exclusive role, here relational variables become more important (Wellman 1983: 155-200; 1988: 19-61).
- Parallel to the development of these concepts and approaches stressing the relational character of social phenomena, a number of social scientists began to apply mathematics to the *formalization and analysis of relational configurations*. The most important methods were graph theory, matrix algebra, multidimensional scaling and structural classification methods such as cluster analysis and block modelling.[20]
- In turn, the development of these *new mathematical and statistical procedures* for relational analysis has undoubtedly been influenced by the development of computer technology in the 60s and 70s, in particular by the speedy diffusion of microcomputing since the end of the 70s.[21]

Currently, network analysis is considered one of the major research tools for structural analysis. Network researchers study elite structures in local

---

19 For overviews see Whetten (1981: 1-28); Glaskiewicz (1985: 281-304). Important contributions are Levine/ White (1961: 583-601); Emerson (1962: 32-41); Evan (1972: 181-200); Benson (1975: 229-249); Metcalfe (1976: 327-343). First application of network analysis in inter-organizational analysis was provided by Aldrich (1979) and Aldrich/ Whetten 1981: 385-408).

20 Harary/ Norman/ Cartwright (1969); Coxon/ Jones (1983); Everit (1983: 226-256); Arabie/ Boorman/ Levitt (1978: 21-63).

21 Very instructive in this context is an article by Coleman (1965) which, however, still reflects the age of mainframe computers. In the meantime, the use of computing technologies in the social sciences has radically changed - and this transformation is just beginning. Only recently has UCINET package and the SONIS system for personal computers appeared. Another network package available for PCs is GRADAP.

communities, actor networks in national policy domains, interrelations between economic firms, and even structural configurations at the world system level. In a state-of-the-art review on the innovative trends in sociology in the 80s, Collins (1986: 1351) considered network analysis one of the five most important innovations for the sociology of the future:

> Network research began as an empirical field, and it has only gradually begun to go beyond description and methodology to acquire some generalizable theory. But although the application of network analysis to theoretical problems is in its infancy, it holds considerable potential, perhaps even of a revolutionary sort.

We are convinced that these methodological tools comprise a great potential for policy research which has not yet been systematically and comprehensively explored. The tools are there but the community of craftsmen is still very small.

4   Types and Dimensions of Policy Networks: A Tentative Definition

In this section, we want to propose a "policy network" concept or definition which, first, accounts for the previously made observations about the changing patterns of policy making and second, is meaningful for contemporary policy analysis on the one hand and for network analysis on the other. We are convinced that the *notion* or the *concept* of *policy networks*, given that it is not used exclusively formally (i.e., as a set of relations of any kind) or metaphorically (e.g. as a synonym for crisscross could be a common point of reference and could have an integrative function. We propose to reserve the concept for a *specific class of policy making structures* with specific attributes. In a complex political world, everything could be represented in graphs or networks - even hierarchies and markets. In order to produce a theoretical surplus, the term network should thus be reserved for specific organizational modes of policy making (cf. Mayntz 1980: 8). Analogous to the use of networks in new institutional economics[22] and in the literature of governance (cf. Schmitter 1989 and Hollingsworth 1990) these structures could be lo-

---

22   Cf. Williamson (1985) and North (1990). See also footnote 31.

cated somewhere beyond or between[23] "policy markets" and "policy hierarchies":

Policy markets may be imagined as completely competitive party systems in which political parties "formulate policies in order to win elections, rather than win elections in order to formulate policies" (Downs 1957: 28). Another market version is Landes and Posner's interest group approach in which legislation is seen as a good supplied by the government or parliament to groups that outbid rival seekers of favorable legislation. Payment takes the form of votes, campaign contributions, etc. Legislation is thus "sold" by the legislature and "bought" by the beneficiaries of the legislation (Landes/ Posner 1975: 877).

The other extreme is policy hierarchies as ideal types of bureaucratic policy making. This means, on the one hand, the electoral hierarchy as a chain of principal-agent relationships from the "people" down to parliament and executive. On the other hand, the parliament-executive-administrative chain is also a hierarchy. Policies are formulated within the parliament by majority voting. The executive and administrative branches are mere implementing agents of those policies.

Policy networks should be conceived as *specific structural arrangements* in policy making. Policy networks are new forms of political governance which reflect a changed relationship between state and society. Their emergence is a *result* of the dominance of organized actors in policy making, the overcrowded participation, the fragmentation of the state, the blurring of boundaries between the public and the private, etc. Policy networks typically deal with *policy problems* which involve complex political, economic and technical task and resource interdependencies, and therefore presuppose a significant amount of expertise and other specialized and dispersed policy resources. Policy networks are mechanisms of political resource mobilization in situations where the capacity for decision making, program formulation and implementation is widely distributed or dispersed among private and public actors.

A policy network is described by its actors, their linkages and by its boundary. It includes a relatively stable set of mainly public and private corporate *actors*. The *linkages* between the actors serve as communication channels and for the exchange of information, expertise,

---

23　Networks as social configurations beyond markets and hierarchies are discussed by Powell (1990), whereas Williamson (1985) understands networks as an organizational form *between* markets and hierarchies.

trust and other policy resources. The *boundary* of a given policy network is not primarily determined by formal institutions but results from a process of mutual recognition dependent on functional relevance and structural embeddedness.

Policy networks should be seen as integrated hybrid structures of political governance. Their *integrative logic* cannot be reduced to any single logic such as bureaucracy, market, community or corporatist association, for example, but is characterized by the capacity for mixing different combinations of them. It is the mixture and not the individual logic per se which accounts for its functioning. This characteristic of policy networks reflects and even generalizes Katzenstein's (1987) policy network idea, which he described in the West German case as a combination of party competition, cooperative federalism and corporatist concertation or interest intermediation. The concrete mixture of different logics which may be present in a specific policy network is an empirical question. A policy network thus could combine domains that are largely self-regulated, but also those where the responsible corporate actors are closely engaged in ongoing bargaining relationships with the state and other corporate actors in corporatist and pluralist patterns. It is thus perfectly thinkable that a policy network has corporatist, pluralist and self-regulatory regions or "provinces" - and it integrates these different modes of political organization. Since the whole complex consists mainly of relatively autonomous action units, the dominant decision rules and decision styles are rather "bargaining" (Scharpf 1989) or "sounding-out" (Olsen 1972) than "confrontation". The logic of confrontation is inherent in voting which polarizes either/or relationships, forcing all the participants into one camp or the other. Bargaining, in contrast, is based more on the logic of "sounding-out", stressing common interests and unanimity. Since the capacity of collective action is very dispersed in networks, the decision making and strategy formation in a network context is thus very time-consuming.

In spite of such limitations, networks have some important virtues. In situations where policy resources are dispersed and context (or actor) dependent, a network is the only mechanism to mobilize and pool resources. An example is "tacit knowledge" such as details and primary experience in a policy program, a form of information that is difficult to codify and to transmit. It is stored in an inexplicit form in the minds of the decision makers who have primary experience within their domain (Starbuck 1970: 318). Such information, in fact, is only accessible through cooperation and exchange. Nobody can be forced to provide intangible information. Implementation processes which depend on the mobilization of such resources, cannot be governed by hierarchical command-and-control relations.[24]

Comparative advantages and disadvantages of policy networks seem to be higher costs in policy formulation (coordination costs, decision costs) but significantly lower costs in policy implementation (monitoring costs, controlling costs). In situations where a given policy task structure implies high interdependencies and where the necessary policy resources are highly dispersed, policy networks seem thus to be more efficient and effective than hierarchical policy configurations.

Policy networks also may be analytically related to the different phases of policy development such as issue definition, agenda-building, policy formulation and implementation. Not every problem or issue will be transformed into a problem of public policy. In order to be considered as a problematic state or situation that could be tackled by policy intervention, a problem has to be placed on the government agenda. Agenda-building may pass over discussions in the public and in mass media, but very often policy issues are raised and defined within restricted networks of habitually involved actors. These actors, or parts of them, may also formulate and implement a given policy. But networks that remain integrated over time, encompassing the entire policy process, cannot be generally expected. There may be other situations in which formulation and implementation networks differ sharply from the network of issue initiators. The stability or change of policy networks in terms of access, repositioning and exit of actors within policy cycles, is an empirical question and cannot be determined *a priori*. If there are structural types of policy networks with clear differences in performance or not, is an interesting question for further research. To identify and measure such structures, network analysis could be a valuable structural tool. In the final section, therefore, we will investigate the question of usefulness of network analytical approaches for the study of empirical policy networks.

---

24 Bohnert/ Klitsch (1980) argue, for instance, that nobody can be forced to provide good information.

5 Network Analysis and the Empirical Study of Policy Networks

Policy Analysis and *Network Analysis* are two relatively coherent families of social research with an important potential for cross-fertilization. Policy analysis, as expressed by Dye (1976: 1), "is finding out what governments do, why they do it, and what differences it makes".[25] Network analysis includes the broad array of methodological tools for the analysis of relational configurations and structures.[26] Although there has been almost no communication between the two disciplinary fields until now, we think that both of these research domains are highly relevant to each other. On the one hand, for network analysts, policy research could become an interesting and relevant "application domain". Policy analysts, on the other hand, could find in network analysis a powerful toolbox to be able to grasp and analyze highly complex structures, relational configurations and actor systems in modern politics.

Network analysis does not provide an "explicit theory" by itself - although it may have a strong affinity to some particular social theories.[27] Some describe this approach as a method looking for a theory (see, for example, Collins 1988). In our opinion, network analysis is no theory *in stricto sensu* but rather a toolbox for describing and measuring relational configurations and their structural characteristics. For a number of theories, such structural arrangements are important elements.

From this perspective there seem to be at least six different applications of network analysis in the study of policy networks:

1. One possible research strategy has been described by Scharpf (1973, 1977) and could be labeled the *normative* or *prescriptive* use: here, network analysis would be used to compare prescriptive networks

---

25 Overviews on policy analysis are given in Dye (1976); Windhoff-Héritier (1987) and Feick/ Jann (1989).

26 For a methodological introduction to network analysis see Knoke/ Kuklinski (1982); Pappi (1987); Burt/ Minor (1982); Marsden/ Lin (1982); Berkowitz (1982). For overviews, trend reports and valuative accounts see Alba (1982: 39-74); Barnes (1979: 403-423); Scott (1988: 109-127).

27 Since measurement and description is always "theory-loaded", network analysis also contains implicit theories. These are especially theories which emphasize the importance of structure for the understanding of social phenomena. For the discussion on the theoretical status see: Laumann/ Knoke (1987: 83-109), Anderson/ Carlos (1976: 27-51), Poucke (1979/80: 181-190), Burt (1982), and Mathien (1988: 1-20).

which map the "objective need" for coordination and cooperation in a policy process (prescriptive patterns of coordination, prescriptive task structure and "objectively required" policy interactions) with existent patterns of exchange and collaboration in *empirical* networks. A further step would be the development of indicators for the "goodness of fit" or "misfit" between both networks. The guiding idea is to detect structural obstacles, failures or stalemates in policy networks.

2. In another strategy, the description and measurement capacities of network analysis would be used for *cross-network comparisons* in order to develop (or test) hypotheses explaining the effect of aggregate characteristics of the policy network on specific interactions. This can be accomplished by cross-national policy network comparisons or by comparisons between different national policy domains or policy processes. This strategy concentrates on building empirical indicators to measure network characteristics (for example, density, connectedness, centralization, asymmetry, fragmentation, etc.) and on building models relating these structural characteristics to the performance or, more generally, the outcomes produced by specific policy networks. Such a hypothesis, for example, could be that the more asymmetrical the exchange or influence network is structured, the higher the capacity for collective action.

3. A third application of network analysis is its use in the construction and testing of *formal models* on policy making processes. In this research strategy, network analysis is employed in the *operationalization* of formal models. An example would be the model developed by James S. Coleman on exchange processes within systems of action.[28] The application of such a model demands plenty of information about structural dependencies and resource flows within a set of policy actors. This information can be collected and the required model indicators can be constructed using network analytic tools.[29]

4. A further application is the use of network analysis to *test hypotheses* of *theories* on *policy making* which include structural propositions.

---

28 A short outline of the model contains Coleman (1986: 85-136). For a more extended elaboration see Coleman (1990).
29 For applications of the Coleman model see Marsden/ Laumann (1977: 199-250); Pappi/ Kappelhoff (1984: 87-117); Laumann/ Knoke (1987). For the application of Laumann and Knoke's data to another model see Stokmann/ van den Bos/ Wasseur (1989).

Corporatist theory, for example, assumes specific relational configurations between large and monopolistic associations, their members and the state - in contrast to pluralist theory which supposes different structural arrangements in the policy process.[30] Additionally, governance theories differentiating between hierarchies and market-like relations[31] contain implicit propositions on structural configurations which can be identified and described more precisely with the help of network analysis.[32] For instance, it could be used to decide whether an empirical structure of cooperation and information exchange represents hierarchical control instead of market coordination - or, more importantly, it could *discover* any other empirical forms of cooperation including hybrid mixtures of different governance forms.

5. A fifth application would be the use of network analytical methods for the identification and reconstruction of complex policy games, i.e., relations or patterns of strategic actions between a set of actors in the formulation and implementation of a policy. In this approach, network analysis would be used as a measurement tool for game-theoretical models. Network sampling methods could be used to specify boundaries of games,[33] to identify aggregate or collective actors[34] and also, to some extent, to identify some of the relationships between players which are constitutive for a given game (e.g. information structures on mutual payoffs).

6. Network analytic methods could also be used to reconstruct network dynamics in terms of structural transformation or stability. By replicating policy network studies at different points in time, for example, the conditions under which the whole set of actors and its status differentiation stays stable or changes, could be studied. Interesting

---

30 For an operationalization of corporatist and pluralist structures of interest intermediation see Schmitter (1974).

31 Hollingsworth/ Lindberg (1985); Campbell/ Lindberg/ Hollingsworth (1991); Schmitter (1989: 173-208).

32 An example is Marsden's (1983) analysis of power structures *within* exchange systems.

33 A n-person game or several interconnected games could be delineated by the identification of clusters of actors which take each others action as mutually relevant (cf. Laumann et al. 1982).

34 "Aggregate actors" in the sense of Scharpf (1990), which are treated as single players in game theoretical models, could be identified with clique-identification methods, cluster analysis or blockmodels. For an application of an empirical identification of collective actors see Marsden/ Laumann (1977).

questions in this analysis would be the entry of new actors, their repositioning and the exit of actors.[35]

This list of application possibilities is by far not exhaustive. It only contains some hints for directions in which a cross-fertilization of policy studies and network analysis might develop.

6 Conclusion

The motivation behind the development of the ideas in this chapter was the feeling that a complementarity exists between first, the description of the contemporary policy making processes, second, the emerging policy network idea which acquired increasing conceptual currency during the 80s, and, third, innovations in methodological tools for analyzing structural configurations. However, this complementarity is still in the state of a potentiality. For the most part, the scholars working in these fields did not yet combine and integrate their efforts enough. The starting point of the chapter was that we believe that such an "alliance" or integration could lead to a better and much more precise description and understanding of contemporary policy making.

The aim of the chapter was to propose a policy network definition which could support this conceptual and methodological integration process. It was not intended to add one or two new facets to the variety of existing network metaphors, but to contract and explicate the number of real phenomena on which these conceptual developments are based, as well as to uncover the key propositions and the essential links and nodes within the existing conceptual diversity. Moreover, we tried to sketch out the methodological toolbox already available for the analysis of highly decentralized and intermeshed policy making actor configurations and some possible research strategies. Consequently, the policy network concept proposed here could offer some operational steps for an integration of conceptual and methodological efforts within in the empirical analysis of policy networks.

---

35 This could be done, for instance, by a kind of "broken-tie analysis" which Palmer (1983) applied to interlocking directorates.

Admittedly, a policy network concept which is operational for the empirical analysis, is not without problems and difficulties. Identifying actors, links and boundaries in networks structures demands sophisticated techniques and large efforts in data-gathering. Such large-scale investments in empirical political analysis is not accepted by everybody within the scientific community since not all systematic structural inquiries lead to breathtaking empirical and theoretical results. Often they confirm more intuitive and "soft" observations of qualitative analysis which also can be obtained by low-budget research. However, it should not be overlooked that an intuitive grasp of actor configurations is rapidly exhausted when the number of actors involved increases. Even a genius researcher would be unable simultaneously to grasp the structure of an actor system with more than a handful actors involved. And often the links between actors are not only *multiple* but also *multiplex*. Theoretical concepts which acknowledge that social and political reality is complex and highly intermeshed, should not confine their analysis to the repetition that "everything is connected to everything" but should engage into efforts to measure and map such political or social structures with satisfactory precision. For an approximation of such long-term goals, we also want to conclude - as it is done so often - that still much research is needed to exploit the combined potential of policy analysis and network analysis in the study of public and private policy making.

References

Alba, R. D., 1982: Taking Stock of Network Analysis: A Decade's Results. In: *Research in the Sociology of Organizations* 1, 39-74.

Aldrich, H. E., 1979: *Organizations & Environments*. Englewood Cliffs, NJ.: Prentice-Hall.

Aldrich, H. E. / D. A. Whetten, 1981: Organization-sets, Action-sets, and Networks: Making the Most of Simplicity. In: P. C. Nystrom/ W. H. Starbuck (eds.), *Handbook of Organizational Design*. Vol. 1. Oxford: Oxford University Press, 385-408.

Anderson B./ M. L. Carlos, 1976: What is Social Network Theory. In: T. R. Burns/ W. Buckley (eds.), *Power and Control. Social Structures and their Transformation.* London: Sage, 27-51.

Anderson, C. W., 1976: Public Policy and the Complex Organization: The Problem of Governance and the Further Evolution of Advanced Industrial Society. In: L. N. Lindberg, *Politics and the Future of Industrial Society.* New York: McKay, 191-221.

Arabie, P./ S. A. Boorman/ P. L. Levitt, 1978: Constructing Blockmodels: How and Why. In: *Journal of Mathematical Psychology* 17, 21-63.

Atkinson, M. M./ W. D. Coleman, 1985: Corporatism and Industrial Policy. In: A. Cawson (ed.), *Organized Interests and the State: Studies in Meso-Corporatism.* Beverly Hills: Sage, 22-45.

Atkinson, M. M./ W. D. Coleman, 1989: Strong States and Weak States: Sectoral Policy Networks in Advanced Capitalist Economies. In: *British Journal of Political Science* 19, 47-67.

Barnes, J. A., 1979: Network Analysis: Orienting Notion, Rigorous Technique or Substantive Field of Study? In: Paul W. Holland/ S. Leinhardt (eds.), *Perspectives on Social Network Research.* New York: Academic Press, 403-423.

Benson, J. K., 1975: The Interorganizational Network as a Political Economy. In: *Administrative Science Quarterly* 2, 229-249.

Benson, J. K., 1982: A Framework for Policy Analysis. In: D. L. Rogers et al., *Interorganizational Coordination: Theory, Research, and Implementation.* Ames: Iowa State University Press, 137-201.

Bentley, A. F., 1967: *The Process of Government: A Study of Social Pressure.* Cambridge, MA.: Harvard UP (Chicago 1908).

Berkowitz, S. D., 1982: *Introduction to Structural Analysis: The Network Approach to Social Research.* Toronto: Butterworths.

Bohnert, W./ W. Klitzsch, 1980: Gesellschaftliche Selbstregulierung und staatliche Steuerung. Steuerungstheoretische Anmerkungen zur Implementation politischer Programme. In: R. Mayntz (ed.), *Implementation politischer Programme. I: Empirische Forschungsberichte.* Königstein/ Ts.: Athenäum, 200-216.

Brodkin, E. Z., 1987: Policy Politics: If We Can't Govern, Can We Manage? In: *Political Science Quarterly* 102(4), 571-587.

Burt, R. S., 1982: *Toward a Structural Theory of Action: Network Models of Social Structure, Perception, and Action.* New York: Academic Press.

Burt, R. S./ M. J. Minor, 1982: *Applied Network Analysis - A Methodological Introduction*. Beverly Hills/ London: Sage.

Callon, Michel, 1986: The Sociology of an Actor-Network: The Case of the Electric Vehicle. In: M. Callon/ H. Law/ A. Rip, *Mapping the Dynamics of Science and Technology. Sociology of Science in the Real World*. Houndmills: Macmillan, 19-34.

Campbell, J. C. L./ J. R. Hollingsworth/ L. N. Lindberg (eds.), 1991: *The Governance of American Economy*. New York: Cambridge University Press (forthcoming).

Carlton, D. W./ J. M. Klamer, 1983: The Need for Coordination Among Firms, with Special Reference to Network Industries. In: *University of Chicago Law Review* 50, 446-465.

Coleman, J. S., 1965: The Use of Electronic Computers in the Study of Social Organization. In: *European Journal of Sociology* 6, 89-107.

Coleman, J. S., 1974: *Power and the Structure of Society*. New York: Norton.

Coleman, J. S., 1982: *The Asymmetric Society*. Syracuse, New York: Syracuse University Press.

Coleman, J. S., 1986: Social Action Systems. In: J. S. Coleman, *Individual Interests and Collective Action*. Cambridge: Cambridge University Press, 85-136.

Coleman, J. S., 1990: *Foundations of Social Theory*. Cambridge, Mass.: Harvard University Press.

Collins, R., 1986: Is 1980s Sociology in the Doldrums? In: *American Journal of Sociology*, 91 (6), 1336-1355.

Collins, R., 1988: *Theoretical Sociology*. San Diego: HBJ.

Coxon, A. P./ C. L. Jones, 1983: Multidimensional Scaling. In: D. McKay et al. (eds.), *Data Analysis and the Social Sciences*. London: Pinter, 171-226.

Downs, A., 1957: *An Economic Theory of Democracy*. New York: Harper & Row.

Dye, T. R., 1976: *Understanding Public Policy*. Englewood Cliffs: Prentice Hall.

Emerson, H., 1962: Power-Dependence Relations. In: *American Sociological Review* 27, 32-41.

Evan, W. M., 1972: An Organization-Set Model of Interorganizational Relations. In: M. Tuite/ R. Chrisholm/ M. Radnor (eds.), *Interorganizational Decision Making*. Chicago: Adline Publishing, 181-200.

Evans, P./ D. Rueschemeyer/ T. Skocpol (eds.) 1985: *Bringing the State Back In.* New York: Cambridge University Press.

Everit, B. 1983: *Cluster Analysis.* In: L. N. Lindberg, *Politics and the Future of Industrial Society.* New York: McKay, 226-256.

Feick, J./ W. Jann, 1989: *Comparative Policy Research - Eclecticism or Systematic Integration?* MPIFG Discussion Paper 1989/2. Köln: Max-Planck-Institut für Gesellschaftsforschung.

Franz, H.-J., 1986: Interorganizational Arrangements and Coordination at the Policy Level. In: F.-X. Kaufmann/ G. Majone/ V. Ostrom (eds.), *Guidance, Control, and Evaluation in the Policy Sector.* Berlin: de Gruyter, 479-494.

Friend, J. K./ J. M. Power/ C. J. L. Yewlett, 1974: *Public Planning: The Inter-corporate Dimension.* London: Tavistock.

Glaskiewicz, J., 1985: Interorganizational Relations. In: *Annual Review Sociology* 11, 281-304.

Grant, W., 1987: *Business Interests, Organizational Development and Private Interest Government.* Berlin: de Gruyter.

Hanf, K., 1982: The Implementation of Regulatory Policy: Enforcement as Bargaining. In: *European Journal of Political Research* 10 (June), 159-172.

Hanf, K./ F. W. Scharpf (eds.), 1978: *Interorganizational Policy Making. Limits to Coordination and Central Control.* London: Sage.

Hanf, K./ B. Hjern/ D. O. Porter, 1977: Local Networks of Manpower Training in the Federal Republic of Germany and Sweden. In: K. Hanf/ F. W. Scharpf (eds.), *Interorganizational Policy Making. Limits to Coordination and Central Control.* London: Sage, 303-341.

Harary, F./ R. Z. Norman/ D. Cartwright, 1969: *Structural Models: An Introduction to the Theory of Directed Graphs.* New York: John Wiley & Sons.

Heclo, H., 1978: Issue Networks and the Executive Establishment. In: A. King (ed.), *The New American Political System.* Washington D.C.: American Enterprise Inst., 87-124.

Hollingsworth, J.R., 1990: *The Governance of American Manufacturing Sectors: The Logic of Coordination and Control.* MPIFG Discussion Paper 90/4. Köln: Max-Planck-Institut für Gesellschaftsforschung.

Hollingsworth, J.R./ L.N. Lindberg, 1985: The governance of the American economy: the role of markets, clans, hierarchies, and associative behavior. In: W. Streeck/ P. C. Schmitter (eds.), *Private Interest Government. Beyond Market and State.* London: Sage, 221-254.

Hucke, J., 1982: Implementing Environmental Regulations in the Federal Republic of Germany. In: *Policy Studies Journal* 1, 130-140.

Jacobson, H. K., 1979: *Networks of Interdependence. International Organizations and the Global Political System.* New York: Knopf.

Jordan, A. G., 1981: Iron Triangles, Wooly Corporatism, and Elastic Nets: Images of the Policy Process. In: *Journal of Public Policy* 1(1), 95-123.

Jordan, A. G., 1990: Sub-Governments, Policy Communities and Networks: Refilling the Old Bottles? In: *Journal of Theoretical Politics* 2(3), 319-338.

Jordan, A. G./ J. J. Richardson, 1983: Policy communities: the British and European style. In: *Policy Studies Journal* 11 (June), 603-615.

Katz, M. L./ C. Shapiro, 1985: Network Externalities, Competition, and Compability. In: *American Economic Review* 75(3), 424-440.

Katzenstein, P. J. (ed.), 1978: *Between Power and Plenty. Foreign Economic Policies of Advanced Industrial States.* Madison: University of Wisconsin Press.

Katzenstein, P. J., 1987: *Policy and Politics in West Germany. The Growth of a Semisovereign State.* Philadelphia: Temple University Press.

Kenis, P., 1991: *The Social Construction of an Industriy - A World of Chemical Fibre.* Frankfurt a.M./ Boulder, CO.: Campus/ Westview.

Kenis, P./ V. Schneider, 1987: The EC as an International Corporate Actor. Two Case Studies in Economic Diplomacy. In: *European Journal of Political Research* 15(4), 437-457.

Keohane, R. O., 1984: *After Hegemony. Cooperation and Discord in the World Political Economy.* Princeton, NJ.: Princeton University Press.

Knoke, D./ J. H. Kuklinski, 1982: *Network Analysis.* Beverly Hills: Sage.

Krippendorf, K., 1989: Cybernetics. In: E. Barnouw et al. (eds.), *International Encyclopedia of Communications.* New York/ Oxford: Oxford UP, 443-446.

Landes, W. M./ R. A. Posner, 1975: The Independent Judiciary in an Interest-Group Perspective. In: *Journal of Law and Economics* 18, 875-901.

Latham, E. 1964: The Group Basis of Politics: Notes for a Theory. In: F. Munger/ D. Price, *Political Parties and Pressure Groups.* New York: Crowell, 32-57.

Laumann, E. O. / F. U. Pappi, 1976: *Networks of Collective Action: A Perspective on Community Influence Systems.* New York: Academic Press.

Laumann, E. O./ P. V. Marsden/ D. Prensky, 1982: The Boundary Specification in Network Analysis. In: R. S. Burt/ M. J. Minor (eds.), *Applied Network Analysis.* Beverly Hills, CA.: Sage, 18-34.

Laumann, E. O./ D. Knoke, 1986: Social Network Theory. In: S. Lindenberg/ James S. Coleman/ S. Nowak (eds.), *Approaches to Social Theory.* New York: Russel Sage Foundation, 83-109.

Laumann, E. O./ D. Knoke, 1987: *The Organizational State. Social Choice in National Policy Domains.* Madison, WI.: Wisconsin University Press.

Lehmbruch, G., 1985: Concertation and the Structure of Neo-Corporatist Networks. In: J. H. Goldthorpe (ed.), *Order and Conflict in Contemporary Capitalism.* Oxford: Oxford University Press, 60-80.

Lerner, D./ H. D. Lasswell (eds.), 1951: *The Policy Sciences.* Stanford: Stanford University Press.

Lévi-Strauss, C., 1969: *Anthropologie structurale.* Paris: Librairie Plon.

Levine, S./ P. E. White, 1961: Exchange as a Conceptual Framework for the Study of Interorganizational Relationships. In: *Administrative Science Quarterly*, 583-601.

MacIver, R. M. 1947: *The Web of Government.* New York: Macmillan.

Mandell, M., 1984: Application of Network Analysis to the Implementation of a Complex Project. In: *Human Relations* 37, 659-679.

Marin, B., 1982: *Die Paritätische Kommission. Aufgeklärter Technokorporatismus in Österreich.* Wien: Internationale Publikationen.

Marin, B. (ed.), 1990a: *Generalized Political Exchange: Antagonistic Cooperation and Integrated Policy Circuits.* Frankfurt a.M./ Boulder, CO.: Campus/ Westview Press.

Marin, B. (ed.), 1990b: *Governance and Generalized Exchange: Self-Organizing Policy Networks in Action.* Frankfurt a.M./ Boulder, CO.: Campus/ Westview Press.

Marsden, P. V., 1983: Restricted access in networks and models of power. In: *American Journal of Sociology* 91, 28-53.

Marsden, P. V./ E. O. Laumann, 1977: Collective Action in a Community Elite. Exchange, Influence Resources and Issue Resolution. In: R. J. Liebert/ A. W. Imersheim (eds.), *Power, Paradigms, and Community Research.* London: Sage, 199-250.

Marsden, P. V./ N. Lin, 1982: *Social Structure and Network Analysis.* Beverly Hills/ London: Sage.

Mathien, T., 1988: Network Analysis and Methodological Individualism. In: *Philosophy Social Sciences* 18, 1-20.

Mayntz, R. 1979: Regulative Politik in der Krise. In: J. Matthes (ed.), *Sozialer Wandel in Westeuropa: Verhandlungen des neunzehnten deutschen Soziologentages.* Frankfurt a.M.: Campus, 55-81.

Mayntz, R. 1979a: Public bureaucracies and policy implementation. In: *International Social Science Journal* 31, 633-645.

Mayntz, R., 1983: The Conditions of Effective Public Policy: A New Challenge for Policy Analysis. In: *Policy and Politics* 2, 123-143.

Mayntz, R., 1985: Die gesellschaftliche Dynamik als theoretische Herausforderung. In: B. Lutz (ed.), *Soziologie und gesellschaftliche Entwicklung.* Frankfurt a.M.: Campus, 27-44.

Mayntz, R., 1986: Corporate Actors in Public Policy: Changing Perspectives in Political Analysis. In: *Norsk Staatsvitenskapelig Tiddsskrift* 3, 7-25.

Mayntz, R., 1987: Politische Steuerung und gesellschaftliche Steuerungsprobleme - Anmerkungen zu einem theoretischem Paradigma. In: Th. Ellwein et al. (eds.), *Jahrbuch zur Staats- und Verwaltungswissenschaft.* Vol. 1. Baden-Baden: Nomos, 89-110.

Mayntz, R./ B. Nedelmann, 1987: Eigendynamische Soziale Prozesse. Anmerkungen zu einem analytischen Paradigma. In: *Kölner Zeitschrift für Soziologie und Sozialpsychologie* 39, 648-668.

Mayntz, R. et al., 1988: *Differenzierung und Verselbständigung: Zur Entwicklung gesellschaftlicher Teilsysteme.* Frankfurt a.M.: Campus.

Mény, Y., 1989: Formation et transformation des policy communities. L'exemple français. In: Y. Mény, *Ideologies Parties and Politiques & Groupes Sociaux.* Paris: Presses de la Fondation Nationale des Sciences Politiques, 355-366.

Metcalfe, J. L., 1976: Organizational Strategies and Interorganizational Networks. In: *Human Relations* 4, 327-343.

Nadel, M. V., 1975: The Hidden Dimension of Public Policy: Private Governments and the Policy-Making Process. In: *Journal of Politics* 37, 2-34.

North, D., 1990: A Transaction Cost Theory of Politics. In: *Journal of Theoretical Politics* 2(4): 355-367.

Olsen, J. P., 1981: Integrated Participation in Governmental Policy-Making. In: P. C. Nystrom/ W. H. Starbuck (eds.), *Handbook of Organizational Design*. Vol. 2. Oxford: OUP, 492-515.

Olsen, J. P., 1983: *Organized Democracy. Political Institutions in a Welfare State - The Case of Norway*. Oslo: University Press.

Olson, M., 1965: *The Logic of Colletive Action . Public Goods and the Theory of Goods*. Cambridge, Mass: Harvard UP.

Ostrom, V., 1983: Nonhierarchical Approaches to the Organization of Public Activity. In: *Annals* 3, 135-147.

Palmer, D., 1983: Broken Ties: Interlocking Directorates and Intercorporate Coordination. In: *Administrative Science Quarterly* 28, 40-55.

Pappi, F. U. (ed.), 1987: *Methoden der Netzwerkanalyse*. München: Oldenbourg.

Pappi, F. U., 1990: Politischer Tausch im Politikfeld 'Arbeit' - Ergebnisse einer Untersuchung der deutschen Interessengruppen und politischen Akteure auf Bundesebene. In: Th. Ellwein et al. (eds.), Jahrbuch zur Staats- und Verwaltungswissenschaft. Vol. 4. Baden-Baden: Nomos, 157-189.

Pappi, F. U./ P. Kappelhoff, 1984: Abhängigkeit, Tausch und kollektive Entscheidung in einer Gemeindeelite. In: *Zeitschrift für Soziologie* 2, 87-117.

Perrow, C., 1989: Eine Gesellschaft von Organisationen. In: *Journal für Sozialforschung* 1, 3-19.

Perrucci, R./ H. R. Potter (eds.), *Networks of Power: Organizational Actors at the National, Corporate and Community Levels*. New York: de Gruyter.

Plowden, W. (ed.), 1987: *Advising the Rulers*. Oxford: Blackwell.

Poucke, W. van, 1979/80: Network Constraints on Social Action: Preliminaries for a Network Theory. In: *Social Network* 2, 181-190.

Powell, W. W., 1990: Neither Market nor Hierarchy: Network Forms of Organization. In: *Research in Organizational Behaviour* 12, 295-336.

Presthus, R. 1962: *The Organizational Society*. New York: Knopf.

Rainey, G. H./ H. B. Milward, 1983: Public Organizations: Policy Networks and Environment. In: R. H. Hall/ R. E. Quinn (eds.), *Organizational Theory and Public Policy*. London/ Beverly Hills: Sage, 133-146.

Rhodes, R. A. W., 1981: *Control and Power in Central-Local Government Relations*. Farnborough: Gower.

Rhodes, R. A. W., 1986: Power dependence: Theories of central-local relations. A critical assessment. In: M. Goldsmith (ed.), *New Research in Central-Local Relations.* Brookfield: Gower, 1-33.

Rhodes, R. A. W., 1990: Policy Networks: A British Perspective. In: *Journal of Theoretical Politics* 2(3), 291-318.

Richardson, J./ A. G. Jordan, 1983: Overcrowded Policy-making. Some British and European Reflections. In: *Policy Sciences* 15, 247-268.

Rogers, E. M., 1989: Network Analysis. In: Erik Barnouw et al., *International Encyclopedia of Communications.* New York/ Oxford: Oxford University Press.

Rokkan, S., 1969: Norway: Numerical Democracy and Corporate Pluralism. In: R. A. Dahl (ed.), *Political Oppositions in Western Democracies.* New Haven: Yale University Press, 70-115.

Ronge, V., (ed.) 1980: *Am Staat vorbei. Politik der Selbstregulierung von Kapital und Arbeit.* Frankfurt a.M.: Campus.

Sabatier, P. A., 1987: Knowledge, Policy-Oriented Learning, and Policy Change: An Advocacy Coalition Framework. In: *Knowledge, Creation, Diffusion, Utilization* 8, 649-692.

Sabatier, P. A./ N. Pelkey, 1987: Incorporating Multiple Actors and Guidance Instruments into Models of Regulatory Policy-making: An Advocacy Coalition Framework. In: *Administration & Society* 19(2), 236-263.

Salisbury, R. H., 1984: Interest Representation: The Dominance of Institutions. In: *American Political Science Review* 78, 64-76.

Scharpf, F. W., 1973: Komplexität als Schranke der politischen Planung. In: Fritz W. Scharpf, *Planung als politischer Prozeß. Aufsätze zur Theorie der planenden Demokratie.* Frankfurt a.M.: Suhrkamp, 73-113.

Scharpf, F. W., 1977: Interorganizational Policy Studies: Issues, Concepts and Perspectives. In: K. Hanf/ F. W. Scharpf (eds.), 1977: *Interorganizational Policy Making. Limits to Coordination and Central Control.* London: Sage, 345-370.

Scharpf, F. W., 1989: Decision Rules, Decision Styles and Policy Choices. In: *Journal of Theoretical Politics* 1, 149-176.

Scharpf, F. W., 1989a: *Games Real Actors Could Play: The Problem of Complete Information.* MPFIG 89/9. Köln: Max-Planck-Institut für Gesellschaftsforschung.

Scharpf, F. W., 1990: *Games Real Actors Could Play: The Problem of Connectedness*. MPIFG Discussion Paper 90/8. Köln: Max-Planck-Institut für Gesellschaftsforschung.

Schmitter, P. C., 1974: Still the Century of Corporatism? In: *The Review of Politics* 36, 85-131.

Schmitter, P. C., 1989: Sectors in Modern Capitalism: Modes of Governance and Variations in Performance. In: *Stato e mercato* 26, 173-208.

Schmitter, P. C. /Lehmbruch, G. (eds.), 1979: *Trends Towards Corporatist Intermediation*. Beverly Hills/ London: Sage, 7-72.

Schneider, V., 1988: *Politiknetzwerke der Chemikalienkontrolle. Eine Analyse einer transnationalen Politikentwicklung*. Berlin: de Gruyter.

Schneider V./ R. Werle, 1990: International Regime or Corporate Actor? The European Community in Telecommunications Policy. In: K. Dyson/ P. Humphreys (eds.), *The Political Economy of Communications. International and European Dimensions*. London: Routledge, 77-106.

Schuppert, G. F., 1989: Markt, Staat, Dritter Sektor - oder noch mehr? Sektorspezifische Steuerungsprobleme ausdifferenzierter Staatlichkeit. In: Th. Ellwein et al. (eds.), *Jahrbuch zur Staats- und Verwaltungswissenschaft*. Vol. 3. Baden-Baden: Nomos, 47-87.

Scott, J., 1988: Trend Report Social Network Analysis. In: *Sociology* 1, 109-127.

Sharpe, J., 1985: Central Coordination and the Policy Network. In: *Political Studies,* 361-381.

Simon, H. A., 1973: The Organization of Complex Systems. In: H. H. Pattee (ed.), *Hierarchy Theory. The Challenge of Complex Systems*. New York: George Braziller, 3-27.

Smith, C. S., 1987: Networks of Influence: The Social Sciences in Britain since the War. In: M. Bulmer (ed.), *Social Science Research and Government. Comparative Essays on Britain and the United States*. Cambridge: Cambridge University Press, 61-76.

Somit A./ J. Tanenhaus, 1970: The "Behavioral-Traditional" Debate in Political Sciences. In: L. D. Hayes/ R. D. Hedlund (eds.), *The Conduct of Political Inquiry. Behavioral Political Analysis*. Englewood Cliffs, NJ.: Prentice-Hall, 45-55.

Starbuck, William H., 1970: Nonmarket Organizations and Organizational Co-Ordination. In: M. N. Zald (ed.), *Power in Organizations*. Vanderbilt: Vanderbilt University Press, 312-321.

Stokmann, F. N./ J. M. M. van den Bos/ F. W. Wasseur, 1989: *A General Model of Policy Making Illustrated Within the US Energy Policy Arena.* Paper presented at the ECPR Joint Session of Workshops in Paris, April 10-15th 1989.

Streeck, W./ P. C. Schmitter (eds.), 1985: *Private Interest Government. Beyond Market and State.* Beverly Hills, CA.: Sage.

Taylor, C. C., 1983: *Why Governments grow.* Beverly Hills, CA.: Sage.

Teubner, G., 1990: Die vielköpfige Hydra: Netzwerke als kollektive Akteure höherer Ordnung. In: W. Krohn/ G. Küppers (eds.), *Emergenz und Selbstorganisation.* Frankfurt: Suhrkamp (forthcoming).

Thorelli, H. B., 1986: Networks: Between Markets and Hierarchies. In: *Strategic Management Journal* 7, 37-51.

Trasher, M., 1983: Exchange Networks and Implementation. In: *Policy and Politics,* 11(4), 375-391.

Trasher, M./ D. Dunkerley, 1982: A Social Exchange Approach to Implementation Analysis. In: *Social Science Information* 3, 349-382.

Traxler, F./ G. Unger, 1990: Institutionelle Erfolgsbedingungen wirtschaftlichen Strukturwandels. Zum Verhältnis von Effizienz und Regulierung aus theoretischer und empirischer Sicht. In: *Wirtschaft und Gesellschaft* 16(2), 189-223.

Truman, D., 1971: *The Governmental Process. Political Interests and Public Opinion.* New York: Knopf.

Tuite, M./ R. Chrisholm/ M. Radnor (eds.), *Interorganizational Decision Making.* Chicago: Adline Publishing, 181-200.

Warner, W. L. 1967: *The Emergent American Society. Vol. 1: Large-Scale Organizations.* New Haven, London: Yale University Press.

Wellman, B., 1983: Network Analysis: Some Basic Principles. In: *Sociological Theory,* 155-200.

Wellman, B., 1988: Structural Analysis: From Method and Metaphor to Theory and Substance. In: B. Wellman/ S. D. Berkowitz (eds.), *Social structures: a network approach.* Cambridge: Cambridge University Press, 19-61.

Whetten, D. A., 1981: Interorganizational Relations: A Review of the Field. In: *Journal of Higher Education* 1, 1-28.

Wildavsky, A., 1974: *The Politics of the Budgetary Process.* Boston: Little.

Wilks, S./ M. Wright, (eds.), 1987: *Comparative Government-Industry Relations. Western Europe, the United States and Japan.* Oxford: Clarendon Press.

Williamson, E. O., 1985: *The Economic Institutions of Capitalism.* New York: Free Press.

Willke, H., 1983: *Entzauberung des Staates. Überlegungen zu einer sozietalen Steuerungstheorie.* Koenigstein/Ts.: Athenaeum.

Windhoff-Héritier, A., 1985: *Politikarena und Policy Netz - Zum analytischen Nutzen zweier Begriffe.* Veröffentlichungsreihe des Internationalen Instituts für Vergleichende Gesellschaftsforschung (IIVG)/ Arbeitspolitik des Wissenschaftszentrums Berlin. IIVG/dp85-212.

Windhoff-Héritier, A., 1987: *Policy-Analyse.* Frankfurt a.M.: Campus.

Winter, G., 1985: Bartering Rationality in Regulation. In: *Law and Society Review* 19(2), 219-250.

Wright, M., 1988: Policy Community, Policy Network and Comparative Industrial Policies. In: *Political Studies* 36, 593-612.

Zijlstra, G. J., 1978/79: Networks in Public Policy: Nuclear Energy in the Netherlands. In: *Social Networks* 1, 359-389.

Part Two

Policy Networks In National Policy Domains

Chapter 3
Organizations in Political Action: Representing Interests in National Policy Making

Edward O. Laumann and John P. Heinz
with Robert Nelson and Robert Salisbury

1   Introduction

State policies are the products of complex interactions among governmental and nongovernmental organizations, each seeking to influence the collectively binding decisions arising from policy making events that have consequences for their interests. In the United States, the incredibly voluminous and disparate character of national policy making activities is only dimly revealed in the tens of thousands of pages officially published every year in the *Federal Register* to describe the myriad actions of hundreds of executive agencies, departments, bureaus, institutes, and establishments, the thousands of Congressional hearings held to evaluate the merits of about 10,000 bills being proposed each biennium, and the thousands of pages devoted to summarizing appellate court actions on a multitude of cases of the most diverse sorts. We must thus seek some way of systematically decomposing this complex totality into more manageable units that can be studied with existing techniques. Following the leads suggested by Laumann, Knoke and their associates (Knoke/ Laumann 1982; Laumann/ Knoke/ Kim 1985; Laumann/ Knoke 1987) in their study of national policy domains, we propose to regard national policy making as subdividable into a number of delimited policy domains. Each of these may be identified by specifying a substantively defined criterion of mutual relevance or common orientation among a

This chapter is a substantially revised and updated version of a paper read at the annual meetings of the American Sociological Association in New York, New York, August 30 - September 3, 1986. We wish to acknowledge our appreciation for the generous financial support provided by the American Bar Foundation and the National Science Foundation (SES 8320275) and for the thoughtful and expeditious research assistance of Tony Tam in performing the data analysis.

set of consequential corporate actors concerned with formulating, advocating, and selecting courses of action (that is, policy options) intended to resolve a delimited substantive problem (Knoke/ Laumann 1982: 256). Obvious examples of national policy domains include education, agriculture, housing, foreign trade, civil rights, defense, energy, and so forth. Participants in domain policy making actions include all public- and private-sector actors whose capacities to affect the collective outcomes of policy decisions must be taken into account by the other participants. In brief, a national policy domain consists of the consequential actors in a delimited subsystem of the State. Our central assertion is that corporate (organizational) actors are the principals who dominate the national policy making process.

If one can meaningfully distinguish substantively circumscribed policy arenas for close study, we are then in the position to identify three critical sets of actors that play distinct roles in the representation of private and public interests. First, there are the clients, found in many organizational guises, who retain Washington representatives to monitor policy developments having consequences for their interests and/or to communicate their preferred outcomes in appropriately influential ways. Then there are the government officials who must deal with these representations; and finally there are the representatives themselves, both lawyers and nonlawyers, employees and fee-charging consultants, who do the myriad tasks required to perform these mediating functions effectively.

The research design is thus based on a tripartite conception of private representation in which client (nongovernmental) organizations retain representatives to contact government officials for the purpose of affecting policy outcomes. The links among the three sets of actors are diagrammed in Figure 1. The connection between client organizations and their representatives involves the decision to hire particular representatives and, thereafter, to monitor and, when necessary, control them. The linkages between the representatives and the targeted officials consist of activities of monitoring and intervention regarding official policy actions. The latter, in turn, produce outcomes that presumably affect the client organizations in some way and may lead, in turn, to some alteration in their relationship with their representatives.

We had two fundamental objectives in devising our study design. First, we wanted to identify a set of policy domains sufficiently diverse on important analytic dimensions that they could be expected to give

Figure 1: Tripartite Conception of Representation

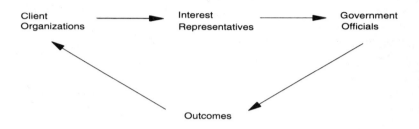

us at least a first approximation of the diversity and range of representational tasks and modes of organization that characterize national policy making deliberations more generally. That is, by judicious selection of the parts, we hoped to get some glimpse of the whole. Secondly, we wanted to devise replicable procedures for validly and reliably identifying the key actors in each domain, who, in turn, would become the objects of closer examination. (For an extended description and rationale for the study design, see Heinz et al. 1987, 1991).

1.1 The Selection of the Policy Domains

The four domains we selected for study - agriculture, energy, health, and labor - have distinctive features that provide theoretical grounds for expecting differences in how policy is formulated and in the roles and impact of representatives. The particular topics included in a given operational definition of a policy domain were determined from a broad reading of the documentary sources pertaining to a particular policy subject. The *Congressional Quarterly*, for example, regularly publishes volumes devoted to reviewing legislative and other initiatives that bear on particular policy topics. The *Federal Register* is also a good source for learning about activities of specific executive agencies, and appellate court cases can be screened for those pertaining to particular policy controversies.

The domains vary in four interesting respects. First, they vary in the constellation of interest groups. Agriculture and energy politics are organized around regionally segmented producer groups (milk, grains, cotton, tobacco, etc., in agriculture; oil, natural gas, coal, nuclear energy in energy) (see, e.g., Hadwiger/ Brown 1978; Guither 1980; Heinz 1962; Davis 1982; Chubb 1983; Laumann/ Knoke 1987). Health and labor are dominated by various nationally oriented brokering institutions, such as the American Medical Association, the American Hospital Association, and the American Association of Retired Persons in health (see, e.g., Marmor 1970; Starr 1982; Laumann/ Knoke 1987); and the AFL/ CIO, the US Chamber of Commerce, and the National Association of Manufacturers in labor (see, e.g., Wilson 1979; Greenstone 1969; Bok/ Dunlop 1970).

Second, the level and form of conflict in the domains vary. Labor policy typically pits two major camps against each other, and indeed, much of the contention between the parties has become institutionalized within the National Labor Relations Board and various agencies of the Department of Labor. Health policy typically has involved disputes over the means of attaining widely shared goals, but has undergone considerable fragmentation in recent years, as the interests of doctors, hospital associations, insurance companies, medical schools, hospital equipment manufacturers, and so forth have diverged (Heclo 1978: 96). Energy and agriculture manifest more explicit competition among alternative producers and between consumers and producers.

Third, the institutional composition and general policies of the domains have changed at much different rates in the last two decades. Agriculture and labor have long maintained a relatively stable set of agencies and broad policies. Energy and health have only recently given rise to new cabinet-level departments and wide areas of policy making. Finally lawyers and legal institutions play different roles across and within domains. Agriculture and health are less "lawyered" domains, both because direct bureaucratic negotiation and policy development are more important processes than are formal adjudicatory, licensing, and rulemaking procedures, and because farmers and doctors compete more effectively for positions of policy making authority in government and private organizations (cf. Nelson et al. 1988).

While both energy and agriculture have policy subdomains concerned with foreign trade and international policy making, our selection of policy domains is heavily skewed toward domestic policy issues. To the extent that domestic policy controversies differ in important ways from those concerned with defense and foreign policy, we may run the risk of overestimating the ease with which interested parties enter into particular policy arenas and have impact on policy outcomes. We may even run a risk of misrepresenting the sorts of actors who come to be influential in policy deliberations.

1.2 Sampling Design

Appropriately modifying the procedures developed by Laumann and Knoke (1987: chap. 3), we adopted a sequential sampling design that successively revealed the three sets of actors we believe play the crucial roles in policy deliberations. To identify the claimant actors in a policy domain, we devised procedures which allowed us to (1) identify the organizations attempting to influence policy in a specific policy domain, (2) assess the level of policy making activity by those organizations, and (3) sample organizations according to their level of activity. Sampling from this comprehensive listing of interested parties, we then asked well-placed informants in the organizations we sampled to tell us the names and positions of representatives they employed or retained in a given policy domain. The population of named individuals was sampled and queried, in turn, about their contacts with specific government officials exercising policy-related responsibilities. This listing of nominated governmental officials constituted our third population of interest: targeted government officials. This chapter restricts attention to the four samples of organizations and their reported participation in 20 selected events between 1977 and 1982 as described by their representatives.

The procedures for identifying organizations active in a domain required a substantial amount of documentary investigation and preliminary interviewing because no single list adequately defines the population of interested parties. Each policy area involves numerous policy making subsystems within the executive, legislative, and judicial branches that attract quite distinctive populations of participants.[1] We thus wanted to use several different methods for locating interested parties. Each method, by itself, had a systematic bias toward finding certain kinds of organizations and neglecting others because it concentrated on particular decision making arenas. By combining nominations from several sources with

---

1   The total numbers of government targets we ultimately identified as relevant and active in the agricultural, energy, health and labor policy domains were 74, 66, 62 and 56, respectively.

different known biases, we hoped to "triangulate" on a comprehensive listing of the population of relevant organizations. We describe below the results of these methods at some length because they uncovered an enormous number of organizational actors that are active in the representation process - a volume of participation of unique corporate actors that has been underappreciated in the literature on interest groups.

Our first method for locating interested actors in a policy domain was attentive to issues attracting mass media attention because of their controversiality and broad popular interest. Such issues are often to be resolved in the Congressional arena. Organizations taking partisan public stands on popular issues are often to be identified by this technique. We conducted a computerized search of stories in national and regional newspapers and magazines dealing with federal policy making in each domain from January 1977 to June 1982, noting the number of stories mentioning each organization. The data regarding newspaper coverage of organizational participation were compiled from "The Information Bank," a data base of the *New York Times* Information Service (NYTIS). To compensate for regional effects, the data base included the following newspapers: Chicago *Tribune*, Houston *Chronicle*, Los Angeles *Times*, New York *Times*, San Francisco *Chronicle*, Seattle *Times*, Washington *Post* and *Time* magazine. The product of the computer search was an extensive set of news story abstracts from the source news media. These abstracts were then searched and tagged for the names of organizations, and lists of organizations in each domain were compiled. The number of mentions for each organization was recorded, a mention for this source being defined as an appearance in one newspaper abstract. Duplicate abstracts of stories reported in two or more news sources were eliminated. The first row of Table 1 reports the number of mentions and the number of unique organizations identified by this method for each domain.[2]

---

2   See Andrew Shapiro (1985) for a more complete description of this procedure and the other three methods used in generating the target population of interested parties.

Table 1: Frequency of Mentions and Unique Organizations Identified by Each Source of Nomination for the Four Policy Domains

| | Policy Domain | | | | | | | | | |
| | Agriculture | | Energy | | Health | | Labor | | Total | |
Source	Mentions/ Count[a]	Ratio[b]	Mentions/ Count[a]	Ratio[b]	Mentions/ Count[a]	Ratio[b]	Mentions/ Count[a]	Ratio[b]	Mentions/ Count[a]	
New York Times Information Service	203/ 153	1.33	1,197/ 297	4.03	421/ 283	1.49	557/ 313	1.78	2,378/ 1,046	
Congressional Information Service	2,426/ 1,406	1.73	2,449/ 1,641	1.49	1,673/ 1,108	1.51	907/ 623	1.46	7,455/ 4,778	
Government Officials	144/ 100	1.44	170/ 117	1.45	125/ 97	1.29	168/ 97	1.73	607/ 411	
Washington Representatives	625/ 625	1.00	1,234/ 1,234	1.00	549/ 549	1.00	230/ 230	1.00	2,638/ 2,638	
Total	2,773/ 2,284	--	3,816/ 3,289	--	2,219/ 2,037	--	1,132/ 1,263	--	9,940/ 8,873	
Unique Organizations Total	2,060		2,595		1,673		1,117		7,445	

a The first number is the frequency with which organizations were mentioned in the source, while the second number is the number of unique organizations identified by that source.

b The ratio is calculated by dividing the number of mentions by the unique count.

Second, we searched the abstracts of Congressional hearings held by committees and subcommittees with jurisdiction in each of the four domains during the 95th through the 97th Congress, noting the number of hearings in which organizations testified. Less publicly partisan and more specialized organizations are revealed by this procedure. In light of the enormous number of hearings covered in the Congressional Information Service (CIS) database, we restricted the search to the first sessions of the 95th, 96th, and 97th Congresses and to a selection of only the major committees active in each domain. The second row of Table 1 gives the aggregate counts of mentions and unique organizations identified by this procedure.

Third, during winter and spring, 1982, we interviewed twenty to twenty-three government officials in each of the four policy domains, and asked the officials to name the organizations that contacted them frequently and organizations representative of those that contacted them episodically. This method is especially likely to identify organizations having direct dealings with particular executive agencies and their regulatory initiatives. Two criteria were used in selecting individuals to be interviewed: (1) the position of the individual in the unit and (2) his or her tenure in the unit. An attempt was made to avoid relying exclusively on politically appointed officials as well as on those with fewer than two years tenure in office. Row three of Table 1 gives the aggregated results of this inquiry.

Finally, for each domain we compiled a list of organizations appearing under the industry heading related to the domain in *Washington Representatives* (1981), an annual publication that canvasses various public sources and surveys organizations in an effort to list organizations represented before the Federal government. Organizations that are self-professed lobbyists before Congress and the Executive agencies are especially likely to be identified. The fourth row gives the count of organizations identified in this way.

Several features of Table 1 are worth noting. First, we can readily see that each source method of nominating organizations for inclusion in the population of claimant organizations has distinctive features that set it apart from the others. If we had relied only on the listing produced by the *Washington Representatives*, we would have underestimated the population of interested organizations by a factor of 2.8 (7445/2638). Secondly, we learn that domains differ substantially among themselves with respect to the amount of newspaper attention given them, the raw numbers of organizations identified as active, and the numbers of organizations engaged in repeated efforts to influence policy outcomes in their respective domains. From various points of view, the energy domain seems to be the largest in terms of the number of organizations attracted to its concerns, with agriculture and health roughly tied in scale of participation with almost a third fewer organizational participants, and labor placing a rather distant third. Thirdly, while the CIS ratios of mentions to counts of unique organizations identified are remarkably stable across the four domains, the NYTIS ratios suggest considerable differentiation across the domains with respect to the presence of repeat players.

For each domain we drew a random sample of 100 organizations, with each of the four sources contributing equally, but with each organization in the first three sources weighted by the number of mentions in that source. Because, for all but the listing from *Washington Representatives*, the probability of selection increased with the number of mentions, our sampling procedure reflected each organization's level of activity in the domain. But we had an even stronger reason to adopt this weighting procedure. Laumann and Knoke (1987: chap. 5) had demonstrated that there was a high correlation between the number of times an organization was named by other organizations as being among the most influential actors in the domain and the number of mentions of the organization in newspaper stories, appearances in congressional hearings, *amici* briefs and interviews with government officials. Hence, there is solid reason to believe that the number of mentions in the various sources is a good measure of perceived organizational influence - an essential feature to know for the analysis more generally. The sampling procedure thus generates a list of organizations that disproportionately includes the most influential organizations in the domain and relatively underselects the least influential organizations. Simple inspection of the samples reveals that we were quite successful in including many of the most prominent and influential organizations, with an admixture of less visible, more peripheral organizations, that will permit us to investigate what, if any, systematic differences are to be observed in their modes of participation in policy deliberations.[3]

---

3   In fact, at least 14 percent of the organizations actually interviewed in the four domains had received ten or more mentions through a combination of our four procedures for identifying participating organizations; and slightly more than 32 percent had received at least 5 mentions. Thus the organizations selected were heavily skewed toward the most

Having sampled the client organizations participating in each domain, we identified the representatives they employed or retained in the domain by conducting telephone interviews with informants in a minimum of 75 organizations in each domain, 316 organizations in all.[4] These informants were identified by using published listings of organization officers, supplemented with direct inquiries of the organizations, to determine who had operating responsibility for the organization's involvement in federal policy in the appropriate domain. The informant so identified was asked to name up to four individuals inside the organization (employees, officers, member-volunteers) and up to four individuals external to the organization (employed in outside firms, trade associations, and so forth, but not falling within the definition of an internal representative) who acted as key representatives for the organization in the policy area. It is this listing of nominated individuals who constituted the population of representatives to be sampled next.

The client interviews generated between 400 and 450 names in each domain, for a total of 1,716 individuals. (Representatives could appear on the lists as many times as they were mentioned; about 5 percent appeared in more than one domain.) Random selection from these lists produced realized samples ranging between 184 and 206 representatives per domain. About two-thirds of the total sample were based in Washington and interviewed there;[5] while another 15 percent were based in other major cities and interviewed there. The remainder of the sample was interviewed by telephone using an adapted format. The overall response

---

active organizations in each policy domain. For comparison, only 1.5 percent of the organizations in the sampling universe had 10 or more mentions, and only 5.3 percent had received 5 or more mentions.

4 The response rate was 75 percent, with 8 percent of the organizations refusing interviews. Another 12 percent of the organizations could not be located, were located overseas, or had ceased to exist. The refusals did not follow a pattern, and therefore, did not constitute a major source of bias. See Shapiro (1985: 12-14).

5 The fact that almost one-third of the persons meeting our definition of a Washington representative are located outside the Washington metropolitan area deserves stressing. Contrary to much received opinion, which has taken particular notice of the rapid growth of the trade association and lawyer populations in Washington over the past decade, Washington does not currently exercise a monopoly over the performance of the representational function. Unfortunately, we lack any historical evidence that would permit us to estimate the extent to which this function has shifted to Washington. Certainly we might expect that different aspects of representation might be done by insiders and outsiders. Our data permit us to evaluate the kinds of roles various representatives perform, but they are not directly pertinent to the concerns of this chapter (see Heinz et al. 1987).

rate of representatives successfully interviewed is 78 percent. About 10 percent of the representatives contacted declined interviews.

It is this sample of representatives that we used to determine the extent and nature of organizational participation in specific decision making events in each policy domain. Each respondent was treated as an informant about the organization that nominated him/her; in many cases, two to four representatives were interviewed from an organization. We pooled the information from multiple representatives regarding the organization's participation in the 20 decision making events. Over two-thirds of the representatives were, in fact, employees of the nominating organizations.

Table 2 provides an overview of the distribution of the types of organizations active in the four policy domains and, by inference, in Washington domestic policy arenas more generally. It also documents the systematic variation in this respect between policy domains.

Table 2: Types of Organizations Active in Four Policy Domains: Percent Distributions

Type of Organization	Policy Domain				
	Agriculture	Energy	Health	Labor	Total
Business	20	54	15	8	24
Citizen issue	14	11	7	4	9
Government	3	5	6	1	4
Labor unions	5	1	3	34	10
Minority group	3	-	14	11	7
Nonprofit	1	4	21	7	9
Professional	1	3	17	4	6
Trade associations	51	22	16	26	29
Other	2	-	1	5	2
Total	100	100	100	100	100
N	80	76	81	74	311

The sort of organization that is most often represented is the trade association, which accounts for more than a quarter of all clients. But there is substantial variation among the domains in this regard. In the agricultural policy area, more than one-half of the clients are trade groups, while only about one-sixth of the health clients are such associations. The agricultural trade associations include not only the organizations of farmers or producers, but also the industry associations of processors and distributors, such as the Grocery Manufacturers Association. Individual corporations are included in the "business" category, which is the next most numerous class of clients, and where a similar variation among the domains is displayed. Overall, nearly a quarter of the clients are businesses, but the range extends from a high of 54% in the energy domain to a low of only 8% in the labor policy area. We have no solid explanation for the finding that clients in agriculture are more often represented as umbrella groups or associations while those in the energy policy domain tend to retain their identity as individual businesses, but this tendency may be explained by the relative "maturity" of the two domains.[6] It may also be due to the relative size of the business entities in the domains (i.e., energy businesses are larger and therefore more capable of acting independently than those in agriculture and health).

As one might expect, the next most numerous category of clients, labor unions, is much more often active in labor policy than in the other domains. Even in the labor domain, however, two-thirds of the clients are not unions, and unions make up only a small proportion of the clients in the other three domains. One might also anticipate the findings that minority group organizations are much more active in labor and health policy than they are in agriculture and energy, and that nonprofit and professional organizations are far more prominent in health policy than in the other domains. State and local governments and "citizen issue" groups[7] are relatively evenly represented across the domains, although they have a smaller presence in labor issues than they do in the other policy arenas.

Most client organizations identified three or four key employees who acted, often exclusively, as their representatives on matters in the four domains. Only 31% of all the organizations surveyed (N = 311) reported that they regularly retained law firms for advice and representa-

---

6 With a few exceptions, agriculture has been the subject of federal regulation for a longer time than has "energy policy" as such. There has thus been a greater opportunity for those organizations with common agricultural interests to coalesce into groups.
7 The term "citizen issue groups" refers to organizations claiming to advance or defend the well-being of the public as a whole regardless of, or in opposition to, what are alleged to be narrower "special interests". These organizations include those concerned with environmental protection, abortion, political campaign reform, and so on.

tion in a policy domain, and more than one-half (51.4%) reported that they *never* used law firms for such purposes.[8] Organizations were much more likely to use trade associations regularly for advice and representation, but almost one-half (49.8%) of the organizations never used such associations - nearly the same proportion as that which never used law firms. Almost two-thirds (63.7%) reported that, apart from their use of law firms, they never used outside consultants, lobbyists, or public relations personnel for representational work, and only a little over one-fifth (22.2%) of the client organizations regularly turned to such outside representatives for assistance. (See Laumann/ Heinz 1985, and Nelson et al. 1988, for a more extensive discussion of these findings.)

2 Organizational Participation in Decision Making Events

One of the key methodological innovations of our study design (first developed by Laumann and Knoke (1987: chap. 1, 9-13)) is the identification of a set of significant decision making events over an extended period of time (in our case, between 1977 and 1982) in which the sampled organizations could choose to participate. By combining a bounded set of organizations and events, we can construct a data set describing the interface of organizations and events that permit us to answer a number of important questions about the organizations' roles in national policy formation. How do the organizations vary in the extent to which they participate across the set of events? What organizational and interorganizational features account for these variations in participation? What features of the events themselves help explain organizational participation? To what extent does an organization's participation in one event predict its participation in another? Asked from quite a different point of view, how are the events linked to one another by common or disjoint patterns of participation? Can the relative degree of event interdependency illuminate the degree of loose or tight coupling within, and across,

---

8   Economically oriented organizations such as business firms, trade associations, and unions are considerably more likely to use law firms for representational tasks than are professional, governmental, or other nonprofit organizations. One fact that might account for this difference in law firm usage would be the considerable difference in the financial resources controlled by the two broad types of organizations.

domain policy making? And perhaps most importantly, to what extent do organizations' preferred outcomes on one event predict their preferences with respect to another? How this last question is answered will lay the foundation for understanding the structure of consensus and cleavage in the policy domain. And finally, how stable are these patterns of consensus and cleavage over time? In this brief report, we can only address several of these questions in a preliminary way, but we believe the results are sufficiently promising and provocative that more thorough-going investigation is amply justified.

Table 3: Illustrative Events being Processed in Each Domain

Policy Domain	Mean Number of Org.s Activated per Event	Time	Event	Number of Org.s Activated	Number of Org.s "For"	Number of Org.s "Against"
Agriculture	24.2	May 1979	2 - House agriculture committee reports HR 2172, increasing federal sugar price supports (Measure is defeated by full House in October)	25	9	10
Energy	24.6	March 1980	7 - Congress passes HR 3919, a Windfall Profits Tax on decontrolled oil	40	9	25
Health	28.4	April 1981	13 - Reagan administration proposes phasing out health planning, PSROs, and federal financing for HMO's	53	21	23
Labor	25.0	July 1981	11 - Budget Reconciliation Act terminates CETA Title 110 and VI public service job programs	33	7	17

Space limitations preclude our listing the 22 events in each policy domain that we investigated. For illustrative purposes, we have selected one event from each domain, with its time of occurrence, brief description of its substantive content, and the number of organizations activated, with the split between those for and against the initiative also indicated. We have also reported the average number of organizations activated per event in each of the four policy domains.[9]

Not only do the 20 events in each domain vary considerably in the number of organizations they attract to deliberate their outcomes, but the individual organizations also vary in the number of events in which they become active. Due to certain design features of the study that focused attention on individual representatives rather than on organizations as the units of analysis, the data collected are not always optimal for measuring features of organizational participation. In the case of estimating organizational activation, these limitations are especially likely to lead to underestimating activation in specific events. Despite this caveat, we note that only a few organizations fail to participate in at least one of our targeted events (and these were excluded from the subsequent analysis). The means and ranges of individual organization participation in the 20 events in each domain are:

	Mean	Range
Agriculture	4.1	1-13
Energy	4.8	2-10
Health	4.7	1-11
Labor	4.7	1-16

9   To facilitate cross-domain comparisons, we included two events common to all four policy domains, the passage of the Economic Recovery Act of 1981 that provided across-the-board reductions in individual income taxes and the rejection of the Regulatory Reform Act of 1982 that would have provided for a legislative veto of proposed agency regulation. For purposes of this chapter, we have excluded these events from the following analysis.

3   Event Linkage or Dependency

The twenty events we identified in each domain obviously possess quite distinct substantive and institutional content, and they occurred over a span of six years. These events might be regarded as free-standing, independent occasions for the sample of organization to attempt to exert their influence, given an interest in the outcome. At least some pairings of events, however, may well have a common core of participants and/or nonparticipants. Such patterned linkages among events might be used to shed light on the degree to which the policy domains, or at least parts of them, were loosely or tightly linked - presumably with implications for the overall coordination of policy outcomes. Our analytic premise here is that pairs of events vary along a continuum of actor participation. (See Laumann/ Knoke 1987: chap. 11, for an extended treatment of this approach.) At one pole, the events may be treated as entirely independent of one another (i.e., participation of actors in one event is random with respect to their participation in the other). At the other, the two events are completely dependent on one another, either in the causal sense that

Figure 2: Event Linkages Defined on the Basis of Participation Patterns

	Event B		
	Participate	Not Participate	Row Total
Event A — Participate	a	b	a + b
Not Participate	c	d	c + d
Column Total	a + c	b + d	N

N = total number of possible organizational participants

the first event is a necessary and sufficient condition for the second or in the strategic or purposive sense that an actor's preference for the outcome of the second event constrains its behavior concerning the first event.

There are four possible ways in which an organization can respond to a pair of events. An organization may (a) participate in the first event and continue to participate in the second event, (b) participate in the first event but drop out in the second event, (c) not participate in the first event but become active in the second event, or (d) remain inactive throughout. To measure the degree of dependency between a pair of events (Y_{ij}), we shall use Yule's Y: $Y = (\alpha-1) / (\alpha+1)$, where $\alpha = (a * d / b * c)$, and a, b, c, and d refer to the cell frequencies in Figure 2.[10]

Table 4 presents selected comparisons of Yule's Y as our measure of paired event dependency or linkage for the four policy domains. Not surprisingly, all four domains manifest average absolute Y's significantly larger than 0, but that is only because we disregard signs in calculating such an average. Each domain, in fact, has a very distinctive pattern of event linkage when we examine the means and percentages of positive and negatives Y's. The labor domain is the only one with a positive bias (i.e., 75.3% of the Y's are positive) in event linkage, suggesting that its system of actors and events are, at least, loosely coupled. It is 8.7 percent more probable, on the average, that an observation of joint participa-

---

10 We have chosen Yule's Y as a measure of association between a pair of events because it is invariant with respect to the relative number of cases that appear in each column or row, i.e., it is insensitive to the number of participants in each event. To control the marginal distribution is of concern because of the great variability in the rates of participation across events.

Yule's Y has a straightforward interpretation as the difference in the probability of being in the diagonal cell and the probability of being in the off-diagonal cell for a standardized 2 x 2 table. The standardized table for a given α is one that has marginal probabilities (.5, .5) for both rows and columns. That is, all marginal effects on the expected probabilities have been "removed." In short, the size of Yule's Y tells us how much more probable it is that an observation will fall into a diagonal cell rather than an off-diagonal cell (cf. Bishop et al., 1975). Since it is a ratio scale measure, with an absolute value bounded between (0, 1), it can be averaged and compared across domains.

Since Y is not commonly employed in the sociological literature, it may be helpful to suggest yet another way of interpreting it. Each Y corresponds to a specific probability of falling into the diagonal cells of the standardized 2 x 2 table. To obtain this probability, simply calculate $P = (Y + 1) / 2$. For instance, if Y is 0.4, then the probability of observations falling on the diagonal (the co-present and co-absent cells) is $(0.4 + 1) / 2 = 0.7$. By subtraction, the probability of being in the off-diagonal cell is 0.3.

Table 4: Selected Comparisons of Yule's Y as Measure of Paired Event Linkage for the Four Policy Domains

	Policy Domain			
	Agriculture	Energy	Health	Labor
Average absolute linkage (|Y|)	.257	.240	.302	.172[a]
Average positive linkage (Y ≥ 0)	.221	.227	.231	.172[a]
Average negative linkage (Y ≤ 0)	-.308	-.253	-.378	-.172[a]
Average linkage (Y)	+.004	-.016	-.063	+.088[a]
% of Positive Y's	58.9	49.5	51.6	75.3[a]
% of Negative Y's	41.1	50.5	48.4	24.7[a]

a In the labor domain, the eighth event had only two participants. As a result, there were many Yule Y's of +1 or -1, which greatly affected the averages. To avoid this, we dropped the pairings which included Event 8 from the analysis reported here. For the sake of strict comparability, the unadjusted averages for labor are .235, .218, -.285, and .094 for the first four row entries in the labor column, respectively.

tion (or joint absence) will occur on labor events than an observation of mixed (present/absent) participation. The agriculture domain has a considerably less strong tendency toward a positive bias of event linkage within its set of events, while both energy and health have roughly equal numbers of positively and negatively linked pairings of events. In the case of energy these balance out so that there is no net bias of linkage (-.016) among the pairings of events - in other words, random linkage among events is the norm. Consistent with this finding of independence among energy events, Laumann and Knoke (1987) present a diverse array of empirical indicators that the energy domain lacked institutionalization of the rules of the game so far as access and participation were concerned. The health domain, on the other hand, has a net negative bias (-.064) in event linkages. Remember that a negative Y represents a systematic dependency between two events in the sense that inactivity in one event is nonrandomly associated with activity in the other. This negative bias in health was observed in the earlier study (Laumann/ Knoke 1987: chap. 4 and 11) as well and can be shown to be related to the fact that biomedical research controversies tend to attract a very different set of actors from those active in the other health-related events - that is, those organizations interested in biomedical research issues participate exclusively in those and avoid all other events, and the converse is also true.

Some degree of patterned participation across sets of events was anticipated, of course, since the events were drawn from domains of presumably interrelated concerns. A similar analysis of participation in events drawn from wholly unrelated policy areas (so that there is no coherent or systematic patterning of actor participation from one event to another) would produce an average Yule's Y approximating zero. A negatively signed Y is likely to occur when the paired events are drawn from disjunctive policy domains where participation in one event precludes participation in the other. Overall, one must be struck by the relative lack of interdependencies among our events, even though they are all drawn from a presumptively common universe of concern.

Much can be learned from a careful examination of the patterning of the Yule's Y across the set of events in a domain (e.g., the existence of relatively sharply demarcated subdomains). We must defer such an examination to another occasion. For present purposes, we need only point out that while the co-presence of actors in pairs of events is sometimes substantially greater than chance, common participation in pairs of events nevertheless involves relatively few actors. This fact gains in significance when we examine the extent to which actors' preferences for particular outcomes co-vary across the events because it tells us that we can expect only small numbers of common actors in randomly drawn pairs of events. To put it another way, if the average rate of participation in events is about 20 percent of the total sample, then we can expect by chance that only 4 percent (.20 x .20) of the actors will jointly appear in any two events having these rates of participation. Since the participation patterns are only modestly tied across events (i.e., the average Y's are somewhat larger than chance), we can expect only a few more common participants across pairs of scenarios than would be predicted by chance.

4   The Structure of Conflict and Consensus

Those concerned with analyzing conflict and consensus in the resolution
of policy issues may well ask how our approach deals with such matters.
In light of the multitude of parties, both public and private, who are
actively engaged in controversies over diverse policy issues, is it possible
to specify principles that organize interested parties in a stable structure
of cleavage and cooperation? Should we expect, on the contrary, a fluid
structure of almost random coalitions and oppositions for each contested
event? Given a system of fluid coalitions, agreement or opposition between any pair of interested parties in a given event would depend
solely on calculations of the marginal advantages and disadvantages of
each policy option. Such calculations are unlikely to provide very consistent bases for ordering preferences across corporate actors, save, perhaps,
for those whose organizational mandate is to be ideologically consistent
even with respect to the most arcane "technical" questions.

To what extent, then, do actors' preferences in one event covary with
their preferences in another? Strictly speaking, this refers to behavioral
or revealed preferences and not to attitudes or "true" preferences. An
actor reveals its preference in a given event only if it participates in its
resolution on a particular side (including an explicit fence-straddling
position). The actor may harbor strong views about most of the events
we asked about, but only those in which it acted will count in the analysis. Each organizational actor was attributed its preferred outcome in an
event on the basis of the consensual report of one or more informant
representatives acting in its behalf.[11] Of the 190 Spearman rank-order
correlations in each domain (20 x 19 / 2), we found only 7.9%, 10.5%,
8.9%, and 41.6% in the agriculture, energy, health, and labor domains,
respectively, that were significant at the $p < .05$ level or less (two-tailed
test). Only the labor domain, by all accounts the most polarized and
ideologically motivated, shows a high proportion of significant correlations between organizations' preferred outcomes across pairs of events.

---

11   If active in an event, an organization was assigned to one of three positions: "1" for
     "pro," "2" for "no position" or "ambivalent," and "3" for "con." Inactive organizations
     were treated as missing cases. Spearman's rho's were then computed for every pairing
     of events to measure the degree to which the jointly active organizations' position in
     one event were associated with its position in the second.

In sum, we observe only modest evidence of linkage among events with respect to participation and preferred outcomes in all four domains. To be sure, a small subset of events are closely interconnected and manifest consistent cleavages - but persistent cleavages appear very much to be the exception to the rule. One interpretation of these results would suggest that technocratic and strategic, rather than systematically ideological, considerations drive actors' participation in most policy controversies in the four domains.

In general, individual organizational actors maintain portfolios of issue concerns in which they have an interest. Each actor's portfolio of expressed interests effectively links these issues to one another in distinctive ways. Actors sharing issue portfolios constitute issue publics that are, in turn, linked in greater or lesser proximity to one another as a result of their variable overlapping interests. Thus linkage of events is in part a function of the concatenation of individual actors' interests. Moreover, the events themselves are linked to other events in the past on various grounds, they overlap in the present with other events that compete for attention or frame political debate, and they are linked to future, anticipated events. In acting strategically with respect to given events, therefore, every actor constructs a unique web of linked events and interests that influences the decision to participate and with what effect.

An alternative explanation for the observed low level of connectedness of participation and preference points to the important distinction between intra-organizationally preferred and publicly revealed preferences. Our data refer primarily to the final stages of long processes in which options proposed by various interested parties are progressively winnowed, leaving only a handful of "viable" alternatives to be placed on the formal governmental agenda. Although actors have well articulated preferences for particular outcomes, participants in the endgame must engage in a form of strategic action in which selecting a course of action entails an evaluation of the implications (linkages) of each option for the actor's other current or future objectives, subject to the constraints imposed by their past actions. Such considerations oftentimes support the strategic endorsement of the winning option despite strong initial and continuing preferences for some other alternative. The actor settles for the least "bad" outcome when it faces the prospect of losing anyway - especially if, by going along, one may win even minor concessions. One may also hope that one can redress the balance of costs and benefits in future interactions on other issues. Calculations that lead to joining the winning side are especially likely in recurrent events under generally nonadversarial conditions. Only events that are episodic (nonrecurrent) and/or have clear winners and losers tend to lead the opposing sides to fight to the bitter end.

To this point, our argument would seem to imply that there is very little coherence or pattern in the multifaceted controversies and selective choruses of agreement arising in the four domains. To the contrary, however, we do expect to observe highly patterned structures of consensus and cleavage in each domain. To appreciate this surprising contention in the face of the relatively low association across events in participation and preferences, we call attention to the linkages among the actors with respect to their policy interests, information exchanges, and involvement in institutionalized decision making arenas. Laumann/ Knoke (1987: chap. 4, 7 and 8) demonstrated that the flow of candid and confidential information follows well worn channels among actors sharing common interests and broadly similar postures toward issues of importance to them. That is, actors regularly turn to trusted others for interpretive and strategic information concerning "what is going on" and "what is to be done." Timely information gained from these confidential exchanges helps to orchestrate the individual actors' strategic policy interventions. The pattern of confidential exchanges in a given policy domain constitutes the *enduring* structure that binds the actors. Analogously, we might speak of such a structure as a crystal that is left intact or subjected to breakage along different fault lines, depending on the blows it receives from various policy-relevant events.

Figures 3 through 6 depict the first two dimensions of the three-dimensional smallest space solutions (Schiffman et al. 1981) for the four policy domains, derived from the input proximity matrices described in the footnote below.[12]

---

12 To calculate the input matrices for multidimensional scaling, we first assigned organizations to their preferred outcomes on each event, as described in footnote 11. The affinity - antagonism based proximities were then estimated in three stages. First, for each of the 20 events in a domain, we constructed two social dissimilarity matrices: one corresponding to the affinity in positions (shared preferences in outcomes) between pairs of organizations and the second corresponding to their opposed positions to one another. For the affinity matrix, the element (i, j) will be "0" if the position of organization i and j are not missing for the event and if their positions match, otherwise the element will be "1." For the antagonism matrix, the element (i, j) will be "1" if either i or j is "for" while the other is "against" the option; otherwise the element will be "0." In both matrices,

Figure 3: Organizations in the Agriculture Domain

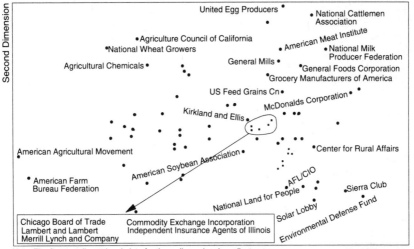

Note: The first two-dimensional plot of a three-dimensional smallest space solution depicting the proximities of 117 organizations with respect to their pro and con positions on 20 selected events. (Kruskal stress = .17, R^2= 85.3%)

Each three-dimensional solution achieved quite acceptable Kruskal stress and R^2 coefficients, despite the large number of points being plotted, indicating good fits between the monotonic transformation of the original proximities and the derived distances.

"0" means similar whereas "1" means dissimilar. Second, we stacked the 40 binary matrices, 20 for affinity and 20 for opposition - i.e., two for each column-wise Pearson correlations to generate the N by N proximity of the 20 events, to form a comprehensive matrix of N by 40 N in size, where N = the number of organizations in the domain. We then computed column-wise Pearson correlations to generate the N by N proximity matrix. This procedure is akin to the analysis of multiple networks with procedures such as CONCOR (Arabie et al. 1978) for blockmodeling. There is one critical difference: The dummy matrices used in our method refer to dissimilarity matrices whereas those of multiple network analysis refer to the presence/absence of ties regardless whether the ties signify social similarity or dissimilarity. Thirdly, the proximity matrix estimated in stage 2 is submitted to ALSCAL (Schiffman et al. 1981) in SAS for nonmetric multidimensional scaling. In general, the fitted distance between two organizations in the resulting spatial solution is inversely related to the degree of structural equivalence of the two organizations in terms of their affinity and oppositional linkages to other organizations in the space.

Figure 4: Organizations in the Energy Domain

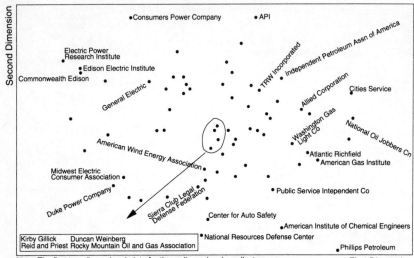

Note: The first two-dimensional plot of a three-dimensional smallest space solution depicting the proximities of 103 organizations with respect to their pro and con positions on 20 selected events. (Kruskal stress = .17, R^2= 78.4%)

First Dimension

In all four solutions, one finds a tight cluster of organizations in the central region that includes the law firms, consulting firms, and certain trade associations that participate relatively infrequently.[13] These organizations are retained or consulted by clients that vary from matter to matter and they are not consistently partisan on the major issues of the domains. By contrast, the peripheral locations ringing the spaces are occupied by major advocacy or claimant organizations that speak, with frequency, for a fairly narrow and consistent range of interests. Since over one-hundred organizations are plotted in each solution, it is difficult to discern the basic pattern in the welter of detail. To facilitate perception of the underlying pattern, we have plotted the locations of all the organizations but have provided the names for only a select few that typify the organizations to be found in a localized region of the space. To imagine the general shape of each solution, one might think of a sphere on whose

13   The Pearson correlations between the number of events in which an organization participated and the distance the organization was located from the centroid of the three-dimensional solution were .85, .79, .85 and .89 for agriculture, energy, health, and labor respectively (p < .001).

Figure 5: Organizations in the Health Domain

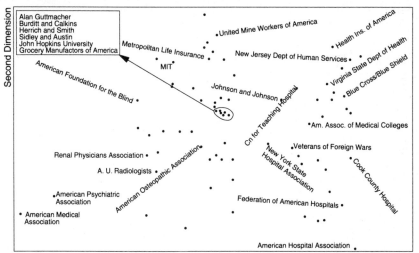

Note: The first two-dimensional plot of a three-dimensional smallest space solution depicting the proximities of 120 organizations with respect to their pro and con positions on 20 selected events. (Kruskal stress = .17, R^2= 84.9%)

surface is distributed the peripherally located actors, with a tight cluster of organizations-usually law and public relations firms-located roughly at the core or central region of the sphere. Throughout the body of the sphere are scattered organizations located at different radial distances from the center of the sphere as a function of their level of event participation - the less active being closer to the center and the more active being farther to the periphery (surface) of the sphere.

For example, in Figure 3, we find the American Agricultural Movement at the extreme lower lefthand side of the space diametrically opposite the National Cattlemen's Association at the upper righthand corner (shades of the range wars!), and the Environmental Defense Fund in the lower righthand corner, thus forming an equilateral triangle of opposing interests in agricultural politics. The Farm Bureau, like its more politically radical neighbor in the space, the American Agricultural Movement, represents grain producers. The Cattlemen's interests are generally aligned with those groups that process and consume grain, including the Milk Producers, General Mills, the Grocery Manufacturers Association, and so forth. The Environmental Defense Fund is the most active of the labor, environmental, and consumer groups that challenge, among other things, the farmers' use of pesticides and water.

Figure 6: Organizations in the Labor Domain

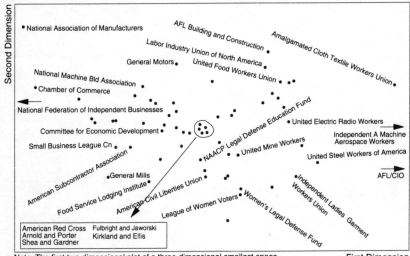

Note: The first two-dimensional plot of a three-dimensional smallest space solution depicting the proximities of 106 organizations with respect to their pro and con positions on 20 selected events. (Kruskal stress = .13, R^2= 92.4%)

First Dimension

With respect to the energy domain (Figure 4), four sectoral quadrants can be roughly delineated, beginning in the upper lefthand corner with the public utilities (and their principal trade association, the Edison Electric Institute), and going clockwise to the upper righthand corner with the big oil interests (and the American Petroleum Institute as their key spokesman), to the lower righthand corner with the natural gas interests (and the American Gas Institute), and, finally, to the lower lefthand side with its environmentalist organizations (including the National Resources Defense Council at the bottom of the space).

The health domain (Figure 5) is also roughly organized into four sectors ringing the center. In the northwest quadrant, we find miscellaneous consumers of health care and labor unions. Moving to the northeast quadrant, we observe the third-party payers of health care costs. The southeast corner is populated by hospitals and hospital trade associations such as the American Hospital Association (an extreme outlier, being one of the most active participants in the policy domain). Finally, in the southwest corner, we find the major professional associations of health-care providers, with the American Medical Association being the extreme outlier.

Figure 6 depicting the labor domain is organized rather neatly, as one might have expected, into a bipolar opposition structure with the unions arrayed on the righthand side and the major employers and their trade associations on the left. The AFL/CIO is the extreme outlier on the right, and the National Association of Manufacturers and the US Chamber of Commerce are diametrically opposite at the extreme leftside of the space. Worth noting is the internal ordering of the two sides. The pairings of sparring partners (e.g., General Motors versus the United Automobile Workers (U.A.W.), General Mills and the Food Service and Lodging Institute versus the United Food Workers) are located diametrically opposite one another, on a rotating axis around the center. Put another way, the employer side arrays its constituent elements from the heavy and intermediate manufacturing companies in the north to the light industry and service businesses, such as construction and food processing, in the south. The converse ordering of the counterpart unions from north to south is to be observed on the union side of the space.

If one treats these solutions as depicting the overall structure of coalition and cleavage among organizations across the diverse array of policy controversies in a domain, one can then examine each policy event separately to see how a particular event split that structure into opposing parts. A detailed examination of the 80 events in hand, in which we identified the regions of support and opposition in each controversy, is highly suggestive about the distinctive politics that characterize each domain. Presentation of such an examination would exhaust the reader's patience, so we must summarize our principal conclusions based on a detailed inspection of these plots. First, we observe that the supporter and opponent sectors are usually delineated in distinctive regions; in only a few controversies are supporters and opponents mixed together in common regions. Yet the patterns of cleavage shift dramatically from event to event as the substantive content changes. More starkly put, with the possible exception of the labor domain where there is evidence of a recurrent polarized axis of cleavage between labor and management, the domains reveal *no single axis of cleavage* that might coincide with an ideological dimension of liberalism/conservatism, defined economically or socially. On the contrary, it appears that an axis of cleavage following the diameter of the spherical spatial solution can be almost indefinitely rotated in any direction as the distinctive features of given controversies differentially capture the attention of organizational interests.

To illustrate this point, let us consider the case of controversies in agricultural policy. One observes a clear split over a proposal to raise acreage limitations on federally irrigated land. Environmental groups are on one side and the United Farm Workers and California farm organizations, beet sugar, cotton, and cattle producers, are on the other. But there is an even more lopsided contest over increased price supports for grain between various grain producers, including the Farm Bureau and regional and local grain producer organizations, and a small number of grain buyers, including CARE, an organization in favor of high production and low prices that was opposed to the higher price supports because it would increase the price of grain on international markets. None of the participants in the controversy over federally irrigated land were active in the fight over grain price supports. On the other hand, proposals to make the Delaney Clause's ban on carcinogens in food additives less stringent were supported by virtually all the food processing interests and opposed by most environmental groups and some labor unions. Two other agricultural events presented yet other interest constellations. Legislation rolling back dairy price supports drew support and opposition from scattered positions throughout the space. The milk producers, dairy state farm bureaus, and national farm organizations were opposed, while retail food and food processor interests were in favor. Cuts in food welfare were passed even though they were opposed by a wide array of producers, environmental, labor, and humanitarian groups and supported by only two or three organizations. Notably absent from this contest were the national farmer groups.

One of the most divisive controversies of the period took place in the health domain regarding hospital cost containment. The issue split the space in half. In the lower half, hospitals, hospital trade associations, and their allies opposed the imposition of mandatory caps on hospital charges. In the top half of the space, third-party payer and consumer groups supported the caps. In the case of cost reporting for Medicare and Medicaid programs, the cleavage line rotated 90 degrees so that opponents of uniform cost reporting - notably the hospital associations and third party payer groups - were arrayed against various consumer groups who wanted to avoid the creation of a two-tiered system of medical reimbursement that discriminated between the poor and the elderly and everyone else. A somewhat different split arose between opponents of the proposed phaseout of health planning schemes, mostly the state and local governmental bodies that derived some influence and control over health care delivery systems in their jurisdictions, and the hospital and medical interest groups that found these planning schemes to be sources of interference. The proposed Delaney Clause revision shows yet another pattern of cleavage that arrayed a tight cluster of food processing interests against a handful of consumer advocates. Finally, the issue concerning prospective medical payments based on categories of illness rotates the axis of cleavage to a vertical plane, where hospital and third-party payers were allied as proponents. The scheme was seen as likely to result in "loose" and highly favorable government-guaranteed payments for services rendered. These interests were opposed by a cross-section of professional medical groups who were concerned about the rigidities likely to arise from categorizing patients on the basis of diagnoses that are subject to change. The energy events display a similar multidimensional combination of structure and fluidity, as was observed for the agriculture and health domains.

While the labor events reproduce the polar antagonism between business and labor, they also reveal differences in the activation of various segments of the oppositional structure depending on the issue involved. Proposals for labor law reform stimulate the entire northern hemisphere of unions and trade associations, plus the AFL/CIO. The question of OSHA enforcement was primarily a concern of industrial employers and unions, but also prompted involvement by women's groups, firefighters, and transportation workers, who typically are not labor militants. The ambivalence of organized labor about civil rights is portrayed in the issue over affirmative action where the unions stood on the sidelines while business groups and civil rights groups did battle.

Returning to the analogy of breaking a crystal, we know that how the crystal splits depends on the strength and precise incidence of the chisel blow, given the structure of the crystal. Similarly, much of the strategic action of event participants, including even the matter of who decides to participate and on what side, depends upon how the issue is framed. The manner of framing may selectively energize the interests and actions of certain domain members and discourage others from entering the deliberations. A consensual chorus results when the accepted frame neutralizes the mobilization of potential opponents by stressing the facilitative, nonadversarial character of the policy question.

5   Structural Stability Across Presidential Administrations

How stable are these configurations of actors? One could easily imagine that new decision making events, arising in different Congresses or Presidential administrations, would result in substantial reorganization of the organizational proximities. Alternatively, stable proximities among organizations might resist change in the face of changing administrations and related historical circumstances. As a first cut at this intriguing question, we propose to use the proximities of organizations estimated from their participation in events during the Carter administration to predict the proximities of these same organizations during the first two years of the Reagan administration. Table 5 presents the correlations of the pairwise proximities for the Carter period (1977-80), using the procedure described as stage 2 in footnote 12, with those estimated on the basis of the events arising during 1981-82.

Table 5: Product-moment Correlations between Organizational Proximities during the Carter Administration and those of the Reagan Administration

	Pearson Correlation	Sample Size [a]	Significance
Agriculture	.19	(N = 6,786)	P < .01
Energy	-.02	(N = 5,253)	P ≈ .06 [b]
Health	.26	(N = 7,140)	P < .01
Labor	.29	(N = 5,565)	P < .01

a Sample size is the number of pairwise proximities in a domain, which is calculated as n(n-1)/2 where n = number of organizations in the policy domain. It is difficult to calculate the degrees of freedom to evaluate the statistical significance of the Pearson correlation because there are, when all is said and done, only n organizations and only n-1 possible partners. In this case we used the original proximity, as calculated in footnote 12, and not the fitted Euclidean distance, which would restrict the degree of freedom to n-2.
b one-tailed

Rather surprisingly, three of the four domains show comparable, but very modest, intertemporal correlations between the two Presidential administrations, with the energy domain displaying essentially no stability. (We are interpreting the strength of the correlation as a rough measure of intertemporal stability. Negative correlations would suggest radical re-organization of the policy domain's structure of consensus and cleavage.) In both the Laumann-Knoke study and this work, the energy domain displays a very low level of institutionalization when compared to the other domains on a number of different indicators. It is worth noting that labor has the highest correlation across time, but even it fails to be especially strong despite its reputation for long-term polarization of the participants into well-defined warring camps.

Since we lack comparable figures for other time periods, it is difficult to draw firm conclusions about the relative volatility of policy making structures over time. The changes alleged to have been wrought by the Reagan Presidency in the conception and implementation of welfare state policies are entirely consistent with the low intertemporal correlations we observe. One suspects, however, that casual observers greatly exaggerate the degree of stability of participation, consensus and cleavage in policy making. Even full-time ideologists would be hard pressed to specify the "correct" position on the myriad "technical" issues demanding resolution. Absent such consistency-producing principles, one should expect to find, as we do, that organizations' preferences are very loosely coupled from event to event because each event is seen as presenting unique or distinct features that must be taken into account and that render them distinguishably different from other events possessing broadly similar content (cf. Laumann/ Knoke 1987: chap. 12, 14).

6   Concluding Remarks

The principal observation of this analysis is the remarkable orderliness in the patterning of consensus and cleavage in the four policy domains. Except perhaps for the labor domain, however, it is not an orderliness that is easily comprehended by one or two broad analytic distinctions. The positions of organizations are not based simply on pervasive ideological disagreements or master corporate identities that are closely associated with known and unchanging interests. The structure is best thought of as a multidimensional set of distinctions that are selectively activated by the particular framing of issue events presented in a certain sequence. Each actor possesses an array of corporate interests, resources, and linkages with others - i.e., strategic considerations - that motivate and constrain the positions it takes. To study such structures more effectively, we must devise more sophisticated methods for capturing the global character of this multidimensionally organized interface of events and actors.

References

Arabie, Phipps/ Scott A. Boorman/ Paul R. Leavitt, 1978: Constructing blockmodels: How and why. In: *Journal of Mathematical Psychology* 17, 21-63.

Bishop, Y./ S. E. Fienberg/ Paul W. Holland, 1975: *Discrete Multivariate Analysis: Theory and Practice*. Cambridge, Mass.: M.I.T. Press.

Bok, D./ J. Dunlop, 1970: *Labor and the American Community*. New York: Simon and Schuster.

Chubb, John E., 1983: *Interest Groups and Bureaucracy: The Politics of Energy*. Palo Alto: Stanford University Press.

Davis, David H., 1982: *Energy Politics*. Third Edition. New York: St. Martin's Press.

Greenstone, J. David, 1969: *Labor in American Politics*. New York: Knopf.

Guither, H., 1980: *The Food Lobbyists*. Lexington, Mass.: Lexington Books.

Hadwiger, D./ W. Browne (eds.), 1978: *The New Politics of Food*. Lexington, Mass.: Lexington Books.

Heclo, H., 1978: Issue Networks and the Executive Establishment. In: A. King (ed.), *The New American Political System*. Washington D.C..

Heinz, John P., 1962: The political impasse in farm support legislation. In: *Yale Law Journal* 71, 952-978.

Heinz, John P./ Edward O. Laumann/ Robert Nelson/ Robert Salisbury, 1987: Private representation in Washington: Surveying the structure of influence. In: *American Bar Foundation Research Journal* (Winter), 141-200.

Heinz, John P./ Edward O. Laumann/ Robert Nelson/ Robert Salisbury, 1990: Inner circles or hollow cores? Elite networks in national policy systems. In: *Journal of Politics* 52 (May), 356-390.

Heinz, John P./ Edward O. Laumann/ Robert Nelson/ Robert Salisbury, 1991: *Hollow Cores. Interest Representation in National Policy-Making*. Cambridge, Mass.: Harvard University Press.

Knoke, David/ Edward O. Laumann, 1982: The social organization of national policy domains: An exploration of some structural hypotheses. In: Peter V. Marsden/ Nan Lin (eds.), *Social Structure and Network Analysis*. Bevery Hills, CA: Sage Publications, 255-270.

Laumann, Edward O./ John P. Heinz, 1985: Washington lawyers and others: The structure of Washington representation. *Stanford Law Review* 37, 465-502.

Laumann, Edward O./ David Knoke, 1987: *The Organizational State: Social Choice in National Policy Domains*. Madison, Wisconsin: University of Wisconsin Press.

Laumann, Edward O./ David Knoke/ Yong-Hak Kim, 1985: An organizational approach to state policy formation: A comparative study of energy and health domains. In: *American Sociological Review* 50, 1-19.

Marmor, Theodore R., 1970: *The Politics of Medicare*. Chicago: Aldine.

Nelson, Robert/ John P. Heinz, with Edward O. Laumann/ Robert H. Salisbury, 1988: Lawyers and the structure of influence in Washington. In: *Law and Society Review* 22: 237-300.

Salisbury, Robert H., 1984: Interest representation: The dominance of institutions. In: *American Political Science Reivew* 78, 64-76.

Schiffman, Susan S./ M. Lance Reynolds/ Forrest W. Young, 1981: *Introduction to Multidimensional Scaling: Theory, Methods, and Applications*. New York: Academic Press.

Shapiro, Andrew, 1985: Sampling procedures. Washington Representative Study, 1982-1985. August 21, 1985.

Starr, Paul, 1982: *The Social Transformation of American Medicine. The Rise of a Sovereign Profession and the Making of a Vast Industry*. New York: Basic Books, Inc.

Wilson, Graham, 1979: *Unions in American National Politics*. London: Macmillan.

Chapter 4
Policy Networks in the German Telecommunications Domain

Volker Schneider and Raymund Werle

1 Telecommunications as a Domain of Public Policy

State control of technology is a topic receiving increasing academic attention. The interest of social science in the role of the state in technology development is rather new, although public policy related to technology can be traced back to the industrial take-off. Especially in all European countries the provision of a telecommunications infrastructure with technologies such as the telegraph, the telephone and also new communications systems such as computer networks, facsimile transmission and interactive videotex has been an undisputed state function and a governmental prerogative that only recently was challenged by a new technological revolution.

The telecommunications domain that has emerged since can be related to a network of technological components enabling communication over distance. However, such a purely technical perspective would overlook the network of actors and the configuration of social forces which are linked by vested interests and various concerns to the purely technical configuration. The telecommunications sector is therefore also a system of actors - an action domain - where specific economic, technical and political interests are at stake, where resources are mobilized and exchanged and where individual and collective strategies are pursued. In addition, telecommunications also provides political and economic arenas

For helpful comments we thank Philipp Genschel, Renate Mayntz, Fritz W. Scharpf, Uwe Schimank and Susanne Schmidt, and for technical assistance we are grateful to Günter Schröder. We also appreciate the assistance of Doris Gau who carried out the interviews concerning the telecommunications reform and Jürgen Bienzeisler who prepared the data set for the analysis and produced a data documentation and a codebook. Thanks to Susan Wylegala-Häusler for linguistic assistance.

structured by established institutions which define "the rules of the game" that shape the actors' interaction, confrontation and cooperation.[1]

The aim of this chapter is primarily to contribute to the analysis of public policy and not to the study of a given technology. Therefore we are not interested in everyday activities in telecommunications such as the use of the telephone or the manufacturing of switching facilities. Our interest, instead, is focused on actor configurations and institutional arrangements shaping public policies in this technology domain. Telecommunications in this sense is not only seen as a general system of action but more specifically as a *domain of public policy* in which relevant actors engage in processes of decision making and resource mobilization which are oriented towards solving economic or social problems gaining political relevance. This may be the provision of a new infrastructure service by the state, but also the structural or institutional redefinition of public functions in this sector.

The entities making up a public policy domain's system of actors are those acting units which are "concerned with formulating, advocating and selecting courses of action that are intended to resolve the substantive problem in question".[2] In contemporary societies these are typically corporate actors - public and private organizations or associations. Since their "capacities to affect the collective outcomes of policy decisions must be taken into account by the other participants", the telecommunications domain must be conceived as a social action system[3] in which the units do not act in isolation but take their respective resources, interests and strategies into account. Such relations of mutual taking-into-acount and resource dependency lead to networks of routinized interaction. Policy domains are constituted therefore by one or more *policy networks*.

---

1   Such rules may emerge out of social interactions, stabilizing and reinforcing the patterns of behaviour, or they may be enacted more or less intentionally and formally. For a discussion of these institutionalist concepts see Langlois (1986) and Scharpf (1989).

2   Cf. Knoke/ Laumann (1982: 256). This *policy* perspective assumes not only a common orientation among a set of actors but also their mutual relevance for each other (see also Wright 1988: 609-610). It contrasts the wider, less specific concept of "relevant social groups" which is employed by some scholars in order to explain the evolution and development of technological *artifacts*. These groups comprise institutions, organizations and all kinds of unorganized groups including consumers or users as long as they "share the same set of meanings attached to a specific artifact" (Pinch/ Bijker 1984: 414).

3   Laumann/ Knoke/ Kim (1985: 2). For a broad and detailed elaboration of the concept of corporate action see Coleman (1990, esp. chapters 16, 19 and 20). See also Mayntz (1986).

The topology and specific configuration of such networks has to be seen as an important structural property of the policy domain.

In the following sections, we will identify different policy networks making up the telecommunications domain. It will be shown that this is not a fluid or amorphous field of actors and events but is shaped by a long history of interaction. An introductory description of the historical emergence and transformation of institutional arrangements and governance structures in German telecommunications will help to understand the current topology of policy networks. We will show that due to technical, economic and political factors, highly differentiated, comparatively large and rather pluralistic policy networks evolved in this sector. This finding will be evidenced in the third and fourth section by two case studies illuminating the actual decision making and interaction structures in two recent "issue areas": Firstly, a policy network which was involved in the introduction of a new service, and secondly, a network which was generated by the recent institutional reform of the German telecom sector. By comparing both networks in the concluding section we will try to conceptionalize the telecommunications policy domain as a sector with differentiated but relatively stable and partly overlapping policy networks which are routinely involved in the processing of policy problems. These networks, however, are not sharply delineated sub-systems but often transcend the classical boundaries of the telecommunications policy domain and overlap with other domains of public policy - without impairing this domain's identity.

2   The History of German Telecommunications: Establishment and Transformation of an "Iron Triangle"

The history of German telecommunications begins with the introduction of telegraphy in the mid-1840s. The telephone emerged about 30 years later. The following major telecom inventions were radio and television in the 1920s and 1930s respectively. Computer-related transmission networks emerged in the 70s and 80s. All these technologies have a common specificity: they are based on network industries relying on the highly coordinated cooperation of different technical and economic actors in the development and operation of the system.[4]

In the early years of telephony, the local systems in some countries were established by private firms, at times with several competing local networks. In most cases, however, early competition quickly turned into oligopolistic or monopolistic market structures.[5] The general trend was thus a horizontal integration of telecommunications networks and the emergence of territorial monopolies. In some countries associational or cooperative management structures were established (Scandinavia and the rural US) but typically telephony developed very early into a hierarchical model of governance, either by private firms or public administration.[6] The tendency toward monopoly pricing by private monopolists as well as the growing infrastructural significance of telecommunication services were the driving forces pushing telephony under governmental control in most countries. Even in a liberal state such as Britain, the state gained total control over this sector in 1911. Although different modes of political governance were employed, basically two dominant forms have emerged. States have either directly engaged in telecommunications creating a public monopoly or they have established specialized agencies and enacted regulations in order to control the behavior of the dominant firms in the sector.[7]

The *state monopoly* in Germany can be traced back to the postal monopolies (royal postal prerogatives: "Postregal") of the late Middle Ages. Although the first telegraph line in Germany was introduced by the military in 1846, telegraphy was soon opened for commercial use and its administration moved from the War Office to the Post Office. This shaped the first steps of German telephone development decisively, because immediately after its invention, the German Post Office (GPO)

---

4   For a general discussion of the concept of "network industries" see Carlton/ Klamer (1983).
5   The most important examples for competitive market arrangements are the US in the period from 1895 to 1907 and Sweden from 1883 to 1918. Economists explain pressures toward monopolization of network industries mainly by the positive externalities of telecommunications networks (along with the number of subscribers, the utility of a network increases for each subscriber) and the related economies of scale; see Rohlfs (1974); Katz/ Shapiro (1985).
6   For the concept of governance that cannot be elaborated in this chapter see Williamson (1985) and Hollingsworth (1990).
7   For a comparative overview on different organizational forms in telecommunications see Pierce (1978) and Schneider (1991).

decided to use telephony as an extension of the telegraph network to rural areas. A few early applications by private businessmen for concessions to run telephone networks were rejected and telephony was declared a part of the official state monopoly. Hence from the very beginning, telecommunications in Germany was under "political control" and administrated by the PTT (post, telegraph and telephone administration).[8]

The status quo of the telephone system as a state monopoly was explicitly legalized in the Telegraph Act of 1892 and confirmed in the Telecommunications Installations Act of 1928. The PTT had the exclusive right to install, operate and maintain the telephone system which included transmission and exchange technology as well as the telephone handsets which were perceived as a constituent part of the technical network.

The PTT as a public administration only reluctantly expanded the system, although after a short time this business turned out to be rather profitable. Among the driving forces were the local and regional chambers of industry and commerce which soon discovered the usefulness of the telephone for business communication. They formed coalitions with the local public administrations to mobilize a minimum number of subscribers which the PTT had declared to be the necessary condition for the provision, construction and installation of a network. Organized business interests thus fulfilled an important function in the identification of demand and the minimization of allocational risks.[9]

The technical components of the telephone system were developed by the manufacturing industry in Germany. The PTT had only minimal technical competence and practically no R&D laboratories to engage in the process of the technical design and production of the system. The equipment was developed and produced by a small group of manufacturing firms in the field of electrical engineering ("the court suppliers").

---

8 The head of the PTT was the Post Office and later the Post Ministry, a branch of the central government. For the early history of the telephone in Germany see Thomas (1988).

9 For this observation see Holcombe (1911: 37-64) who concludes, "... the German system of a special representation of economic interests, and their cooperation with the public authorities in the management of business undertakings, has worked well. ... Thus the organizations of economic interests have an educational as well as administrative value. To this agency the German public trusts not only to get what it wants, but also to learn what it ought to want" (Holcombe 1911: 64).

Their tendency toward cartelization was accepted if not supported by the PTT. The problems of compatibility and network management required the PTT to opt for strict uniformity of all technical components (Einheitstechnik).[10] Consequently, the procurement policy was directed toward purchasing a specific item from a dominant manufacturer holding patent or other proprietary rights for the blueprint of this product. In order to prevent dependency on a single manufacturer, the PTT obliged the respective producer to grant patent rights to at least one national "competitor". As compensation, the firm was guaranteed a relatively high proportion of orders by the PTT.

The *emerging network* of actors may be represented by a simple *triangle*. The PTT as an integrated part of the central government cooperated and bargained on the one side with the local Chambers of Industry and Commerce, but especially with their peak association, the German Chamber of Industry and Commerce (Deutscher Industrie- und Handelstag, DIHT). Dominant issues were the quality of the telephone service, tariffs and other problems typically related to the use of the system. On the other side, there were close contacts to the equipment producers, especially to the large companies like Siemens. Here, problems of investment policy and technical research and development were important topics. In this triangle, the PTT was the dominant actor. After the 1920s, the triad became slightly more differentiated but in principle remained stable during the decades that followed.

With the Reichspost Budget Law of 1924, the legal status of the PTT was transformed from a government department, fully integrated into the central treasury, to a corporate-like public administration with its own property and budget separate from the central budget. The PTT was allowed to retain its revenues and to borrow money from the general capital market. This led to greater organizational autonomy and a reorganization and formalization of political control. An *Administrative Council* with up to 41 members, conceived as a quasi-parliament, consisted of political representatives from the central parliament (Reichstag), the chamber of the *Länder* (Reichsrat) and one from the Finance Minister of the central government. But also the employees of the PTT and the associations of industry, trade, commerce and agriculture were invited to send delegates to this council, so functional as well as territorial politi-

---

10 Also financial constraints and a continuing lack of adequately qualified technical staff brought the PTT to favor this option.

cal interests were represented in this *corporatist body*. The main function of the administrative council was controlling financial affairs and economic activities of the PTT.

The minister of the PTT was the political head and the executive manager of the telecommunications administration. He was charged with regulatory and operational competence in telecommunications. Political control of the PTT by actors other than the minister in charge was not formalized with the exception that the Minister of Finance had the right to approve all relevant financial affairs.

The Administrative Council did not replace the more *clientelist networks* of direct interaction between the PTT and the private manufacturing firms. It rather allowed for an institutionalized mix of political and economic elements of control in telecommunications. *The overall policy network in this sector became slightly more differentiated* and intricate, although the central position of the PTT remained unchanged or was even strengthened. A number of political actors, the manufacturers and the commercial users of the telephone system, were interested in a greater formalization of the intermediation of interests in telecommunications policy making.

The situation rapidly changed in the period of Nazi rule when matters of economic performance of the telephone system were clearly subordinated to political and military priorities (Thomas 1988: 197-202). The general strategy of the dominating party, the NSDAP, pushing the "unity of party and state" resulted in cutting down informal political networks and liquidating intermediary organizations. Concerning telecommunications, the Administrative Council was abolished. This measure was intended to reduce the organizational autonomy of the PTT by producing a hierarchical command structure and decision making process, and setting the organization free from economic considerations. Paradoxically, however, this partly increased the autonomy. Correlating this development, the PTT drifted into a situation of *isolation* - deteriorating technical innovation and sophistication (except for military purposes) - and also economic inefficiency.

After the Second World War, with the foundation of the Federal Republic of Germany, a federal PTT Ministry was re-established and in the early 1950s a very moderate political discussion started about the institutional reconstruction of the telecommunications domain. The state monopoly was not challenged at all but was perpetuated on the basis of the Telecommunications Installations Act of 1928. The question of reorganizing the PTT was answered rather quickly. In 1953, the model of the Reichspost Budget Law was transformed into a slightly modified new version called the PTT Administration Act. The separation of the PTT budget from the federal finances was confirmed as was the Administrative Council and its central competence. Though the number of members was reduced to 24, the composition of the re-established corporatist body changed only slightly.[11]

It should be noted that the PTT Administration Act ensured more elaborated rights of intervention for other ministers in the PTT affairs than the old Budget Law had done. The Minister of Economics had to approve the charges and utilization conditions for the telecommunications services and the Minister of Finance had to approve the PTT's budget (including debts, plans for investments etc.). On the other hand, the more informal interdependence of the PTT and the manufacturing industry remained unchanged by the Act, although the formal model of the PTT Administration Act was based on a conception of rather tightly coupled political and economic activities in telecommunications. Figure 1 shows the structure of the political-economic network in telecommunications as it had evolved in the 1950s and 1960s before major technological and economic changes triggered a network expansion and an increased separation of the political and economic sphere (cf. Werle 1990: 143).

As a public monopoly, the management and operation of the telecommunications system was not only oriented towards economic goals but was clearly a product of political processes, too. The *policy network* engaged in the major political decisions shaping telecommunications policy *during the* more than 20-year *post-war period was rather small.* Besides the formally involved political actors like the federal cabinet, several ministries (first of all the PTT Ministry), the Federal Parliament (members of Parliament and certain committees) and the Federal Council, only the political parties (especially through their activities in parliamentary committees), the postal workers' unions and the DIHT continuously participated. The equipment manufacturing firms did not play a significant political role but restricted their direct participation to economic

---

11 The Federal Parliament (Bundestag) and the Federal Council (Bundesrat) could send 5 representatives each into that assembly. Another 5 delegates were recruited from industry, trade, commerce and agriculture. The council was completed by 7 members representing the staff of the PTT and two experts in telecommunications technology and finance respectively.

Figure 1: The Political-Economic Actor Network in the Early 1970s

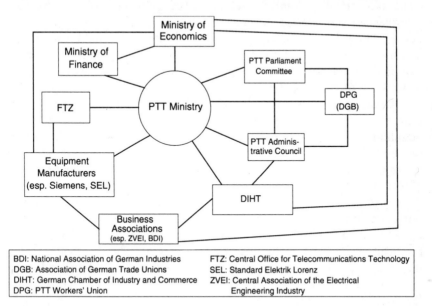

BDI: National Association of German Industries
DGB: Association of German Trade Unions
DIHT: German Chamber of Industry and Commerce
DPG: PTT Workers' Union
FTZ: Central Office for Telecommunications Technology
SEL: Standard Elektrik Lorenz
ZVEI: Central Association of the Electrical
Engineering Industry

activities. Here, they could rely on informal links among themselves and with the PTT Ministry and its engineering center, the Central Office for Telecommunications Technology (Fernmeldetechnisches Zentralamt, FTZ), which had been revitalized and stabilized after the war during the years of close cooperation when the future telecommunications system had to be designed.

In a first step the policy network grew moderately in the 1960s when telephony gradually expanded in residential areas, too. The PTT's problems in meeting the growing demand for telephones on the one hand, and the increasing political significance of the industrial activities in telecommunications on the other, triggered the engagement of additional actors. Especially the equipment-manufacturers in the electrical industry and its Central Association (Zentralverband der Elektrotechnischen Industrie, ZVEI) but also the peak association of industrial firms, the Federation of German Industry (Bundesverband der Deutschen Industrie, BDI) appeared on the stage although the DIHT remained the most visible representative of economic interests in telecommunications outside the PTT.

During the expansion process of the telephone system, it became more obvious that political and economic decision making processes intermeshed and overlapped but only few actors participated in all processes. Many actions had to be legitimized politically and economically and their effects were difficult to project. Raising telephone charges, for example, could either provoke political protest and a loss of votes or a decrease of usage and dissatisfaction with the service, or both.

An effort to reduce these problems by an institutional separation of regulatory and operational functions in telecommunications failed at the beginning of the 1970s. But it became obvious that with the increasing number of actors in telecommunications not every actor was able and willing to engage in all kinds of activities. At the beginning of the 1950s, only a handful of actors participated in the discussion of the PTT Administration Act; about 15 years later, the debate on the reform of this act activated approximately 10 associations (including two workers' unions) outside the official circle of political actors (government officials, political parties etc.) and almost a dozen experts. The equipment manufacturers and other economic actors remained in the background.

This suggests that - as a consequence or at least as a correlate of the process of expansion and differentiation in the area of telecommunications services and equipment - differently composed actor networks have evolved to deal with either more political or more economic problems in this sector. This differentiation does not necessarily imply total separation of networks and actors. But it clearly led to the emergence of relatively autonomous clusters of interaction based on the division of labor in complex societies.

As long as purely economic decisions affect public policies, governmental agencies will also try to influence, and participate in these decision making processes and not restrict themselves to politics. One therefore should expect that the PTT Ministry holds central positions in almost all of the co-existing networks. In the following sections we will look at two of these actor networks which evolved in the process of growth and differentiation in telecommunications.

3   Policy Networks in the Introduction of a New
    Telecommunications Service: The Case of Videotex
    (Bildschirmtext)

Bildschirmtext (Btx) is a new telecommunications service which combines
the telephone, video and computer technology.[12] Its purpose is to make
the exchange of visually displayed information between videotex terminals possible. The core of the system is an information data base and
a number of text communication facilities (electronic mail). This idea
of an easy-to-use electronic data service for the mass public emerged
in the mid-70s and inspired politicians and businessmen to see this technology as the communications infrastructure of the future, giving everybody access to the world of computer information. However, in most
countries, with the exception of France, these hopes did not come true
and the use of videotex is still restricted to specialists.

The German Bildschirmtext system was introduced between 1975
and 1984 and this introduction was heavily promoted by the German
PTT and a number of industrial actors.[13] The primary interest of the PTT
was, firstly, to get a new, future market which could complement the
almost saturated telephone business in the long run, and secondly, to
increase the utilization of the existing telephone network especially outside peak hours. After the first official demonstration of the system (initiated by the PTT in 1977) restricted trials began in 1978 involving the
PTT, certain equipment producers and about one hundred information
providers. In these pilot experiments, field trials were conducted from
1981 to 1983 which aimed at anticipating possible social and economic
consequences of the new service. Finally, the service was to be officially
started in the autumn of 1983, but due to technical snags, implementation
was delayed for almost one year.

In 1984, there still were great expectations: It was believed that at
the end of the decade, several millions of subscribers would be connected
to this service. Up to the end of 1990, however, Btx gained only about
250,000 users. Compared to the initial expectations and to the about 5

---

12   In other countries it is known by the names viewdata, videotext, Prestel, Teletel, and
     Telidon.
13   For a more detailed and comprehensive analysis of the introduction of videotex in Germa-
     ny see Schneider (1989).

million participants in the French videotex system, this service introduction was certainly not a success.

Although there is clearly no single explanation of the fatal German situation, an important determinant of the different development in the two countries is undoubtedly related to the institutional structures by which these service introductions were governed. In both countries, the preexisting public telecommunications monopoly turned videotex introduction - despite its commercial character - into a matter of public policy, involving the general political decision making machineries. Due to the German federalist decision making structure and also to the fact that the participating industry in Germany was much more autonomous and fragmented than its French counterpart, Btx could not be implemented with the same decisiveness that the French have demonstrated with their Minitels.

An important factor in the politicisation of the introduction of Btx was the relation of this new communication service to media policy. Since Btx allows not only the transmission of messages, but essentially provides an electronic infrastructure for the distribution and communication of information, it was thought to affect a number of actors in the traditional media sector. In Germany, this was the press, the broadcasters, and especially the *Länder* (federal states) as the authorities responsible for the German radio and television system. Other actors appeared from outside the media policy domain advocating data protection and consumer protection with respect to concerns of social groups which were anxious about negative impacts of the videotex technology on their life style and social situation.

During the Btx introduction in Germany, the PTT played a dominant role as coordinator and "system leader": It initiated the undertaking, shaped the core decisions of systems architecture, coordinated the establishment of the central computer network, controlled the installation of specialized telecommunications connections and led and coordinated to a large extent the public relations activities.

Despite this central position, the German PTT was far from achieving hierarchical control over the overall actor set. Btx not only interfered with other public policy domains but also in its indigenous field the PTT had to rely more and more on the cooperation of private firms competing under market conditions. The procurement of Btx terminal equipment was completely liberalized. In the first years of Btx development, the PTT was not even allowed to provide any terminals. This was not only due to its technical concept of Bildschirmtext relying on the normal TV set[14] but also to the growing demand for deregulation and liberalization (see next section). During the early 1980s, it became very difficult for the PTT to continue its traditional terminal procurement for new services. Since the "French strategy" of a completely state-led terminal diffusion[15] was "politically not feasible" in Germany,[16] the Bundespost had to use an indirect approach which was not entirely unsuccessful. Despite a lack of traditional ties to private TV set manufacturers or to the press, the German PTT was able to motivate a larger number of actors for cooperation by a series of financial incentives, organizational and informational support (e.g. research funding, coordination of trials and presentations, support by extensive marketing activities, etc.).

Similar problems arose in the information business since the PTT as a "common carrier" could not offer information services itself. The growth of an information market within the videotex system thus depended on the successful motivation and stimulation of private firms, primarily from the print media sector, to engage in this new market.

Seen from the perspective of governance, the German Btx was introduced within a mixture of market arrangements, hierarchical coordination by the PTT and associational coordination through business associations in consumer electronics and the new information provider domain. In this situation, the traditional, only slightly extended triangle in German telecommunications began to expand into a complex network of heterogenous actors.

---

14 When the German Bundespost initiated videotex introduction in the mid-1970s, it was believed that the use of the home TV set with an adapter would be the most economic solution and the Bundespost had therefore to cooperate with the German TV industry. Since this sector is organized as a private and highly competitive market, a liberal terminal policy was the logical consequence.

15 In France, the PTT bought several million videotex terminals from its telecom industry and distributed the terminals for free (Mayntz/ Schneider 1988).

16 This is indicated by a statement of officials of the PTT Ministry in an interview: "We could do it, for instance, like the French: We commission one million terminals and give them away for free. Then we would have 1 million subscribers in a short time. This would be nice - but this is not feasible in the Federal Republic. We expect that the terminals will be provided by industry and bought by the users. ... We also discussed these problems with our French colleagues. They think that one has to give the industry a fixed order - otherwise this will not work. If we would have taken up their proposal and have ordered, say, 500,000 decoders, we would have been swamped with reproaches. We would not have survived the subsequent political discussion" (Diebold Management Report Nr. 6/7-1985, 12. Translation by author).

The structure of the Btx network was shaped by the existing institutions, some key decisions in the technical area, and the actors' perceptions. The legally relevant definitions of the new medium played an important role for the inclusion in or exclusion from the policy network. At the end of the 1970s, it was not clear whether Btx should be considered as a form of *broadcast communication* or as an *individual telecommunication* like the telephone or data transmission. Such a distinction had important consequences in Germany because quite different regulatory structures in telecommunications, broadcasting and the press exist. Whereas telecommunications is a state monopoly run at the federal administrative level, the broadcasting system is controlled by the German *Länder*.[17] In the press sector, finally, governmental regulation (by *Länder* legislation and by a "regulatory framework" at the federal level) is very limited.

In this context, the *Länder* saw Bildschirmtext mainly as an *electronic mass medium* and feared that it could introduce market forces in their traditional domain. The press, in contrast, perceived the intervention of the broadcasting authorities as intended to extend their regulatory powers into the area of new electronic media.

The fact that the provision of terminals was liberalized, that media policy became involved and that Btx created other social issues (rationalization, data and consumer protection) triggered the engagement of a rather inclusive set of actors. The *technical and organizational built-in requirements* for system development (resource mobilization, systems operation, administration, standardization, guarantee of access, content regulation, information provision) thus activated many more actors than traditional telecommunications policies. In addition, a number of actors got involved by anticipating certain "external" effects or social impacts[18] of the Btx technology. Thus, the *perceived technical and organizational functions and anticipated externalities* "generated" a network of actors who considered each other directly or indirectly relevant for the system. Although this structure was not the result of a common and homogenous perception of the technological system (competing purposes, competing

---

17   In the 1980s the German Broadcasting System was partially opened to private radio and
     TV stations which are also generally regulated by the states' governments.
18   Examples are: privacy and security, consumer protection and effects on employment
     and industry structure.

usage perceptions), the different visions, nevertheless, converged into a single structure of mutual relevance on the actors' level.[19]

Besides an intuitive and qualitative account of this interaction system, the network of mutually relevant Btx actors can be identified and analyzed more systematically by network analytical methods.[20] For this purpose we applied a research strategy similar to that of Laumann/ Knoke (1987). In the first step we identified about 140 organizations which had been considered relevant for the introduction of Btx by a group of experts. Then, from this large set we selected the subset of the 40 most influential organizations and this subset was interviewed with a standardized questionnaire.[21]

From the pre-selected subset each respondent was asked to mark organizations listed in the questionnaire which had particular influence in the technical and institutional "shaping process" of Bildschirmtext. The respondents also reported, using a standardized form, whether they cooperated and exchanged information with the other actors on the list.

Influence reputation, cooperation and information exchange can be interpreted as the major facets of a structure of mutual relevance. An impression of this structure is given in Table 1. For the sake of simplicity of presentation, we only display the average value each actor received concerning influence, exchange of information and cooperation. In order to make comparisons easier, the indices have been rescaled to give the actor with the highest score the maximum value 1.00.[22]

19 "Mutual relevance" implies that actors take each other into account in their actions. They have to have a certain degree of power to influence the policy making process. Mere inaction does not necessarily indicate irrelevance or marginality, since others may take the interest of one "passive" actor into account (Knoke/ Laumann 1982: 257).

20 For an overview of network analytical methods see Knoke/ Kuklinsky (1982) and Pappi (1987).

21 The list of these 40 actors was presented to the interviewees. They could add relevant actors not included in the list and eliminate those they considered irrelevant. The resulting population to be analyzed in this section comprises 42 actors.

22 The influence reputation scores are slightly different from those reported in an earlier version of this chapter and in Schneider (1989: 205). This is a result of different recoding procedures, which were employed in the two analyses. This fact should prevent us from overinterpreting the influence positions. The formal precision of the computation clearly suggests a greater validity of the measurement than one can really achieve by means of a questionnaire.

Table 1: Influence Reputation, Cooperation and Information Exchange in the Videotex (Btx) Introduction

Name of Actor	Category	Influence Reputation	Cooperation	Information Exchange
PTT Ministry (BMP)	PTT	1.00	1.00	1.00
FTZ	PTT	0.96	0.92	0.74
Btx-AV	Assn. of IPs	0.93	0.87	0.85
IBM	Producer	0.93	0.87	0.35
Loewe Opta	Producer	0.88	0.76	0.35
Siemens	Producer	0.83	0.68	0.38
Press	IP	0.80	0.63	0.29
Dornier	Producer	0.76	0.58	0.29
DIHT	IP/Users/Pol.	0.76	0.55	0.38
Bosch (Blaupunkt)	Producer	0.72	0.45	0.29
ZVEI	Prod./Pol.	0.71	0.50	0.35
Länder	Politics	0.68	0.53	0.18
Mupid	Producer	0.67	0.37	0.18
SEL	Producer	0.67	0.37	0.35
RAFI	Producer	0.66	0.42	0.24
HHI	Science	0.65	0.42	0.24
Philips (PKI)	Producer	0.65	0.32	0.27
HDE	IP/Users	0.62	0.34	0.18
Mail Order Firms	IP/Users	0.62	0.34	0.18
Banks	IP/Users	0.62	0.34	0.24
Nixdorf	Producer	0.61	0.32	0.27
Danet	Producer	0.57	0.29	0.27
BIFOA	Science	0.57	0.34	0.29
BDI	Prod./Pol.	0.51	0.21	0.12
GDD	Data Protect.	0.51	0.21	0.03
ZDH	IP	0.49	0.16	0.12
VDMA	Prod./Pol.	0.49	0.18	0.09
Grundig	Producer	0.46	0.13	0.18
Forschungsmin. (BMFT)	Politics	0.46	0.11	0.12
Münchner Kreis	Science	0.45	0.18	0.21
Bundestag	Politics	0.45	0.13	0.12
Insurances	IP/Users	0.45	0.18	0.06
SONY	Producer	0.43	0.13	0.18
Computer Centers	IP	0.41	0.11	0.06
Wirtschaftsmin. (BMWi)	Politics	0.41	0.13	0.09
Telefunken	Producer	0.40	0.11	0.21
DGB/DPG	Trade Unions	0.37	0.11	0.03
SPD	Politics	0.25	0.08	0.03

Note: The table contains only actors with an influence reputation score of at least 0.25. All indices were rescaled to the maximum 1.00. IP = Information or service provider.

As it is shown in Table 1, the actors with the greatest *influence reputation* were the German PTT Ministry and its technical agency (FTZ). Among the producers, IBM was considered most influential since it designed and established the network of computer databases. Also the small and innovative TV set producer Loewe Opta was considered to be very influential. This firm strongly stimulated the development of the terminal market by its innovative capabilities. That Siemens - the largest telecommunications producer in Germany - also held a strong "reputational position" was expected. On the user and application side, the information providers' association Btx-AV (Btx-Anbieter Vereinigung), ranking as high as IBM, the press and the DIHT have been considered to have the highest influence reputation.

It is interesting that purely "political actors" such as the party with the highest influence scores (the SPD), the Federal Ministry of Research and Technology (Bundesministerium für Forschung und Technologie, BMFT), the Bundestag, those responsible for data protection at the federal and the *Länder*[23] level etc. received relatively low rankings, whereas producers and the major information providers were positioned more at the upper end of the influence reputation scale.

The PTT Ministry was not only the most influential actor but also the most frequently nominated partner of *cooperation* in Btx. All in all, Table 1 shows that the rank order of cooperation is very similar to that of influence.

Considerable similarity between the actor's positions also exists with regard to *information exchange*. The PTT Ministry ranked highest and the FTZ and the Btx-AV were very frequently mentioned partners in information exchange processes, too. All the other actors have significantly lower scores. But this does not mean that there was no clearly structured network of information exchange. This can be demonstrated by a block model procedure,[24] a network analytical tool in the narrower sense. Using this procedure, the whole network of information exchange can

23 Their relatively highest (twelfth) position is due to the fact that for a longer period, Btx was also perceived as an electronic mass medium.
24 The block model was produced by the COBLOC-procedure (Carrington/ Heil 1981) with the program system SONIS (Pappi/ Stelck 1987).

be reduced to the essential "strings" and "nodes"[25] where the actors with highly similar communication profiles are condensed into single actor blocks.

Figure 2: The Policy Network in Videotex (Btx)

Blocks	1	2	3	4	5	6	7	8
1	83	48	44	100	53	91	100	44
2	23	38	40	7	11	64	0	0
3	0	4	0	0	0	46	0	0
4	6	2	11	3	23	67	8	0
5	20	0	0	40	0	70	45	0
6	42	21	42	71	35	91	100	0
7	25	14	42	46	15	100	41	0
8	0	14	11	0	0	58	0	0

Note: Each matrix entry reports the degree (in percent) of information exchange from the perspective of the row-block actors.

The theoretical maximum is 100%.

◯ Density > 30%

- - -▶ asym. information exch. (>30%)
▬▬▶ sym. information exch. (>30%)
Size of circles indicates aggregate influence reputation

Figure 2 represents such a compressed communication structure with eight actor blocks. Here, the three most frequently mentioned partners of information exchange, together with the association of the telecommunications equipment manufacturers (ZVEI), occupy the most central position in the network. The role of this group can therefore be labeled as the "coordinator and system leader". This central group has direct ties to four blocks of producers and main information providers. The group of "political actors" which were mainly responsible for the media, con-

---

25 Because every actor was asked to specify the actors with whom he had an especially extensive information exchange during the Btx introduction, we received an asymmetrical matrix representing the communication linkages in our population. This matrix is the basis (input) of the block model procedure.

sumer and privacy regulations occupies a rather peripheral position in the network. This structure suggests that *technical and economic problem perceptions clearly dominated political considerations.*

The "infrastructure" of this information and coordination network consisted, on the one hand, of direct informational and cooperative relations in the field trials and of promotional alliances for public relations activities and, on the other hand, also of the membership and participation in a series of formal committees within the PTT and the information providers association (Btx-AV). The latter was very influential because it accomplished an organizational framework for the cooperation between the PTT and the most important information providers. Beyond this economic organization of Btx development, a number of formal political institutions organized and channelled the influence of the *Länder*, the intervention of data protection authorities, and the voice of the consumers and other affected groups in the regulation of this new electronic medium.

To summarize and visualize the structure of mutual relevance in the introduction of Btx each actor position with respect to influence reputation, information exchange and cooperation is displayed in a three dimensional scattergram (Figure 3). It shows the outstanding positions of the PTT, its technical agency (FTZ) and the Btx-AV. Between these three actors and all the others there is a relatively large gap - especially with regard to information exchange and cooperation.

At the beginning of this section, we pointed to the failure of the Btx diffusion and indicated that these development problems have to be related to the structure of the Btx policy network during its introduction. A comparative examination of the introduction of videotex in France and the UK[26] indicates that such a relationship clearly exists. In the three countries, governance structures of videotex introduction differ in three respects:

1. the weight of political actors representing "regulatory policy issues" in the media policy domain and in consumer protection;
2. the degree of vertical control the PTT had in each system (from equipment and terminal production to systems operation and information provision);

---

26 For a comparison of different videotex introduction strategies see Mayntz/ Schneider (1988) and Vedel (1989).

Figure 3: The Structure of Mutual Relevance in Videotex (Btx)

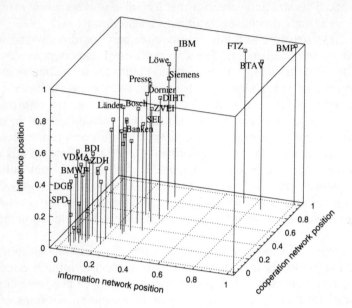

3. the degree to which the systems provider had a monopoly in the service provision or was submitted to market competition (horizontal control).

In Britain, the "political actors" had the lowest weight because political regulation never became an issue there. An important reason was that the old British Post Office had been able to "buy off" potential opposition from the press by giving up its claims on information provision and by incorporating press organizations into the videotex project. This meant, on the other hand, that the Post Office's direct "vertical" control of Prestel, the British videotex system, was rather low because it was not only dependent on the cooperation of terminal producers but also on the information providers. In addition, when British telecommunications became completely liberalized in the early 1980s, the new British Telecom also lost the "horizontal" control and Prestel had to fight with new competing services.

The French videotex introduction, in contrast, was under almost complete horizontal and vertical control of the French PTT. The French telephone authority Direction Générale des Télécommunications (DGT) provided the service, distributed the terminals (for free!) and controlled the most important information service, the electronic directory.

Similar to the British, the German terminal domain and the information sector were market controlled but Btx never had to compete with other videotex services. On the other hand, it was shaped and partly restricted by the regulation of potentially negative externalities. Although the different actors demanding this kind of regulatory intervention had a rather low influence reputation, they managed to impose the (from their perspectives) necessary minimal regulations confining Btx, for example, to "interactive" usage between either terminals or terminals and a data base. However, the most important facet of Btx introduction was undoubtedly the low degree of vertical control, despite the PTT Ministry's central position in the Btx network. Aside from the PTT Ministry, there were other rather influential actors with different interests in the "coordinator and system leader" block. The same holds true for the blocks of dominantly economically oriented producers. The group of political actors, although not very influential after a restrictive political definition of Btx had been reached, "remained" in the network - ready to keep watch that the definition was not violated by the PTT Ministry.

The German videotex development became locked into a kind of chicken-egg dilemma. Potential users waited for cheap terminals and attractive services but terminal prices and the utility of information services depended to a large degree on the investments of private business firms. These actors, however, were only willing to invest when there was already a critical mass of users. The PTT, which might have financially been able to cut the vicious circle by subsidizing terminals, telecommunications tariffs and perhaps even the provision of information services during the early years of Btx introduction, could not manage it.

Obviously, the direct approach used by the French to establish a system from scratch over night was not feasible in the German context. But institutional constraints and the concrete structure of the actor network were not deterministic causes of the relative failure. The strategy of the PTT to introduce Btx in a cooperative mode together with autonomous actors, respecting the given institutional boundaries and the delimited economic domains, was not bound to fail automatically. If the accumulation of technical coordination and timing problems had not created serious technical snags, the strong expectations which almost everybody had during 1982 and 1984 could have pushed the growth of the user community beyond the necessary critical mass within a short period. Complications produced by international standardization processes and the tendency to over-engineering in German telecommunications made the whole undertaking very time-consuming and resulted, among other things, in too expensive Btx terminals. When the expected "take-off" of the system did not take place, Btx's reputation was further damaged. All in all, this finally led to the failure of the PTT's introduction strategy, recovery from which will be very difficult.[27]

4   The Policy Network of the Institutional Reform in Telecommunications

In contrast to the case of videotex policy making which demonstrated the impact of the institutional setting on the economic prospects of the service, the policy process of institutional reform was driven by the goal to change and restructure this setting. Success or failure of such a process can be assessed on a long-term or a short-term basis.[28] A short-term indicator could be the mere capacity for collective action, i.e. whether the initiators and proponents of the reform succeeded in mobilizing support to transform the proposals for institutional change into an enacted law. "Objective problem pressure" alone does not trigger reform initiatives, nor is there only one way out of the problematic situation. "Change agents" with convincing arguments and sufficient formal political power as well as informational and reputational resources to form coalitions to overcome institutional inertia are always needed.

After the failure of a first reform initiative in the early 1970s, it took about 8 years until the dissatisfaction with the status quo led a few actors to call for a liberalization of the telecommunications market. Computer manufacturers like IBM and Nixdorf, a dynamic German company which later was sold to Siemens, demanded free entry into the terminal equipment market which through the PTT's restrictive approval practice

---

27   After this failure was acknowledged in 1987, the PTT was allowed to enter the terminal market.

28   Medium- or long-term success of the structural changes in telecommunications would be indicated by better performance, higher efficiency and innovativeness which was explicitly intended by the reform.

was a well protected domain of the traditional suppliers of the German PTT. But also liberal CDU ministers of economics in the *Länder*, especially Lower Saxony, began to criticize the growing monopoly power of the PTT which, as a consequence of the confluence of computers and telecommunications, at least indirectly interfered in the traditionally unregulated market for computer equipment.

In a first spectacular step in 1980, the German Monopolkommission (antitrust commission) analyzed the procurement policy of the PTT and the structure of the telecommunications equipment market which in many segments was dominated by the purchasing power of the PTT. In its report, the commission questioned the PTT's double role as player and umpire in the market (Monopolkommission 1981: 91-110). The commission demanded far-reaching liberalization measures in the terminal market and a certain degree of service competition within the public telecommunications network. The PTT successfully rejected the proposals, but its position had already become weakened because of some strategic errors made in previous years (Dang Nguyen 1985: 112-114). Especially the fact that the PTT still supported the development of an obsolete analogue electronic switching system while the world was going digital had provoked severe criticism. This case was seen as evidence of bureaucratic and monopolistic inertia.[29]

As these problems did not directly or visibly affect the quality or availability of telephone service, the general public did not challenge the PTT's monopolistic position which seemed to guarantee universal service at reasonable costs. In addition, radical reforms like privatization of the telecommunications branch of the PTT were practically excluded by the Basic Law postulating the PTT to be state-owned. The new federal government - a coalition of the Christian Democrats (CDU/CSU) and the Liberals - coming into office in 1982, had to take this into consideration. The new PTT minister, who had formerly criticized the PTT monopoly frequently, was willing to initiate a reform at all costs. In this respect, he could count on the liberals, who demanded far-reaching changes in

---

29 The decision was not cancelled until 1979 when it had become obvious that fully digitized systems were technically and economically superior to analogue technology (Werle 1990: 249-263).

telecommunications, whereas his own party, especially the Bavarian wing
(CSU), was not so enthusiastic.[30]

Although technical changes - digitization, satellite and mobile communication - and an international trend toward liberalization and deregulation exerted pressures for reforms,[31] a series of legal and political complications in Germany favoring veto coalitions against any kind of transformation of the status quo demanded a well prepared concept. The
government therefore established an independent commission which was
composed of almost all relevant social groups, i.e. trade and industry,
science and politics.

In 1987, the Commission of the European Communities (CEC) issued
a "Green Paper on the Development of the Common Market for Telecommunications Services and Equipment" demanding a "restructuring
of national markets" to permit competition in the market for terminal
equipment and for value added services.[32] Only a few months later, the
German government commission published its report on the possibilities
of "improving the fulfillment of tasks in telecommunications".[33] A 9:2
majority of the commission proposed a "Restructuration of the Telecommunications System" strikingly similar to the EC proposals. Major points
were organizational separations of

- the telecommunications branch from the other branches of the PTT,
- the regulatory (sovereign) functions from the operational (entrepreneurial) tasks.

The PTT TELEKOM was to keep its network monopoly and also the
monopoly of the telephone service, but all other services would be offered in competition with other providers. The market for terminal equipment would be completely liberalized.

The reform act, drafted by the government a short time later, was
based on the commission's report. But the government not only intended

---

30 For a comparative study of institutional reform in telecommunications, emphasizing
    political aspects see Grande (1989).
31 Especially the US administration - after the divestiture of AT&T - attacked the German
    "protectionist" policy in telecommunications.
32 For the strategic role of the CEC in the European process of telecommunications liberal-
    ization see Schneider/ Werle (1990).
33 That is: "The most effective promotion of technical innovation, the development and
    observance of international communication standards and the safeguarding of competition
    on the telecommunications market" (Witte 1988: 9).

to organizationally separate TELEKOM, it explicitly wanted to split the PTT into three public corporations (TELEKOM, Banking, Postal Services) under the roof of a directorate (Direktorium) with mainly coordinating competence. The reform was declared a necessary adaptation to international and technological developments contributing to more efficiency and variety within the telecommunications infrastructure and to a strengthening of the German industry in the world market.

The parliament's committee on post and telecommunications organized two hearings, the first dealing with the EC's Green Paper and the second with the reform act. A wide range of political and economic actors and many experts were invited to give statements and to answer a series of questions formulated by the committee. More than fifty individuals or organizations participated. Compared to earlier legislative and administrative processes in telecommunications, the mere number of interested or affected actors had grown considerably.

After the reform law had passed the legislative bodies in summer 1989, we carried out a survey among all these actors but excluded scientists and other experts not directly affected by the reform.[34] Once again, standardized questionnaires were used, and the general data collection procedure was similar to that of the videotex network.

The first step of the data analysis concentrates on the structure of mutual relevance as it was perceived by the actors in the process of institutional reform. We saw, in the previous section, that the PTT Ministry held a central position in the process of introducing Btx. One might argue that this was typical for a technical innovation process in which economic considerations predominated. Service providers and producers of terminal equipment and network technology were more relevant than, for example, political actors, and the PTT Ministry as the central financier of the technical infrastructure of the new service had to carry a high risk. Compared to Btx, the telecommunications reform was much more political in the sense that parts of the institutional basis of this sector were to be redesigned and restructured. This was far more dangerous for the PTT because the organization was directly and fundamentally

---

34 Because of the higher degree of formalization of this reform process compared to the introduction of Btx, the identification of the relevant actors was less complicated. In addition to the actors who participated in the hearings, the relevant political parties and ministries were included in the survey. The number of actors analyzed in the following amounts to 38.

affected by every detail of the reform. Obtaining control over this process was a vital question for the PTT. Table 2 shows that the PTT Ministry indeed succeeded in getting such a central position in the reform network.

As in the case of Btx, all respondents were asked to give an estimation of the *influence* of every organization included in a list we presented. All but one respondent rated the influence of the PTT Ministry as "very strong" or "strong". After rescaling the influence reputation, the PTT Ministry displays the maximum value of 1.00.[35] The PTT Ministry also was most frequently mentioned as a partner in *information exchange and cooperation* by the other actors. Its relative dominance becomes evident when we, as in the case of Btx, display the position of each actor in the "three dimensional" space of influence reputation, information exchange and cooperation in Figure 4.

Table 2 and Figure 4 also show, as could be expected, that the most influential actors in the reform process were political organizations such as parties, other ministries, workers' unions and manufacturers' (producers') associations. The largest and most important German equipment manufacturer, Siemens, only ranked fifteenth in the influence-reputation scale.

Although in the beginning a general consensus seemed to exist that the German telecommunications sector had to be restructured, neither the government commission nor the PTT Ministry managed to reach an agreement among all relevant actors when the concrete details of the reform had to be designed. The liberal party (FDP), the BDI (Federation of German Industry) and the computer manufacturers represented by the Association of German Machinery Manufacturers (Verband Deutscher Maschinen- und Anlagenbau, VDMA), but partly also the Ministry of Economics and the DIHT demanded further liberalization, in particular the elimination of the PTT's network monopoly.

The postal workers' unions (especially the Deutsche Postgewerkschaft, DPG), the SPD and also the majority of the (smaller) telecommunications equipment manufacturers in the Central Association of the Electrical Industry (ZVEI) considered the liberalization as too far-reaching or the speed of the restructuring process to be too fast. The most prominent

---

35 In an earlier presented version of this chapter, the rescaling procedure was not employed and a couple of questionnaires had not been returned at that time, so the figures are slightly different.

Table 2: Influence Reputation, Cooperation and Information Exchange in the Telecommunications Reform

Name of Actor	Category	Influence Reputation	Cooperation	Information Exchange
PTT Ministry (BMP)	PTT	1.00	1.00	1.00
Wirtschaftsmin. (BMWi)	Politics	0.85	0.76	0.61
DGB/DPG	Trade Unions	0.85	0.44	0.46
CDU/CSU	Politics	0.83	0.68	0.68
FDP	Politics	0.77	0.54	0.65
Finanzministerium (BMF)	Politics	0.68	0.46	0.38
SPD	Politics	0.68	0.41	0.53
Länder	Politics	0.68	0.64	0.51
DIHT	IP/Users/Pol.	0.68	0.68	0.67
Bundeskanzleramt	Politics	0.67	0.46	0.37
BDI	Prod./Pol.	0.67	0.67	0.57
Innenministerium (BMI)	Politics	0.66	0.41	0.32
EG-Kommission (CEC)	Politics	0.64	0.48	0.42
ZVEI	Prod./Pol.	0.62	0.64	0.55
Siemens	Producer	0.54	0.51	0.42
IBM	Producer	0.52	0.44	0.41
DPV/DBB	Trade Unions	0.52	0.25	0.26
VDMA	Prod./Pol.	0.51	0.52	0.47
Data Protectors	Politics	0.47	0.33	0.26
SEL	Producer	0.47	0.49	0.39
ZDH	Producer/Pol.	0.46	0.40	0.38
Philips (PKI)	Producer	0.44	0.52	0.44
Nixdorf	Producer	0.44	0.51	0.40
CPG/CGB	Trade Unions	0.43	0.18	0.17
Banks	Users	0.42	0.38	0.32
Bosch (Blaupunkt)	Producer	0.39	0.40	0.38
VAF	Producer/Pol.	0.39	0.38	0.32
Krone	Producer	0.36	0.41	0.34
Cities Association	Users/Pol.	0.32	0.25	0.25
VdP	Users/Pol.	0.32	0.19	0.22
DeTelecom	Users/Pol.	0.32	0.25	0.26
Grüne	Politics	0.27	0.16	0.20
AgV (Consumers)	Users/Pol.	0.25	0.14	0.12

Note: The table contains only actors with an influence reputation score of at least 0.25. All indices were rescaled to the maximum 1.00.

opponent was the DPG, a union organizing more than 80% of the PTT employees. The DPG attacked the reform as a first step towards privatization and criticized the organizational division of the PTT as a measure to impede cross-subsidization. According to the DPG this would result in increased rationalization pressure and layoffs in the postal branch. Another important concern was the presumed weakening of its organizational integration, although the workers' unions were conceded one third of the seats on the boards of the three corporations.

Figure 4: The Structure of Mutual Relevance in the Telecommunications Reform

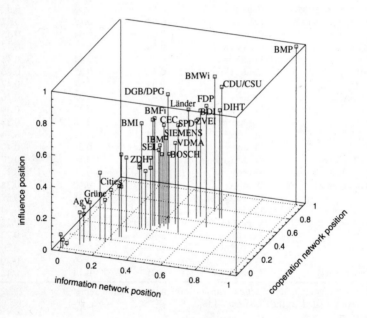

The *Länder* also criticized the reform draft. Those governed by SPD majorities tended to reject any reform initiative launched by the federal

"Wende"[36] administration. This brought Bavaria, governed by an absolute majority of the CSU (the Bavarian "sister" of the CDU), into a strategically strong position. Its votes in the Bundesrat (Federal Council) were needed to secure a majority over the SPD *Länder*. Bavaria, a state with industrial conglomerates but also large peripheral rural areas, traditionally stressed the infrastructural significance of the PTT complex and demanded more political control of this sector. Most of the other *Länder* wanted to keep a position of minimum influence which was in danger of diminishing because the reform draft contained no substitution for the eliminated Administrative Council.[37]

The short description of the position of several relevant actors may create the impression that their attitudes and interests varied considerably. Their image of the reform process, however, was not very divergent. The three issues of liberalization (of the markets for terminals, services and networks) and the issue of organizational division of the three old PTT branches were perceived to be closely linked. The complex reform problem has only one underlying issue dimension. This can be demonstrated by a principal component factor analysis which shows high loadings of all four items on one single factor (see Table 3). This factor, comprising 75% of the total variance of the four input variables,[38] represents a latent variable measuring the actors' attitudes toward the global *"liberal reorganization issue"* in telecommunications.

To identify *similarities and differences of interest positions* toward the liberal reorganization of telecommunications in Germany, we also applied network analytical methods. We asked the actors to give a global statement relating their own stance to those of the other actors. The resulting matrix was examined by means of a block model procedure (COBLOC)[39] in order to extract sets of actors with relatively similar interest positions. At least four groups of actors perceiving each other's positions as similar could be identified. The largest group comprises "supporters" of a definite but, at least in the first step, rather moderate

---

36 The change in government from the 13-year SPD/FDP coalition to the CDU-CSU/FDP coalition in 1982, which was considered a fundamental change in West German politics, has become known as "Die Wende".

37 According to the old PTT Administration Act, the states delegated five representatives into the Administrative Council.

38 Perception of the liberalization of the markets for (1) terminals, (2) services, (3) networks and of (4) the organizational division.

39 For a short description of this procedure see previous section.

Table 3: A Factor Analysis of the Actors' Attitudes toward the Telecommunications Reform

	Factor Loadings
Liberalization of Terminal Equipment	.81
Liberalization of Services	.91
Liberalization of Networks	.88
Organizational Separation	.87
Variance 75.2% (N=30)	

(Scale: 1 = Reform is much too radical, 2 = is too radical, 3 = ok, 4 = should have been more radical, 5 = should have been much more radical)

reform. They concentrated their efforts on what appeared to be feasible. To this group belonged, among others, the PTT Ministry, the Ministry of Economics, the CDU/CSU and the EC Commission. Another larger cluster is that of "opponents" who criticized the reform as a whole or central elements of it. Their dominant perspective was that of the affected PTT workers and the individual non-commercial users of telecommunications services. The DPG, the SPD and also the Green Party belonged to this group which at least wanted to retard the reform. A smaller group of actors, comprising the BDI and the FDP might be called the "pushing" coalition. They demanded far-reaching liberalization of the telecommunications sector. A fourth group, including rather heterogeneous actors, generally agreed with the reform but demanded a few specific changes with respect to very special interests. The *Länder* are, for instance, members of this fourth group of "stipulators". They tried to get more political control of the infrastructural component of the telecommunications sector. In this respect, they succeeded in imposing one of the few changes of the reform draft providing the establishment of an "infrastructural council" (Infrastrukturrat) with representatives of each of the *Länder* and an equal number of delegates from the Federal Parliament. This council can decide (or make proposals) whether the three PTT corporations should be obliged to provide certain services with a high infrastructural significance regardless of the market situation.

Figure 5: The Policy Network in the Telecommunications Reform

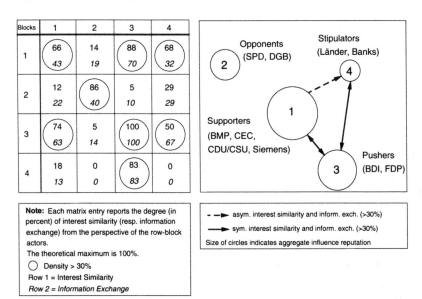

Blocks	1	2	3	4
1	66 / 43	14 / 19	88 / 70	68 / 32
2	12 / 22	86 / 40	5 / 10	29 / 29
3	74 / 63	5 / 14	100 / 100	50 / 67
4	18 / 13	0 / 0	83 / 83	0 / 0

Note: Each matrix entry reports the degree (in percent) of interest similarity (resp. information exchange) from the perspective of the row-block actors.
The theoretical maximum is 100%.
○ Density > 30%
Row 1 = Interest Similarity
Row 2 = Information Exchange

- ─► asym. interest similarity and inform. exch. (>30%)
──► sym. interest similarity and inform. exch. (>30%)
Size of circles indicates aggregate influence reputation

Figure 5 gives an impression of the *actor network* in the process of the institutional reform with regard to interest similarity. The matrix on the left reports the information exchange relations within and between the groups.[40] The four groups differ with regard to the aggregate influence reputation, their internal homogeneity of interests and their relative similarity with the other groups. We can see that the "supporters" are

---

40 This time - in contrast to the last section, where we had no information about the similarity of interest positions - not the information exchange activities, but the perceived interest similarities were used as input variables for the COBLOC analysis. So the information exchange relations only provide an additional information of a structure which is constituted by interest positions.

very influential and internally rather homogeneous. They perceive the stance of the "pushers" as corresponding highly with their own position. The "pushers" do not see any similarity to the "opponents" and vice versa. This latter group is internally relatively homogeneous but there is only little affinity to the position of any other group. In addition, the "opponents" are not very well integrated into the information exchange network of the four actor groups.

The network of interest similarity suggests that the group of "opponents" was in conflict with all other actors and that there was almost no chance to join a coalition with one of the other groups. This impression is confirmed by multidimensional scaling[41] (see Figure 6). This procedure results in a two-dimensional solution with one dimension clearly dominating. In this "liberal reorganization issue" dimension - the horizontal axis of Figure 6 - the most prominent opposing actors are located far on the left-hand side whereas the pushers can be found on the other side, but they are more visibly intermeshed with the great group of supporting actors.[42]

While most of the actors in the supporting group perfectly agreed with the results of the reform process, it is not surprising that the pushers and more so the opponents articulated discontent when asked for a summarizing statement. However, the deviation of the opponents and the pushers from the main stream was not radical enough to provide a basis for a veto-coalition. The pushers, who - as we could see in Figure 5 - were with regard to information exchange and interest similarity, not too strongly separated from the supporters, came to the conclusion that the reform could be interpreted as a small but not the final step in the right direction. So, eventually, they preferred this provisional solution to blocking the whole undertaking. The opponents, on the other hand, were rather isolated not only with respect to their interest positions but also to information exchange and their power resources were too small to impede the institutional change.

In this section, our interest was not only directed at the specific reform problem and the way it was handled but also at the type of actors playing the dominant roles. Although the changes were motivated by

---

41 The dissimilarity of actors with respect to their interest positions was computed as the Euclidian distance.
42 Input variables in this analysis are the atomistic interest positions and not the perceived interest interrelations.

Figure 6: The Actors' Postitions Toward the "Liberal Reorganization of Telecommunications" (Results of Multidimensional Scaling)

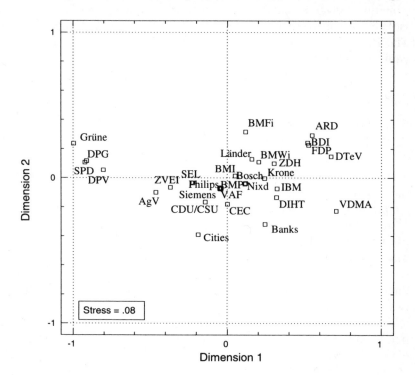

economic and industrial policy considerations and designed to improve the economic performance of this sector, they directly entailed a new definition of the role of the "state" and the respective political actors in this field. It turned out that *political and not economic issues dominated* and political actors constituted the most relevant actor networks in the reform. Within these networks, the PTT Ministry held the strongest position. It was perceived as the politically most powerful organization and was effectively integrated into the networks of cooperation and information exchange. The Ministry could present a well prepared draft of the reform act which preserved relevant parts of the old monopoly and, at the same time, opened the sector for more competition. The law appeared to be a necessary adaptation to an international trend, not too liberal and not too restrictive. Although the pushers as well the opponents had considerable power resources, they neutralized each other or became so isolated that there remained only small chances for coalition formation. The PTT Ministry therefore could maintain a maximum of control and could mobilize the allies it needed to get the law passed.

5   Issue Networks and the Inner Circle in the Telecommunications Domain

The German telecommunications sector was run as a state monopoly for more than a century. Its governance structure in this period was rather simple: a stable triangle including the PTT as a public administration, a small family of equipment manufacturers and the German Chamber of Industry and Commerce cooperated in a clientelist and corporatist mode. Their common interest was to build up the telephone network respecting each others domains and interests. Economic and political interests appeared to be rather congruent, and when they conflicted, politics had primacy. After the war, this triangle remained the backbone of telecommunications policy but around this core a gradually more differentiated policy network containing more actors and divergent interests emerged.

Only at the beginning of the 70s with the expansion of telecommunications, with the proliferation of new services and the rapid technological change did the number of actors begin to explode. This development led to an enlargement of the "policy area" and the "policy community" in telecommunications.[43] At the same time, however, the domain was subjected to significant structural changes. As demonstrated in the two case studies in the previous sections, clearly differentiated actor networks emerge depending on the problem situation and problem perception.

Primarily economic problems like the introduction of the new telecommunications service videotex especially mobilize economic interests and the network of relevant actors predominantly contains private firms

---

43   The concept of policy domain implies these two elements which are distinguished by some scholars (esp. Wilks/ Wright 1987: 299-301). For a discussion of several concepts relating to that of policy networks see also Jordan (1990) and Rhodes (1990).

as manufacturers of equipment, information providers for the new service, specialists for technical development etc. Predominantly political problems like the institutional reform of the German telecommunications system towards more liberalization especially activate the general core of "high politics" like political parties, workers' unions, peak associations of business etc. Thus, political problems seem to create and activate other policy networks than economic problems would. The networks may even be issue-specific and issue-dependent.[44] It appears, however, that variation of networks between "classes or 'functional' types of problems" (i.e. economic vs. political) is greater than between issues within one class. Despite such variations and changes, it should be kept in mind that an important aspect of policy networks is their contribution to continuity and stability in political interactions.

Our two cases indicate that within a policy domain there is always a multiplicity of policy networks which partly overlap and partly diverge. When there is an "inner circle" of actors that are generally influential in the telecommunications policy domain, those actors would be present in all of the coexisting policy networks. In our case, they would form the intersection of both analyzed configurations. A plot of the actors' influence reputation scores in the two networks indeed shows that there was a core of actors having considerable influence in both policy networks (Figure 7).[45]

Those actors positioned respectively on one of the two axis were absent in the other network,[46] whereas the PTT Ministry - placed in the upper right corner of the diagram - played the most dominant role in both. But also the other actors in the upper right square, having an influence reputation of at least .40 in either case, can be considered "members" of the "inner circle" of the telecommunications domain. We see that almost all German manufacturers of telecommunications *and* computer equipment and also their associations belong to the core, although (or

---

44 For the concept of "issue networks" see Heclo (1978).
45 We confined this presentation to the indicator of influence because, on the one hand, not all informations are directly comparable in both cases (similarity of interests) and we wanted, on the other hand, to avoid redundancy. This procedure is confirmed by a computation of the correlation coefficients between influence reputation, information exchange and cooperation. In the case of videotex the *lowest* coefficient amounts to .78 (between influence and information), and in the telecommunications reform the *lowest* coefficient even reaches up to .89 (influence and cooperation).
46 A few of them "stem" from other policy domains and were only mobilized by the specific issues to be dealt with.

Figure 7: Influence Reputation, Cooperation and Information Exchange in Videotex (Btx)

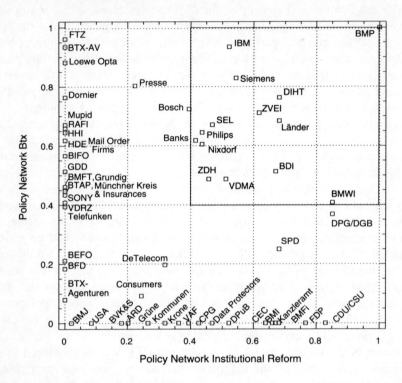

because) they have diverging interests. Also the federal states (*Länder*) with - in contrast to other domains - a rather weak formal (legal) competence in telecommunications have a strong *de facto* position. The traditionally highly influential status of the DIHT has survived all economic and political changes as is reflected in the diagram. Other generally relevant actors are the Federation of German Industry (BDI), the Central Association of German Craft and Trade Enterprises (Zentralverband des Deutschen Handwerks, ZDH)[47] and the Ministry of Economics, the latter not only because it had the right to approve the charges and utilization conditions for the telecommunications services but also as a protector

---

47   Many of their member firms are charged by the PTT to install, maintain or repair cables, terminals etc.

of "free markets" and competition. The banking associations are relatively influential because the banking sector is not only a very important and extensive user of telecommunications services but also because banks compete with some of the financial services offered by the PTT.

The interpretation of Figure 7 should not be overstretched because it is only based on two case studies. However, it clearly shows that the "inner circle" of influential actors has become relatively large and rather "pluralist". We assume that this network also functions as a "translator" of technical into economic and economic into political problems. It is only through this ability that the technical, political or economic implications and consequences of institutional changes or the introduction of new services or other activities in the telecommunications domain can be adequately assessed.[48] Core actors are not always more influential than those who only appear on the stage when specific issues are to be handled. Moreover, as they have partly contradicting interests, the core actors may neutralize each other in conflict situations.

Although formal institutional changes cannot be expected to generate totally novel networks, the telecommunications reform will affect the future actor constellation and their influence positions. In this sense, Figure 7 displays the "old order" of this sector. This order will not become completely obsolete but the intended "depoliticization" of economic and technical issues and the clearer separation of the different "functions" in telecommunications assumingly will lead to a further specialization of actor networks and to new problems of coordination and "translation" between networks.

References

Carlton, D. W./ J. M. Klamer, 1983: The Need for Coordination Among Firms, with Special Reference to Network Industries. In: *University of Chicago Law Review* 50, 446-465.

---

48 See Heclo (1978). This does not necessarily generate a consensus but it may help to clarify positions and to figure out what is feasible and what is not feasible. Therefore, it improves calculability in complex environments.

Carrington, P. J./ G. H. Heil, 1981: Cobloc: A Hierarchical Method for Blocking Network Data. In: *Journal of Mathematical Sociology* 8, 103-131.

Coleman, J. S., 1990: *Foundations of Social Theory.* Cambridge, MA.: Harvard University Press.

Dang Nguyen, G., 1985: Telecommunications: A Challenge to the Old Order. In: M. Sharp (ed.), *Europe and the New Technologies.* London: Pinter, 87-160.

Grande, E., 1989: *Vom Monopol zum Wettbewerb? Die neokonservative Reform der Telekommunikation in Großbritannien und der Bundesrepublik Deutschland.* Wiesbaden: Deutscher Universitäts Verlag.

Heclo, H., 1978: Issue Networks and the Executive Establishment. In: A. King (ed.), *The New American Political System.* Washington: American Enterprise Institute for Public Policy Research, 87-124.

Holcombe, N.A., 1911: *Public Ownership of Telephones on the Continent of Europe.* Cambridge MA: Harvard University Press.

Hollingsworth, J. R., 1990: *The Governance of American Manufacturing Sectors: The Logic of Coordination and Control.* MPIFG Discussion Paper 90/4. Köln: Max-Planck-Institut für Gesellschaftsforschung.

Jordan, G., 1990: Sub-Governments, Policy-Communities and Networks. Refilling the Old Bottles? In: *Journal of Theoretical Politics* 2, 319-338.

Katz, M. L./ C. Shapiro, 1985: Network Externalities, Competition, and Compatibility. In: *American Economic Review* 75, 424-440.

Knoke, D./ J. H. Kuklinski, 1982: *Network Analysis.* Beverly Hills: Sage.

Knoke, D./ E. O. Laumann, 1982: The Social Organization of National Policy Domains: An Exploration of some Structural Hypotheses. In: P. V. Marsden/ N. Lin (eds.), *Social Structure and Network Analysis.* London: Sage, 255-270.

Langlois, R. N., 1986: Rationality, Institutions, and Explanation. In: R. N. Langlois (ed.), *Economics as a Process.* Cambridge: Cambridge University Press, 225-255.

Laumann, E. O./ D. Knoke, 1987: *The Organizational State. Social Choice in National Policy Domains.* Madison, WI.: University of Wisconsin Press.

Laumann, E. O./ D. Knoke/ Y.-H. Kim, 1985: An Organizational Approach to State Policy Formation: A Comparative Study of Energy and Health Domains. In: *American Sociological Review* 50, 1-19.

Mayntz, R., 1986: Corporate Actors in Public Policy: Changing Perspectives in Political Analysis. In: *Norsk Statsvitenskapelig Tidsskrift* 3, 7-25.

Mayntz, R./ V. Schneider 1988: The Dynamics of Systems Development in a Comparative Perspective: Interactive Videotex in Germany, France and Britain. In: R. Mayntz/ T. P. Hughes (eds.), *The Development of Large Technical Systems*. Frankfurt a.m.: Campus, 263-298.

Monopolkommission, 1981: *Die Rolle der Deutschen Bundespost im Fernmeldewesen*. Sondergutachten der Monopolkommission. Vol. 9. Baden-Baden: Nomos.

Pappi, F. U. (ed.), 1987: *Methoden der Netzwerkanalyse*. München: Oldenbourg.

Pappi, F. U./ K. Stelck, 1987: SONIS: Ein Datenbanksystem zur Netzwerkanalyse. In: F. U. Pappi (ed.), *Methoden der Netzwerkanalyse*. München: Oldenbourg, 253-266.

Pierce, J. R., 1978: The Telephone and Society in the Past 100 Years. In: I. d. S. Pool (ed.), *The Social Impact of the Telephone*. Cambridge, MA.: MIT Press, 159-195.

Pinch, T. J./ W. E. Bijker, 1984: The Social Construction of Facts and Artefacts: Or How the Sociology of Science and the Sociology of Technology Might Benefit Each Other. In: *Social Studies of Science* 14, 399-441

Rhodes, R. A. W., 1990: Policy Networks. A British Perspective. In: *Journal of Theoretical Politics* 2, 293-317.

Rohlfs, J., 1974: A Theory of Interdependent Demand for a Communications Service. In: *Bell Journal of Economics and Management Science* 15, 16-37.

Scharpf, F. W., 1989: Decision Rules, Decision Styles and Policy Choices. In: *Journal of Theoretical Politics* 1, 149-176.

Schneider, V., 1989: *Technikentwicklung zwischen Politik und Markt: Der Fall Bildschirmtext*. Frankfurt a.m.: Campus.

Schneider, V., 1991: The Governance of Large Technical Systems: The Case of Telecommunications. In: T. R. La Porte (ed.), *Responding to Large Technical Systems: Control or Anticipation*. Dordrecht: Kluwer Academic, 18-40.

Schneider V./ R. Werle, 1990: International Regime or Corporate Actor? The European Community in Telecommunications Policy. In: K. Dyson/ P. Humphreys (eds.), *The Political Economy of Communica-*

tions. International and European Dimensions. London: Routledge, 77-106.

Thomas, F., 1988: The Politics of Growth: The German Telephone System. In: R. Mayntz/ T. P. Hughes (eds.), *The Development of Large Technical Systems.* Frankfurt a.M.: Campus, 179-209.

Vedel, T., 1989: Télématique et Configurations d'Acteurs: Une Perspective Européenne. In: *Technologies de l'Information et Société* (T.I.S.) 2(1), 15-32.

Werle, R., 1990: *Telekommunikation in der Bundesrepublik: Expansion, Differenzierung, Transformation.* Frankfurt a.M.: Campus.

Wilks, S./ M. Wright, 1987: Conclusion: Comparing Government-Industry Relations: States, Sectors, and Networks. In: S. Wilks/ M. Wright (eds.), *Comparative Government-Industry Relations.* Oxford: Clarendon Press, 274-313.

Williamson, E. O., 1985: *The Economic Institutions of Capitalism.* New York: Free Press.

Witte, E. (ed.), 1988: *Restructuring of the Telecommunications System. Report of the Government Commission for Telecommunications.* Heidelberg: R. v. Decker.

Wright, M., 1988: Policy Community, Policy Network and Comparative Industrial Policies. In: *Political Studies* 36, 593-612.

Chapter 5
Policy Networks and Change: The Case of High-T$_c$ Superconductors

Dorothea Jansen

1 The Discovery of High-T$_c$ Superconductors

In September 1986 two European physicists from the Zurich Lab of IBM published a paper in the German *Zeitschrift für Physik* on "Possible High-T$_c$ Superconductivity" in a ceramic material. Superconductivity is the phenomenon, first discovered in 1911, that certain pure metals and alloys lose their electrical resistance when they are cooled beneath a certain temperature, the "critical temperature" T$_c$. Superconductivity is conditional on very low temperature near absolute zero. It requires complex cryocooling technologies and expensive liquid helium as a cooling medium. Despite hard efforts to raise the critical temperature from these very low temperatures, no progress had been made since 1973, when niobium germanium with the T$_c$ of 23 Kelvin, i.e. 23 degrees above absolute zero, was discovered. There were even theories predicting that superconductivity above 30 K was impossible. Again and again different physicists claimed to have found high-T$_c$ superconductivity (HTS), but all the sensational reports turned out to be false. Now Müller and Bednorz claimed to have discovered an oxidic material, LaBaCuO (lanthanum-barium-copper oxide) with a T$_c$ of 30 K. By December 1986 their experiments were replicated by two groups in Japan and the US. Soon it became clear that the so-called "Zurich oxides" were no exception - there were other oxidic superconductors with even higher critical temperatures. In January 1987, the US group succeeded in preparing a material which soon dominated HTS research: YBaCuO (yttrium-barium-copper oxide). It allows cooling with simple technologies and cheap liquid nitrogen.

With the discovery of YBaCuO, announced in a press conference (even before publication of the scientific paper) in mid-February 1987, a worldwide race in the science and technology of HTS was set off. Feverish activity dominated not only the scientific frontier, but also politics. As early as February 1987 governmental agencies in Japan started funding and organizing the field. Japan declared HTS a basic future technology and part of the MITI-Program "Technologies for the Next Generations' Industries".

Parallel to these Japanese activities, American congressmen started a campaign to commercialize superconductivity. America feared that they might win again in science while losing in the technological competition with Japan. The superconductivity campaign finally culminated in July 1987 in President Reagan's "Superconductivity Initiative", one point of which was to restrict the flow of information from American National Labs to foreign scientists.

The discovery of HTS triggered huge activities in science, industry, and science and technology policy. A very small scientific and technical field (in 1986) suddenly grew by a factor of ten and even more. This particular event offered researchers of science & technology the unique chance to study how a developing field gets organized, which actors use which strategies in policy formation, whether and how this is dependent on their previous position in the field and on special scientific and technological trends.

This chapter provides an analysis of the German HTS policy. It is based on both secondary data on public funding for superconductivity research before and after HTS, and on structured, open-ended interviews with HTS researchers from ten research groups at universities, research institutes and industry, with representatives of the main funding agencies and with members of an advisory committee established by the Bundesministerium für Forschung und Technologie (BMFT = Federal Ministry of Research and Technology).[1] The goal is to explain the formation of

---

1   The interview data were collected during summer 1988 (research groups) and winter 1988/89 (funding agencies, committee) in a project at the Max-Planck-Institut für Gesellschaftsforschung in Cologne in collaboration with the Institut für Wissenschaftstheorie und -forschung in Vienna, which will analyze these data along with data on Austria and Switzerland under a comparative perspective. A research report on the German case is forthcoming (Jansen 1991). Previous versions of this chapter were presented at the policy networks conference and at the ECPR Joint Sessions of Workshops, held at the Ruhr-Universität Bochum, 2-7 April 1990. The chapter benefited from the discussions at the conferences and with colleagues at the institute. I would like to mention Jürgen Häusler, Renate Mayntz, Andreas Ryll, Uwe Schimank and Raymund Werle for valuable discussions and comments. For technical assistance, I would like to thank Marie Haltod-Hilgers,

the HTS policy by showing the points of intersection between scientific and technological opportunity structures and between the relevant actors' different policy strategies.

2   An Outline of the General Approach: Policy Networks and their Adaption to Change

Since the seventies political scientists have been departing more and more from the traditional view of the state as a planning and regulating authority, implementing political decisions that were taken by parliaments. The end of the planning euphoria resulted in research into implementation devoted to finding out why policy programs did not work as they were intended to. Societal actors that possessed information and resources that the state was lacking were detected. A closer look at the implementation process even made clear that the distinction between policy implementation and the definition of policy goals and programs is often artificial. Blurring boundaries between public and private were observed. The top-down approach of traditional implementation research was questioned. "Implementation structures before implementation" were discovered that created policy issues and played an important role in policy formation. As a consequence the interest of policy analysts turned away from state regulation and hierarchical control towards forms of interest mediation, bargaining and collective decision making, towards the role of the state as a participant in these processes or as a designer of institutional arrangements, and towards the question of how these processes and institutional designs are related to the achievement of public goals. On the national level concepts like corporatism and private interest government emerged, on the level of sectors or sub-sectors concepts like meso-corporatism, policy community and policy network came up.

In the area of science and technology policy the problems of the attempt to use science for societal ends ("Finalisierung der Wissenschaft") are well known. The discussions on autonomy versus guidance of science have provoked endless debates (Polanyi 1951, 1968; Bernal 1970; Luhmann 1968; Böhme et al. 1972, 1973; Daele et al. 1975, 1977, 1979;

Cynthia Lehmann and Günter Schröder. The remaining faults are of course the author's, who alone rests responsible for the content of the chapter.

Küppers et al. 1978; Krohn et al. 1987; Keck 1984; Schimank 1988). Scientists are committed to defending the autonomy of science. Research institutes again and again exhibit the tendency to escape state guidance and to define their work on their own. The typical problems of top-down implementation are especially virulent in science and technology. Scientists are the only ones who have access to crucial information for the evaluation of their work. This gives them large discretion in defining their tasks according to their interests and equipment. They tend to define their objectives in intra-scientific terms since this is often the only way of structuring the task that is available. Basic science in particular is characterized by fundamental uncertainties on promising research directions and methods that cannot be overcome by project descriptions and policy goals.

What actually happens in science and technology policy is that goals and programs are negotiated and finally set up in a concerted process between science, industry and politics. Wittrock, Lindström and Zetterberg in their analysis of energy research policy have coined the word of implementations structures before implementation proper, which "exist in the sense of informal networks of interested parties before implementation" and "might well be active in defining and forming a program that will later reach the implementation stage" (Wittrock et al. 1982: 133). Another concept is that of "technical systems" (Figure 1) introduced by Shrum, which he defines as "centrally-administered networks of actors oriented to the solution of sets of related technological problems. They are characterized by relatively large size, cognitive complexity, sectoral diversity, occupational pluralism, and formal organization" (Shrum 1984: 63). Arguing against a superficial autonomy of science Shrum and his colleagues see technical systems as initiated and administered by the state with the aim of solving broad technical problems of social concern (Shrum et al. 1985: 47).[2]

---

2   See the differentiation between the competitive modality of network formation and the cooperative mode by Laumann et al. (1978: 466ff.). While the relations between the corporate actors in the competitive mode are basically antagonistic and linkages are based on resource dependencies, the implicit philosophy in the cooperative modes of network formation is the attainment of a collective purpose, for which the interorganizational field has responsibility, by conscious cooperation of various organizations. Especially the case of "mandated cooperation" seems to respond to the "technical system" concept of Shrum, in which governmental organizations are central control agencies.

Figure 1: Ideal Type Technical System

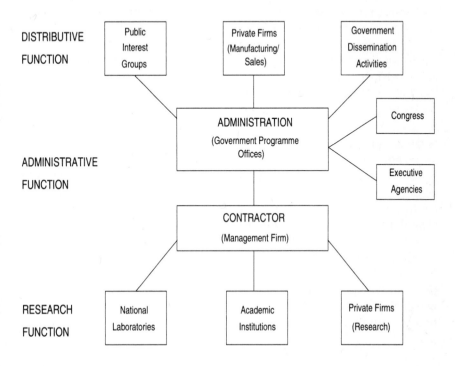

Source: Shrum 1984: 83.

I will use the concept of a policy network as a tool for the analysis of the relationship between interests and governmental departments/ agencies in the process of policy formation in the case of HTS. Kenis and Schneider suggest the definition, "A policy network is described by its actors, their linkages and by its boundary. It includes a relatively stable set of mainly public and private corporate *actors*. The *linkages* between the actors serve as communication channels and for the exchange of information, expertise, trust and other policy resources. The *boundary* of a given policy network is not primarily determined by formal institutions but results from a process of mutual recognition dependent on functional relevance and structural embeddedness." (Kenis/ Schneider, this volume above).

Compared to other policy process concepts like corporatism, meso-corporatism, negotiated economy, iron triangle, pluralism, policy community, issue network, policy universe etc. that are crowding the literature, the policy network has the advantage of being rather neutral. It can be used to denote several kinds of functions of the network (the pluralism/ corporatism debate, lobbying vs. participation in policy formation and implementation) and different levels of analysis (macro, meso and micro). Varying numbers, types and mixes of actors (individual firms/organizations vs. interest groups/associations vs. chambers with compulsory membership/representational monopoly; mixes ranging from only public [= intergovernmental networks, statism] to public and private actors and, finally, to only private actors [= private interest government]) can be considered. Networks can be characterized by varying degrees of conflict/competition and consensus/cooperation between the actors, by the degree of state domination or interest domination, of formalization/institutionalization and by the degree of closure of the network (pluralism/open access vs. elitism/closure).[3] While Kenis and Schneider seem to exclude individual actors from participation in policy networks, I would like to include them. In sectors which lack a high degree of "corporatization" and where personal expertise and reputation is important, like in science, the question of corporate versus individual actor has to be treated as an empirical one.

One of the problems of policy networks that is widely discussed is their resistance or adaption to change. Numerous policy studies show how established networks try to defend the status quo and fail to cope with external, mainly economic changes (see Midttun 1988a on heavy industry and Grant 1985, 1987, 1990, Farago 1985 and Waarden 1985 on agricultural policies). Within an established network regularly a special definition of the problems and issues involved emerges. Networks become cohesive and tend to have a definite view about what and who belongs to their field. New issues and actors are likely to face resistance

---

3   For a more encompassing discussion of the dimensions of policy networks and a location of some of the more common concepts into a typology using number and type of actors, function of the network and the power relation between state and interests see Waarden (1990: 5ff.). For a discussion of the use of the concept in the British literature, see Marsh/ Rhodes (1990).

and exclusion from the network. This problem of adaption, of inclusion or exclusion of new issues and actors is especially relevant in the case of research and technology policy, which typically has to react to the discoveries of basic science providing new knowledge. The explicit goal of policy programs in this area is to scan scientific developments for potential applications. The very quick exploitation of new opportunities is crucial for international competitiveness in high-tech fields which are characterized by cumulativeness, steep learning curves (Dosi 1982: 154; 1984: 86ff.) and first mover advantages (Williamson 1975: 34f.). Any inertia of networks in research and technology policy to respond to new opportunities created by scientific and technological breakthroughs thus poses serious problems.

My chapter will deal with the question of how the German superconductivity policy network reacted to the sudden breakthrough in superconductivity research. It shows first why and how the established network included the new issue - ceramic high-T$_c$ superconductors - in its agenda in a very specific way that is determined by the existing network structure and resources. And it shows secondly why and how an actor from outside tried to enter the network, why it succeeded and how it shaped the structure and policy of the transformed network. The analysis deals with the transformation of the whole policy network and the formation of an HTS policy program as a consequence of the intersection of actor strategies and new opportunity structures[4] that are offered by scientific and technological change.

For the formation of the superconductivity policy I take as explanatory variables (1) the structure of the old superconductivity policy network, (2) the opportunities opened up by scientific and technological change (see section 3), and (3) the intentions and resources of the actors involved. To begin with, the set of actors is defined by the old network. New actors can enter the scene in accordance to the scientific and technological opportunity structure. With respect to the actors, I distinguish between three types: scientists interested in working on scientifically rewarding problems and in raising funds for their research, industrial

---

4   My use of the term "opportunity structure" departs from the use of Laumann et al. (1978: 471), who define an opportunity structure as a subnetwork within which exchange relations tend to be confined for several reasons. I use the term to denote the structure of opportunities which are exogenous to the network and are brought about by scientific, technological and market changes.

R&D (Research & Development) managers interested in defending old markets and developing new high-tech products and, finally, between them I see the state and its science and technology agencies, interested in guiding scientists to technologically relevant basic research, in organizing effective technology transfer from science to industry and in guaranteeing the competitiveness of the national industry.

3   HTS: Changes in Scientific and Technological Paradigms

Scientific paradigms (Kuhn 1962) form a frame of reference that guides researchers on their way to promising research questions and research objects. "Normal science consists in the actualization of that promise, an actualization achieved by extending the knowledge of those facts that the paradigm displays as particularly revealing, by increasing the extent of match between those facts and the paradigm's predictions, and by further articulation of the paradigm itself" (Kuhn 1962: 24).

Before HTS was discovered, superconductivity research was a declining field in science. The golden era of superconductivity in the sixties and seventies was over. Scientists turned to more promising fields, especially to semiconductor physics. Normal science in superconductivity was guided by the "BCS theory", developed in 1957 by Bardeen, Cooper and Schrieffer (and named after their initials), who were awarded the Nobel prize in 1972. Since the sixties, normal science consisted in proving the special mechanism of superconductivity, the "electron-phonon interaction" in various uncommon superconductors. Numerous competing explanations of superconductivity were almost all ruled out by experimental evidence in the course of "normal" superconductivity science. The search for superconductors with higher critical temperatures had been frustrated since 1973 when niobium-germanium with $T_c = 23$ K was found. The established electron-phonon mechanism even explained why all the attempts to discover superconductors with higher critical temperatures were in vain. The theory was thought to imply that superconductivity above 30 K was impossible. The only puzzle for the BCS approach was the superconductivity of "heavy fermions"[5] discovered in the seventies, which did not seem to match up with the predictions. The appearance of HTS fundamentally challenged the BCS theory and changed the course of superconductivity research. Experimental evidence on a traditional key experiment (isotope effect) processed with the new material is inconclusive. Until now no one has succeeded in designing a crucial experiment confirming or ruling out BCS theory. It is far from clear whether superconductivity in HTS is based on the traditional mechanism. Many alternative theories have appeared on the scene.

HTS not only opened up new scientific frontiers for physicists - experimental and theoretical - but also caught the interest of other natural sciences, namely of chemistry and material science. The race for the discovery of room-temperature superconductors was on, the dogmatic limit of 30 K had been overrun. Chemists and material scientists were highly motivated, because the winners would be sure to reap great scientific (and economic) rewards. Other disciplines with different conceptualizations of superconductivity got involved; a chemical theory of HTS, for instance, was proposed (cf. Simon 1987). Soon it became obvious that the complex chemical structure and the ceramic nature of the new materials made an interdisciplinary approach of physicists, chemists and material scientists necessary, not only in applied science but also in basic science. The ongoing race for new materials implies that only those physicists who collaborate with the best preparative groups will have the finest samples of materials and will have them in time. On the other hand, only those preparative groups that collaborate with the best measurement groups with arcane know-how and equipment will get their samples characterized in every respect. This will guide them in their search for new materials or material improvement. These are strong intrascientific incentives for the various disciplines to cooperate.

Another important feature of HTS research compared to traditional superconductivity research is the closeness of basic and applied research. While the heavy fermions - in the center of basic research in 1986 - were technologically absolutely irrelevant, any know-how on HTS materials is of direct technological value. Work in basic and applied research

---

5   Heavy fermions are f-electrons which have effective masses up to 10^2 times greater than normal electrons. Some of the materials containing heavy fermions are superconducting. The micromechanism for the superconductivity of heavy fermions is considered to be spin-fluctuations (Fachlexikon ABC Physik 1989).

often only differs in perspectives and conclusions but not in the actual approach. For instance, thin films are necessary for many basic physical experiments, but they are also the fundamental base of HTS electronics.[6]

In summary, the change in the scientific paradigm of superconductivity can be shown in three dimensions:

-   the challenge of the physical theory of superconductivity,
-   the incorporation of other natural sciences into the field with different theoretical concepts, different know-how and equipment,
-   the jump of basic research close to technological exploitation.

The change of direction in basic research also caused a change in the technological paradigm of superconductors. The term "technological paradigm" was coined by Dosi (1982) in analogy to the definition of a scientific paradigm. "We shall define a 'technological paradigm' as a 'model' and a 'pattern' of solution of 'selected' technological problems, based on *selected* principles derived from natural sciences and on *selected* material technologies. ... In other words a technological paradigm (or research program) embodies strong prescriptions on the *directions* of technical change to pursue and those to neglect" (Dosi 1982: 152).

Within superconductivity, technological research had been restricted to metallic alloys, and the methods employed had been metallurgical ones. Researchers had almost given up searching for materials with higher critical temperatures, and engineers had resigned themselves to the ongoing struggle with the very low temperatures and the complicated helium infrastructure required when working with low-temperature superconductors. Applications in electric power (superconducting cable, superconducting switches, transformers, energy storage) turned out to be feasible but not competitive. In the seventies the German project to develop a superconducting magnetic train was abandoned in favor of a different system. Superconducting magnets were only used where extraordinary power was necessary and costs were secondary as in magnet technology for the fusion project developed at the Kernforschungszentrum Karlsruhe

---

6   This is illustrated by the following example. To perform the "tunnel experiment", which is essential for explaining the micromechanism of HTS, one must have a "tunnel element". This is made up of a sandwich of a substrate, a thin superconducting film, a very thin insulating film and another superconducting film. Under certain conditions, the electron pairs in the superconductor can "tunnel" their way under the insulator. This tunnel element, vital to basic HTS research, serves at the same time as a magnetic sensor or a switching device in applied research.

(KFK, a national research lab) or in magnet technology for high-energy accelerators. In the eighties, to everyone's surprise, magnetic resonance imaging (MRI) magnets used in medical diagnosis turned out to be the first respectable market for superconducting equipment.[7] Besides applications in electric power since the seventies, there were efforts to use the "Josephson Effects"[8] of superconductors. Josephson junctions can be used as very fast switching devices with almost no power dissipation or as hypersensitive detectors of magnetic fields, for instance, in medical diagnosis. While the application efforts of superconductors in electronics did not succeed - IBM gave up the Josephson computer project in 1983 work on superconducting sensor technology was still going on. Estimates of the world market for superconductor equipment before HTS are around DM 500 million annually, more than half of this being devoted to medical application in MRI tomography (magnetic resonance imaging). The industry involved belongs to the electrical and the electronics sector. In Germany the main directions of research in 1986 were the improvement of existing superconducting materials (niobium-tin, niobium-aluminum), new applications in the sensor technology, new cooling concepts, magnet technology, application in magnetic-resonance-imaging devices for medical diagnosis and the construction of a superconducting electrical power generator.

The arrival of ceramic high-T_c superconductors not only brought back into consideration long-abandoned projects such as superconducting power transmission, superconducting trains, superconducting supercomputers. It also opened up new opportunities, for instance, in high frequency applications, sensor technologies, cooling technologies. Market estimates for the year 2000 range between DM 3 billion and DM 75 billion.

What is more far-reaching is that ceramic materials require special chemical preparative know-how and processing techniques which are available not in the electrical and electronics industry, which used to work on superconductors, but in the chemical industry. The chemical industry also has a long tradition in the search for new technologically relevant materials (and is eager to be the first to patent them).

---

7   Siemens, which has been working on superconductivity technology since the sixties, was able to take up this opportunity very quickly and for a long time was the market leader in magnetic body scanners.
8   Brian Josephson who predicted these effects was awarded the Nobel prize in 1973.

To sum up, the change of the technological paradigm concerns the material aspect of superconductors as well as the application aspect of superconductors:

- New and completely different materials open up the patent race for higher T_cs and even for room-temperature superconductors.
- New and completely different materials require different preparative and processing technologies.
- The high-T_c superconductors - and, to an even greater extent, potential room-temperature superconductors, provided they meet technical requirements - will make many old application ideas for superconductors profitable, mainly in the area of power engineering.
- High-T_c superconductors - and, to an even greater extent, potential room-temperature superconductors, provided they meet technical requirements - will open up new opportunities, mainly in the area of electronics/sensor techniques.

These changes in the technological trajectory of superconductors bring about several consequences:

- The market for existing superconducting equipment is challenged.
- The market for power engineering is challenged by the threat of potential substitution by superconducting equipment.
- New market opportunities arise for electronic/sensor applications of HTS.
- New market prospects open up for providers of the best superconducting system (appropriable by patents or licenses) and for providers of preparative and processing technologies making the "system" a useful material.

So, HTS technology crisscrosses the conventional sector structure of industry. The turn to ceramic materials challenges the old superconductor industry and gives an opportunity to sectors with ceramic know-how and production facilities to find their way into superconductors.[9]

---

9   See for instance Jaffe (1989), who analyzes the technological position of firms within the traditional sector structure of industries and who links them to R&D successes.

4   Identification of the Superconductivity Policy Network

The reconstruction of the existing superconductivity policy network can begin with an analysis of research funding in the area of superconductivity in Germany in 1986.

Superconductivity funding in Germany is dominated by BMFT-financed programs in 1986. The Bundesministerium für Forschung und Technologie (BMFT = Federal Ministry of Research and Technology) is the central state actor in the field of science and technology in Germany. Mission-oriented research (Fachprogramme of the BMFT), such as research on nuclear and alternative energy, space research, medical research and also technologically oriented research, belongs to the domain of the BMFT. It is conducted either at universities, industrial labs or non-university research institutes including the "Großforschungseinrichtungen" (= GFE, big science centers, comparable to national laboratories in the US). While universities, industry and research institutes get special grants from the BMFT earmarked for certain projects, the thirteen Großforschungseinrichtungen are institutionally funded.

There are four BMFT programs dealing with superconductivity, one science-oriented "Basic Research Using Large Equipment", and three programs on market-oriented research. The latter make for more than two thirds of the total funding budget in 1986. These are programs for the development of superconducting MRI devices in the medical field, for the development of a superconducting power generator and the more basic program on superconductivity technology within the scope of the special program "Physical Technologies".

Since the task of funding HTS research later was assigned to the latter program, a closer look at it may be worth while. After the change in government the general strategy of the BMFT in direct project funding of market-oriented science and technology research was the concentration of efforts on basic research in key technologies like information technology, material research, biotechnology and physical technologies, that might generate large positive external effects legitimizing state intervention.[10] The funding concept was redesigned as to incorporate and concentrate on basic research and to bring together science and industry

---

10   In general, direct funding was decreased while indirect means of R&D subsidies were intensified in the course of deregulation. Budgets for direct funding of industrial projects have been cut down by DM 1 billion since 1982.

in so-called joint research projects (Verbundforschung). "Verbundforschung" is intended to address problems in R&D too large for one firm, institute or university alone. In a joint project two or more firms and several academic researchers are to work together in precompetitive research on the principle of division of labor. Thus, existing R&D resources can be employed more efficiently, public funding can be concentrated on major projects, and structures promoting technology transfer can be built up (Mennicken 1988; BMFT 1987a: 53ff.; Kulina 1988; Chesnais 1988: 54). Funding for industry was deliberately intended to be subsidiary to industry's own efforts and to be degressive over time (see BMFT 1988b: 20).

The "Physical Technology" program in general and the superconductivity part in particular were lagging behind this general strategy of the BMFT. The program had the lowest rate of funding in the form of "Verbundforschung". In 1986 only 14.9% of the industry funding in this field was given in this form. By 1987 the rate increased to 31.6% still well below the mean of 56% for all market-oriented technology programs. 32 joint projects were in progress in 1987, in contrast to 96 individual research projects. Parallel with the increase of joint projects the share of funding for industry declined. In 1984 before the joint projects, industry got 67% of the budget; in 1987, the rate of funding for industry had declined to 52% with 32 joint projects.

The part of the program concerning superconductors was even more dominated by large firms from the electrical and electronics industry. Its share in the budget in 1984 was 84%. In 1984, the BMFT decided that the program's orientation was not clear enough and reorganized it. As a consequence, the participation of academia increased from 16% in 1984 to about a quarter in 1986, the year before HTS appeared. Joint projects did not play an important part in the program; there was only one joint research project out of 10 projects in 1986.

Besides the BMFT there are two science-oriented funding agencies involved in superconductivity research. The Volkswagen Foundation, a private foundation founded in 1961 by the Federal Republic and the state (Land) Lower Saxony, funded some projects on cryoelectronics in 1986, as part of their program "Microstructure technology", which was to be completed by 1988. The Deutsche Forschungsgemeinschaft (DFG) funded two special research areas (Sonderforschungsbereiche = SFB) in 1986. One of them was created especially for a research group studying heavy fermions, the other was to be finished in 1988. A new program was, of course, intended by that research group. These programs were devoted partly to superconductivity research and related phenomena. The DFG also funded very few individual research projects in the "Normalverfahren" (normal procedure), mainly theoretical work on heavy fermions. Unfortunately, figures on this kind of funding are not available. The following table gives an impression of the funding intensity of the six programs in 1986:

Table 1: Superconductivity Project Funding in Germany in 1986

	in million DM
BMFT Superconducting Medical Equipment	5.2
BMFT Superconducting Power Generator	3.3
BMFT Superconductivity in "Physical Technologies"	3.7
BMFT Basic Research Using Large Equipment	0.8
VW Foundation Program Microstructure Technologies	0.6
DFG Special Research Programs	3.6

These figures do not include institutional funding for superconductivity at the Großforschungseinrichtungen. In 1986 institutionally funded superconductivity research was done at two institutes of the Kernforschungszentrum Karlsruhe. The Institut für nukleare Festkörperphysik (INFP) focused on basic research on materials and the micromechanism of superconductivity. The Institut für technische Physik (ITP) worked on high-field materials and magnet technology for the European fusion project. Figures on their superconductivity budgets are not available.

On the basis of the funding information, I will now try to give a picture of the relevant superconductivity network in Germany in 1986 before HTS was discovered (Figure 2). The two BMFT programs devoted to prototype development in medical instruments and power generators were excluded since these programs could not react to HTS because of their advanced stage, and the four participating firms are or were involved in the basic program anyway. I regard funding, information exchange and explicit collaboration on research projects to be linkages between the corporate actors that participate in the remaining programs. I assume that actors within the same program have some information exchange as is indicated by the boxes around each program. This can be validated at least for the VW program, within which conferences for information exchange on cryoelectronics were held regularly, and for the BMFT program "Physical Technologies", where meetings of the project leaders were common, too. The arrows indicating collaboration within each box are confirmed by funding information, and those crossing the program boundaries are confirmed by interview information. Only one collaboration tie was mentioned in an interview (by Siemens to the University of Munich) which was not covered by the actor network derived from the funding information.

Figure 2: The German Superconductivity Network in 1986

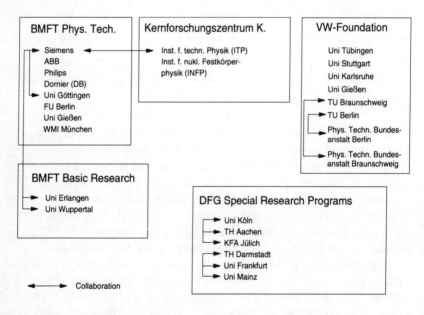

The central actor is clearly Siemens. They collaborate with three universities as well as the more technologically oriented institute of the two at the KFK involved in superconductivity research.[11] All researchers collaborating with Siemens are funded by the BMFT, either by project funding or by institutional funding. Siemens is the only actor whose collaboration ties cross the program boundaries. All the other collaborations of academic actors stay within program boundaries.

5   The Policy Formation: Defining an HTS Funding Program

5.1   The Reaction of the Established Policy Network

In June 1987 - surely influenced by the superconductivity technology war between USA and Japan - the BMFT made up its mind to start a national research effort in HTS. They were extremely dependent on the evaluation of HTS by the leading scientists from academia. In January 1987 the program managing agency for the 'Physical Technologies' held one of the regular meetings of experts and project leaders in the superconductivity funding program. The ministry's and the agency's officials had already learnt about the breakthrough in superconductivity from newspaper articles. They wanted to get some evaluations from the scientists in order to decide about the future directions of the program. Contrary to their expectations, the scientists were very skeptical about high-T_c superconductivity. Obviously, nobody had yet succeeded in replicating the findings, but this was not admitted freely. Nobody was ready to change his research program and no one asked for special funds. This situation was to change soon. Exactly on the day of the meeting a group around Politis at the KFK succeeded in replicating the Müller/ Bednorz results (Politis 1987: 121). This was the starting signal to the superconductivity community in Germany. Now they began to trust the sensational news from the US.[12] The KFK arranged a meeting of the German superconductivity researchers at the KFK on February 19, 1987, in order to evaluate the findings and to discuss organizational and research strategies. They did invite the BMFT to this meeting but turned

---

11   In the seventies the ITP was also funded by the program "Physical Technologies" for the development of cryogenic infrastructure.

12   See Knorr-Cetina (1988) for an explanation of physical closeness and body-presence as factors in the creation of scientific belief and certainty.

to the department for 'Material Research' where they had personal contacts. The BMFT department 'Physical Technologies' was informed only at the very last minute.

Since participation in the first days of the superconductor race was not very expensive, no demands for large funding programs came up at the first meeting of about thirty scientists. Only the university researchers who were suffering from decreasing institutional budgets could not even afford to buy the chemicals needed, to telephone with overseas colleagues or to cover travel expenses. They asked for some seed money, and on the basis of the established program the BMFT was able to respond to these demands rather quickly. In April a small 300,000 DM special program on HTS was lanced, that distributed small amounts of money to 30 university institutes. Most importantly, the BMFT and especially the program managing agency, the "VDI-Technologiezentrum" (VDI-TZ = the Technology Center of the Association of German Engineers), acted as a mediator and information broker on the scene, organizing information letters and meetings, screening people and equipment and attending the European HTS conferences.

The BMFT's final decision on a larger HTS program was based on an intensive discussion of the technological potential of HTS and of German science and industry resources within the "implementation structure before implementation". An important date in this process that may have convinced the BMFT as well as the superconductor industry of the technological importance of HTS despite the basic science nature of this research was an IBM result showing that superconducting thin films were able to carry currents as high as 10^5 A/cm^2. This finding became known in the first days of May 1987. On May 8, 1987, the project managing agency and the KFK invited the whole superconductivity scene, including science, industry and politics, for a discussion aimed at establishing the important research questions and priorities. In June the minister himself met with leading scientists. They strongly urged for the extension of BMFT funding to basic science questions in HTS. Given the applied orientation of the research done at the labs of the traditional superconductor industry this meant funding of university research projects. In July the final version of the HTS program was checked in a meeting with leading experts from science and technology.

When it became clear that the BMFT was going to engage in the funding of basic university research in the case of HTS, the two science foundations deliberately decided to leave this field to the BMFT largely.

This was conditional on the very serious shortage of funding budgets in both foundations caused by the strong demand of the universities for project funding in the course of restrictions in the institutional budgets of the universities. They both followed a policy of keeping only a small but excellent part of their domain, namely two special research areas and a large interorganizational project on Josephson junctions.[13]

On July 23, 1987, the BMFT announced funding for application-oriented basic research in HTS. The funding condition was that local researchers from various university institutes and disciplines cooperate on a common research project. The announcement was clearly addressed to the universities, but industry was invited to participate under the condition that they would fund their own part of a joint project or would cover a substantial amount of the costs of the academic researchers.

Compared to the old superconductivity program this was a completely new approach, a definite turn to basic research, to university research and to interdisciplinary research. The BMFT plan in summer 1987 was about three to five years of funding of interdisciplinary basic research at universities and afterwards a long-term (7-10 years) phase of application-oriented industrial projects (BMFT 1987c).

The BMFT saw an opportunity of taking part in the international superconductor race successfully, since German academia and industry had a long tradition of superconductor research and technology. Faced with extreme international competition and protectionist measures even in the basic science stage, the BMFT realized it was necessary to intensify and coordinate a national basic research effort. The electrical industry of the old network was lacking experienced personnel for the handling of the new ceramic materials. This problem could be overcome by relying on university scientists which were able to take up the topic quickly and on a broad scale. There were strong intrascientific incentives for the collaboration between various disciplines.

The physicists of the old community managed to catch the interest of many colleagues from chemistry, crystallography, material science and engineering sciences who were ready to start an HTS project. By September 1987, a total of eleven university-centered research groups had formed. Fifteen institutes from the old network are non-industrial and

---

13 In 1990, the DFG again has lanced a program on the chemical edge of superconductivity research, a special research program on unusual valence states in solids (ungewöhnliche Valenzzustände in Festkörpern).

non-GFE research institutes: Almost two thirds of them became the cores of nine out of the eleven BMFT-funded groups, while another two have received grants for individual research projects. There are only two new groups (Saarbrücken and Regensburg) which are not based on an old network institute.

The engagement of the university scientists from the old network in the building of the joint projects was not only motivated by the funding opportunities offered by the HTS program. Another reason for their involvement was that HTS was a unique chance for them to establish the core of a material science institute at their university which for long had been prevented by faculty interests and the unwillingness of the faculties to give up any competencies. Such institutes were - this was their opinion - well suited for attracting funds of industrial corporations and state agencies in the future.

The BMFT and the program managing agency were well aware of the problems concerning interdisciplinary research in universities, so they gladly took the opportunity to establish interdisciplinary research projects at the universities without facing any resistance of the scientists. The foundation of a special HTS institute that might have provided the best conditions for interdisciplinary work was deliberately disregarded. It would have required a general political consent on the site and the design of the institute, as well as a search for adequate buildings, directors and researchers. All this was too time-consuming and - after all - too risky, since the technological future of HTS was far from being clear. Another reason for deciding against an institute may have been the consideration that once they get established, research institutes tend to define their research tasks rather autonomously while universities funded by earmarked money showed to be more responsive to the demands of application. This view was widely shared by the industry involved. What was needed was a quick and cheap solution that could be revised at a later stage. The best course of action was to take advantage of the existing infrastructure and personnel at the universities. For the university researchers a centralized approach would have created the situation of "the winner takes all". Thus, a decentralized program was better able to find their consent, too.

What remains to be explained is why the industry of the superconductivity policy network accepted the turn of the BMFT program towards university funding at the expense of the industry. In 1986 more than three-fourths of the program budget (DM 3.7 million) went to industry.

As HTS research began to expand in 1988, industry's share in the increased budget (DM 13.2 million actually spent in 1988) declined to 18%. Although this was still an increase in absolute terms, the firms could have been expected to object to their relative standing within the program, but they did not, and their response to the BMFT's offer to the industry to participate in the university projects was meager. Only one of the old network firms joined one of the eleven university joint projects that were founded in summer 1987. The large corporations decided to start own research groups relying on their established informal contacts to the university researchers of the old network. Why didn't they try to get public funding for their own research efforts? Why did they support the university-centered approach chosen by the BMFT? In my opinion there were several reasons:

- Industry as a collective actor was interested in building up an infrastructure for HTS research at the German universities.
- The industrial actors were aware of the relative advantage of interdisciplinary university research groups in the beginning of the superconductor race compared to their own research groups which were specialized for metallic superconductors and not for ceramic ones. They were interested in maintaining the national position in the international competition. This was possible only by giving public funds to the universities who could not work without such funding.
- The German electrical industry opted for a wait-and-see strategy in the beginning. They set up only small groups within the corporations leaving the first steps of research to the state-funded universities. They were prepared to start larger efforts if a technical breakthrough occurred, at which point they would be sure to get substantial public support (see the BMFT time schedule for HTS research in June 1987, BMFT 1987c).
- The industry, along with the whole superconductivity community, awaited a major increase in the public budgets for superconductivity research. This made the distribution of funding a non-zero-sum game. But this increase in funding was expected to be conditional on the quick formulation of a sound program. This put large pressure towards consent on the whole policy network.

5.2   The Challenge of the Established Superconductivity Network

The break in the scientific and technological paradigm of superconductivity challenged the established network to incorporate the chemical and material science questions posed by HTS. This problem was handled within the old network by relying on university researchers that established interdisciplinary university groups. But there were other answers to this problem. The break in the technological paradigm of superconductors offered new opportunities not only to university scientists possessing ceramic and chemical know-how, but also to chemical industry. Hoechst, a large German chemical firm, took up this chance and succeeded in entering the established network.

Hoechst is one of the three leading German chemical corporations which are known for their very high rate of self-financing of R&D (98%), as well as for their high rate of in-house basic research (6.3%, see Häusler 1989) and their good connections to the chemical departments of German universities (Rilling 1986; Grant et al. 1987; Krempel 1988).

In the eighties, world-wide competition and restricted resources forced high-technology firms to think about new research strategies. Even the largest corporations were no longer able to get along with internal R&D efforts alone (Fusfeld/ Haklisch 1985). The ability of any firm to build up the basis for innovation and economic growth on its own steadily decreased. Technological change shortened product cycles and thus the time available for amortization on R&D expenses. High-tech products and processes depended more and more on the combination of know-how and technologies from different fields. This made R&D more expensive and, what is more important, considerably decreased the likelihood of one company's possessing all the necessary know-how and equipment. High-tech corporations responded to these challenges in two ways:

- They strengthened the cooperation with external research institutes and universities, and
- they began to think about collective R&D, i.e. collaboration with competitors in precompetitive research (Fusfeld/ Haklisch 1985; Chesnais 1988; Hagedoorn 1989).

Hoechst was one of the first German high-tech corporations to draw conclusions from changing conditions for technical innovation. In 1981 Hoechst attracted the public's attention by deciding to finance a biochemical laboratory at Harvard University, and in 1985 it decided (along with other chemical companies) to participate in the long-term, basic-research-oriented BMFT programs on material research and on biotechnology. The material research program was the first major state-funded research in which the German chemical industry participated. It became the paradigm for the new concept of "Verbundforschung" (joint industrial research projects); it encompassed 120 joint projects by 1987 (compared to only 20 single research projects), more than in any other special program. The project managing agency is not the VDI-TZ responsible for superconductivity technology, but the Kernforschungsanlage Jülich (KFA), one of the big national labs of the BMFT. The industrial firms involved in the material research program are generally large chemical firms. Planned for ten years, the program's goal is to promote long-term, scientifically and economically risky research projects. The scientific and technical potential of German researchers within academia and within industry shall be focused on selected questions by means of joint projects.

Probably due to the misrouted information within the BMFT - the department for material research was invited to the first meeting of scientists on HTS -, the R&D department of Hoechst found out about HTS and the meeting. Looking for new products and new markets, the R&D managers decided to attend the meeting as an information base. After the Karlsruhe meeting, the Hoechst R&D management decided to invest heavily in HTS research immediately. They saw HTS as a long-term material research project with considerable market potential. In the eyes of the managers the kind of approach that would be necessary to make high-T_c superconductors a technologically useful material fitted well together with the general concept of the material research program of the BMFT. In Germany, Hoechst had not only the greatest chemical expertise but also the best-suited equipment for developing the materials that could enter (and win!) the superconductor patent race. Aware of their competitive edge, they took immediate advantage of their inside information to secure themselves an excellent starting position.

Hoechst realized quickly that in order to participate in the worldwide patent race for HTS it needed to acquire knowledge about superconductivity in general and processing technologies, such as wire and thin-film fabrication, in particular. This clearly could not be done by an internal research group alone. In the very competitive patent race, it is especially crucial to have a variety of approaches, since no one can tell which approach will be successful in the end. At the same time, collaboration with competitors was impossible in the search for alternative superconductors. Too much was at stake.

Since knowledge about superconductivity was not available within the company, Hoechst managers could foresee that learning processes would require some time and external support. They decided to follow a strategic networking approach to the problem, which made Hoechst a factor that the BMFT and the old superconductor firms had to reckon with in the evolving HTS scene. Within two months after the Karlsruhe meeting they had an internal task force for HTS research made up of about six researchers from the ceramics department and from the department of technical physics. They augmented this in-house task force by making cooperation contracts with scientists from universities and research institutes as a strategy of minimizing risk, of getting access to knowledge and equipment and of recruiting experienced personnel. The criterion for choosing scientists as collaborators was expert know-how in either superconductivity, processing techniques or solid-state/structural chemistry which might provide clues for the search for new superconductors. By April 1987 the research management of Hoechst had concluded contracts with twelve scientists from outside in a concerted action with their patent department. HTS projects of collaborating scientists for about DM 9.2 million were planned. Hoechst partly followed the joint research model of collaboration between industry and science that had been established in the material research program. Obviously they were convinced that HTS would become a subject of this program soon. They deliberately departed from the joint research approach as far as collaboration with competitors in the material patent race was concerned. In spite of this violation of competitive neutrality, they presumed that their approach would be approved by the BMFT. They intended to provide part of the funding for the scientific research program and assumed that the BMFT would pay for the rest.

Figure 3, showing the Hoechst collaboration network, is reconstructed mainly according to interview information. While the scientists in the upper boxes of the network are new in superconductivity research - they are providing the chemical and ceramics know-how - all the scientists in the three lower boxes come from the old superconductivity network. Having managed to choose scientists from each program and even from the two Großforschungseinrichtungen that were involved, Hoechst has clearly succeeded in maximizing know-how and information flow. Surprisingly, there are two institutes among Hoechst's new collaborators, the University of Erlangen and ITP-KFK (the Institute for Technical Physics at the KFK), which collaborate with Siemens in conventional superconductivity research.

Figure 3: Superconductivity Network of Hoechst, April 1987

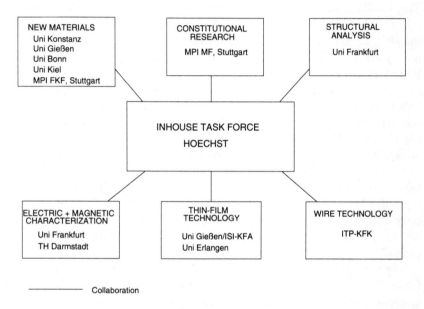

Hoechst was successful in taking advantage of the opportunity presented by the break in the technological trajectory of superconductors. Success in entering a new technological field depends on organizing quick access to knowledge and equipment, and success in the patent race is dependent on following a variety of different approaches while preventing competitors from doing the same. Collaboration with academic scientists was the fastest and easiest way for Hoechst to achieve these goals. They reacted to the challenge of HTS with the construction of a corporation-centered research network in both fields.

Within the BMFT, the department of Physical Technologies was able to establish its competencies for the new field of high-T_c superconductivity very quickly. Their budget for superconductivity research could easily be expanded to include HTS. Not later than in July 1987 the research management of Hoechst had to realize that HTS was not within the domain of the material research program but belonged to the program "Physical Technologies", which had not included the chemical industry up to that date. They realized that this program was dominated by electrical industry, namely by Siemens, and that material science questions were rather new. Joint research projects still were uncommon in this area. The BMFT's decision to concentrate funding on basic research in this context also meant the exclusion of industry from funding, at least in the field of material research. Nevertheless Hoechst insisted on the optimality of their industry-centered approach and tried to convince the BMFT that it was necessary for industry to include industrial joint projects on the material science questions from the beginning. For the established superconductivity policy network the solution to delegate the material science questions to university research groups was viable, but not for Hoechst. They tried to make clear that research on superconducting *materials* was their genuine domain. Hoechst was in an excellent position to bargain with the BMFT, having its own task force with fifteen scientists in contact with twelve elite academic institutes. The chemical firm reminded the BMFT of its general philosophy of industry-university cooperation and technology transfer, and warned that the ministry's failure to fund this extraordinary group would give the wrong signal politically.[14]

In September 1987 Hoechst took the initiative and applied for a grant for a joint Hoechst + collaborator research project, although the July announcement clearly did not include funding for industry. Just two weeks later, on September 23, 1987, the BMFT announced a second funding program for industrial joint projects on the technical potential of HTS. The design of the program followed the usual concept of joint projects, with two or more firms joining academic researchers for a common project, and industry receiving a maximum of 50% of their countable project costs and paying for 25% of the costs of their academic partners. So the BMFT formally adopted Hoechst's position and departed

---

14 Hoechst warned the ministry's officials that they were ready to complain about a failure to include an industrial material research project in the HTS program on the highest level. The fact that the minister of research and technology, Heinz Riesenhuber, belongs to the "family of chemists" - he has a doctoral degree in chemistry - probably played an important role in the considerations of both sides.

from its initial "university-funding-only" policy. It augmented the university-centered approach with an industry-oriented program.

6   The Transformation of the Policy Network: Compromise on the Funding Priorities and the Emergence of an HTS Industry Consortium

The BMFT department "Physical Technologies" had been forced by Hoechst to expand its funding to include an industry-oriented program, but the thrust of the strategy changed only slightly - from "universities only" to "universities first" - and the motivation remained the same. Basic research in a completely new field (ceramic superconductors as opposed to metallic ones) was needed, in which, from the point of view of the old superconductivity policy network, only the universities could provide expertise and people. Know-how not yet embodied in equipment was in the heads of experts who were not available in industrial labs at the beginning. Universities were leading in research in summer 1987 and needed public funding. Industry, especially the old superconductor industry, needed some time to adapt to the new situation, to recruit solid-state experts necessary for the new research questions. And the large corporations that were able to go into basic HTS research were strong enough from the BMFT's point of view to finance their research expenses without public subsidies.

The BMFT had managed to get DM 12 million extra for HTS research for 1988, supplementing the existing low-temperature superconductivity budget of DM 4 million. Further budget increases were not to come until 1989 and the following years. Refusing to split the 1988 budget between cheap university and expensive industry research, the BMFT decided that universities would come first. Although it formally announced an industry-funding program, no money was actually set aside for this program. In autumn 1987, the old superconductors industry sent their applications (abridged versions) to the BMFT. Among them were large projects by Siemens and by AEG, the second-largest electrical corporation in Germany now belonging to Daimler-Benz. All the industrial applications were simply postponed by the BMFT.[15] The old superconductor industry consented to this, but the chemical industry objected strongly. In December 1987, the BMFT set up an advisory committee on HTS as a conflict-managing strategy. Members of this committee came from industry (Siemens, AEG, Philips, Hoechst), from the two involved national labs (KFK and KFA) and from two of the universities of the old network (Karlsruhe and Darmstadt). Hoechst was the only newcomer in the committee and presumably took an isolated position. This committee was intended to work out recommendations for the HTS science and technology policy of the BMFT. It also served the BMFT as an information and coordination instrument for the developing HTS network, especially for industry and national labs which were not or not yet involved in BMFT projects. The committee also allowed the BMFT to gain consent for its strategy - members were deliberately selected not so much because of expert know-how but because of position and influence - and to integrate the only opponent, Hoechst, into the new network. By adopting this co-optation procedure, the BMFT managed to absorb the newcomer Hoechst into the leadership of the HTS policy network and averted threats to the otherwise accepted strategy of "universities first". This is quite evident in the committee's decision, finally approved by all industry members, to reserve 1988 funding for universities and postpone funding for industry until 1989 when more resources would be available. Instead of struggling over the own share in the funding budget, the efforts of the committee were focused on the provision of political legitimacy for the whole HTS program in order to expand future funding.

In summer 1987, even before the BMFT had applied for special money for HTS, the parliamentary committee for research and technology (Bundestagsausschuß für Forschung und Technologie) granted DM 12 million extra money for HTS research for 1988. This was a sort of national effort in reaction to the international competition and to newspaper reports. The parliamentary committee connected this special grant with the stipulation that a funding program for HTS research be submitted soon. The HTS advisory committee of the BMFT took part in the formu-

---

15   The BMFT only offered letters of intent to the industry. These LOIs were sent out in May 1988, stating that industry was expected to provide advance financing for HTS research for 1988 which would be reimbursed if there were funds left over in the ministry's budget at the end of the fiscal year.

lation of this funding program for HTS research which went through several checks during 1988 and was finally published by the project managing agency in February 1989. As far as can be investigated, the amount of public funding that was considered to be necessary by this funding recommendation was raised from DM 167 million to DM 390 million and the program duration from four years to seven years. This expansion of the program was a strong incentive for consent and compromise among conflicting interests within the committee representing the enlarged policy network.

In summer 1987 the old superconductor industry became aware of the newcomer Hoechst on the HTS scene. They realized that HTS was not only a domain of electronics and electrical industry but also a potential market for chemical corporations that could provide ceramic knowhow. In contrast to its strategic exclusion of other chemical firms, Hoechst was very much interested in collaboration with component producers, with whom the competitive overlap was very small. Hoechst wanted to sell semi-finished products, wires, ribbons or films that the electrical and electronics industry would then use to manufacture devices (Chesnais 1988: 105; Fusfeld/ Haklisch 1985). Meetings between Siemens and Hoechst on possible collaborations started. Some time later Daimler-Benz/AEG indicated to Hoechst that they were interested in collaborating. Negotiations on the board level between the three corporations were initiated.

In autumn 1987 the BMFT was confronted with research applications from Hoechst, Siemens and AEG among others, which were similar in many respects. While parallel university research was definitely allowed (though under scrutiny) in the HTS program, parallel industrial research can not be financed by the BMFT. The high costs are prohibitive. The BMFT wanted to combine several projects to form large joint research projects, which would mean that all the firms involved would have access to each other's research results. They also wanted to ensure the compatibility of the research objectives of chemists and ceramists from the chemical industry and of physicists and engineers from the electrical industry. Faced with the problem of having to cut the proposals in some way to eliminate overlaps, the BMFT realized that its own informational base regarding strengths and interests of the corporations was too restricted and decided to ask the corporations themselves. They were all members of the advisory HTS committee, which may have been the site for some bargaining between BMFT and industry and within industry. The attempt of the BMFT to stimulate collaboration between the firms and between firms and university groups met with some resistance of industry, which was concerned about its autonomy in defining cooperative ties. They did not want to take advice from the ministry. The BMFT's stated aim was only to arrange the proposals in order to form joint research projects. This aim, along with the formation of the advisory committee, with the prospects of increased public funding for a national effort in HTS and with the companies' search for synergetic advantage and risk-minimizing approaches, finally triggered the formation of the German HTS consortium. In spring 1988 Hoechst, having consulted with Daimler-Benz/AEG and Siemens, gave a press conference and presented the research consortium, within which Hoechst once again has a central position. Collaboration with AEG/DB and Siemens is relatively easy for Hoechst (exception: Vakuumschmelze, a subsidiary of Siemens which manufactures superconducting wires), while cooperation between AEG and Siemens, which are direct competitors, is far more problematic. This is reflected in the later development of the consortium. The contract was finally signed by Hoechst and Siemens, while Daimler-Benz/AEG decided to have just an option to come in later. Hoechst not only is central in the industry network but also in the surrounding academic network. Hoechst has collaborative ties to fourteen academic partners, Siemens to seven partners and Daimler-Benz/ AEG to six partners. Even if one does not take into account the five partners for the search for new materials, Hoechst remains the corporation with the greatest access to external scientific experience in HTS research.

Hoechst has succeeded in building up a central position in the academic network and in becoming a member of an industrial consortium, pooling resources and minimizing the uncertainties of basic research, while at the same time remaining the only chemical firm in the network. Within the industrial collaboration they occupy a gate position that allows them to maximize the information flow, which is critical for success in basic research. They had this opportunity when they got to know about HTS very early by chance, and they took this chance without hesitating. While old network people were still recovering from the shock of HTS, Hoechst was making contracts with the top university researchers. From this position they were able to convince the BMFT of the necessity of funding joint industrial-university projects. Although the first plans to incorporate HTS into the material research program failed, the networking strategy proved to be error tolerant. It allowed Hoechst to enter the established network and to achieve a central position in the industrial consortium.

7 Summary and Perspectives

The discovery of HTS and the related changes in scientific and technological paradigms triggered a transformation of the old superconductivity policy network and gave rise to a new approach to HTS research policy. The HTS programs set up by the BMFT were largely determined by those actors who took advantage of two special opportunities created by the break in the superconductivity paradigm.

The change in the scientific trajectory could be handled within the old superconductivity policy network. It gave the impetus for the BMFT to set up a basic and interdisciplinary research program based on the university researchers of the old network. The external conditions for this network building by the BMFT were that the necessary combination of chemical/ceramic and solid state know-how was not available within the industry from the old network and that these firms agreed to rely on university research in a first program phase devoted to material science questions.

The second new opportunity deals with the break in the technological paradigm of superconductors that offered chances to sectors which had not been concerned with superconductivity before. Hoechst's arrival in the HTS network was partly a result of chance and even misconceptions - they found out about the first HTS meeting by chance, and were motivated by the false assumption that HTS would become a subject of the material research program. In the material research program, the superconductor industry would have been the newcomer; as it was, Hoechst was the newcomer to the superconductivity network. Despite this status, Hoechst shaped the evolving network with its strategic networking approach. The patent race and a technology exceeding the boundaries of any single industrial sector were the arguments for Hoechst to build up a network of collaboration with academic scientists. This starting position together with the technological importance of the chemical industry enabled Hoechst to convince the BMFT to set up a second program on industrial research, to monopolize the "new materials" aspect of HTS and to acquire a central and unquestioned position within the HTS industry consortium.

This chapter showed how an established policy network adapted to changes in the environment, in this case to a scientific and technological breakthrough. Old definitions of who and what belongs to the field could only be overcome by an extremely powerful and strategically planning actor entering the scene and pushing forward its definition of the problem. Further research in the analysis of the German HTS policy should be oriented to the question of whether public goals can be achieved within the structure that has emerged from this intersection of actor strategies and scientific and technological trajectories. In my view, there are two main problems:

-   the efficient coupling of the various disciplines cooperating (and competing) in the university joint projects, and
-   the efficient coupling of scientific and technological progress.

Contingent factors in the history of the HTS policy network have led to the emergence of two partly competing research programs and research networks: university-centered joint projects on the one side, and the industrial HTS consortium on the other. Whether the rather loose interaction between industry and university groups will result in an effective exchange of information and know-how is not yet clear. With one exception (ABB = Asea Brown Boveri, an electrical firm), the corporations refused the offer to join a university joint project, preferring to pick out some institutes for collaboration in the frame of their industrial projects. While the BMFT is interested in facilitating the transfer of scientific and technical know-how from the state universities to medium-sized and small firms that are expected to join the HTS program later, the large corporations are afraid of losing control over their know-how. Reluctant to collaborate with a wide range of university groups, the large corporations prefer to choose their partners on their own in order to limit the number of participants and to reduce coordination and control problems. They are not interested in creating the conditions of technology transfer in general but only in particular, in so far as the own company's concerns are affected.

Further research should be devoted to this relation between public and private goals in HTS research policy and to the role of network structures in their achievement.

References

Bernal, J.D., 1970: *Wissenschaft.* Reinbek bei Hamburg: Rowohlt (first edition 1954).

BMFT (ed.), 1987a: *Handbuch der Projektförderung.* Bonn.

BMFT (ed.), 1987b: *Förderkatalog 1986.* Bonn.

BMFT (ed.), 1987c: *Supraleitung - faszinierende Forschungsergebnisse und vielversprechende Perspektiven.* Pressemitteilung 49/87 vom 30.6.1987. Bonn.

BMFT (ed.), 1987d: *Neue Hochtemperatur-Supraleiter in der Diskussion.* Pressemitteilung 66/87 vom 18.8.1987. Bonn.

BMFT (ed.), 1988a: *Förderkatalog 1987.* Bonn.

BMFT (ed.), 1988b: *Bundesbericht Forschung 1988.* Bonn.

BMFT (ed.), 1989: *Förderkatalog 1988.* Bonn.

Böhme G./ Wolfgang van den Daele/ Wolfgang Krohn, 1972: Alternativen in der Wissenschaft. In: *Zeitschrift für Soziologie* 1, 302-316.

Böhme, G./ Wolfgang van den Daele/ Wolfgang Krohn, 1973: Die Finalisierung der Wissenschaft. In: *Zeitschrift für Soziologie* 2, 128-144.

Boswell, P.G./ R. Dornhaus, 1987: *The Economic Impact of High T_c Superconductors - a Materials Substitution Analysis for Potential Markets.* Frankfurt a.M.: Battelle.

Buckel, Werner, 1984: *Supraleitung. Grundlagen und Anwendung.*Third edition. Weinheim: Physik Verlag.

Burt, Ronald S., 1979: A Structural Theory of Interlocking Corporate Directorates. In: *Social Networks* 1, 415-435.

Chesnais, Francois, 1988: Technical Co-operation Agreements Between Firms. In: *STI-Review* No. 4, December 1988, 51-119.

Daele, Wolfgang van den/ Peter Weingart, 1975: Resistenz und Rezeptivität der Wissenschaft. In: *Zeitschrift für Soziologie* 4, 146-164.

Daele, Wolfgang van den/ Wolfgang Krohn/ Peter Weingart, 1977: The Political Direction of Scientific Development. In: E. Mendelsohn/ Peter Weingart/ R.D. Whitley (eds.), *The Social Production of Scientific Knowledge.* Dordrecht: Reidel, 212-242.

Daele, Wolfgang van den/ Wolfgang Krohn/ Peter Weingart (eds.), 1979: *Geplante Forschung. Vergleichende Studien über den Einfluß politischer Programme auf die Wissenschaftsentwicklung.* Frankfurt a.M.: Suhrkamp.

Dosi, Giovanni, 1982: Technological Paradigms and Technological Trajectories. In: *Research Policy* 11, 147-162.

Dosi, Giovanni, 1984: *Technical Change and Industrial Transformation.* London: MacMillan.

Elmore, Richard F., 1980: Backward Mapping: Implementation Research and Policy Decisions. In: *Political Science Quarterly* 94, 601-616.

Elmore, Richard F., 1985: Forward and Backward Mapping: Reversible Logic in the Analysis of Public Policy. In: Kenneth Hanf/ Theo A.J. Toonen (eds.), *Policy Implementation in Federal and Unitary Systems.* Dordrecht: Nijhoff, 33-70.

Fachlexikon ABC Physik, 1989, ed. by R. Lenk. Vol. 2. Frankfurt a.M.: Deutsch.

Farago, Peter, 1985: Regulating milk markets: corporatist arrangements in the Swiss dairy industry. In: Wolfgang Streeck/ Philippe Schmitter (eds.), *Private Interest Government. Beyond Market and State.* London: Sage, 168-181.

Fusfeld, Herbert/ Carmela S. Haklisch, n.d.: Kollektive Industrieforschung. In: *Harvard Manager. Innovationsmanagement,* Vol. 1. Hamburg: Manager Magazin Verlagsgesellschaft, 121-128 (English: Cooperative R&D for Competitors. In: *Harvard Business Review* 63 (1985), No. 6).

Galaskiewicz, J. 1985: Interorganizational Relations. In: *Annual Review of Sociology* 11, 281-304.

Grant, Wyn, 1985: Private organizations as agents of public policy: the case of milk marketing in Britain. In: Wolfgang Streeck/ Philippe Schmitter (eds.), *Private Interest Government. Beyond Market and State.* London: Sage, 182-196.

Grant, Wyn, 1991: Models of Interest Intermediation and Policy Formation - Applied to an Internationally Comparative Study of the Dairy Industry. In: A. Grant Jordan/ Klaus Schubert (eds.), *Institutions, Structures and Intermediation of Interest.* Special Issue of the European Journal of Political Research. Amsterdam: Elsevier (forthcoming).

Grant, Wyn/ William Paterson/ Colin Whitston, 1987: Government-Industry Relations in the Chemical Industry: an Anglo-German Comparison. In: Stephen Wilks/ Maurice Wright (eds.), *Comparative Government-Industry Relations.* Oxford: Clarendon Press, 35-60.

Häusler, Jürgen, 1989: *Industrieforschung in der Forschungslandschaft der Bundesrepublik: Ein Datenbericht.* MPIFG Discussion Paper 89/1. Köln: Max-Planck-Institut für Gesellschaftsforschung.

Hagedoorn, John, 1989: *Economic Theory and Analyses of Cooperation and Alliances in R&D and Innovation.* MERIT 89-006. Maastricht:

Maastricht Economic Research Institute on Innovation and Technology.

Hanf, Kenneth/ Theo A.J. Toonen (eds.), 1985: *Policy Implementation in Federal and Unitary Systems*. Dordrecht: Nijhoff.

Hazen, Robert M., 1988: *The Breakthrough. The Race for the Superconductor*. New York: Summit Books.

Hjern, Benny/ D.O. Porter, 1981: Implementation Structures: A New Unit of Administrative Analysis. In: *Organization Studies* 2, 211-227.

Hjern, Benny/ Chris Hull, 1982: Implementation Research as Emprical Constitutionalism. In: *European Journal of Political Research* 10, 105-115.

Institut für Sozial- und Bildungspolitik Hamburg e.V., n.d.: Abschlußbericht des Projekts *"Förderung der Zusammenarbeit zwischen Hochschule und Wirtschaft"*. Hamburg.

Jaffe, Adam, 1989: Characterizing the "technological position" of firms, with an application to quantifying technological opportunity and research spillovers. In: *Research Policy* 18, 87-97.

Jansen, Dorothea, 1991: *Die Supraleitungsforschung und -förderung in der Bundesrepublik Deutschland nach der Entdeckung der Hochtemperatursupraleitung*. Research Report. Köln: Max-Planck-Institut für Gesellschaftsforschung (forthcoming).

Keck, Otto, 1984: *Der schnelle Brüter: Eine Fallstudie über Entscheidungsprozesse in der Großtechnik*. Frankfurt a.M.: Campus.

Kluge, Norbert/ Christoph Oehler, 1986: *Hochschulen und Forschungstransfer*. Kassel: Wiss. Zentrum für Berufs- und Hochschulforschung der GH Kassel.

Knorr-Cetina, Karin D., 1988: Das naturwissenschaftliche Labor als Ort der "Verdichtung" von Gesellschaft. In: *Zeitschrift für Soziologie* 17, 85-101.

Krempel, Lothar, 1988: *Netzwerke zwischen Forschungsorganisationen: Bericht aus einem Forschungsprojekt*. Manuscript. Köln: Max-Planck-Institut für Gesellschaftsforschung.

Krohn, Wolfgang/ Küppers, Günter 1987: *Die Selbstorganisation der Wissenschaft*. Wissenschaftsforschung Report 33. Bielefeld: B. Kleine.

Küppers, Günter/ Peter Lundgren/ Peter Weingart, 1978: *Umweltforschung - die gesteuerte Wissenschaft?* Frankfurt a.M.: Suhrkamp.

Kuhn, Thomas S., 1962: *The Structure of Scientific Revolutions.* Chicago: University of Chicago Press.

Kulina, Peter, 1988: Probleme und Perspektiven der industriellen Verbundforschung. In: *Technologietransfer. Forschung - Industrie.* Jülich: Dostall, 42-46.

Laumann, Edward O./ Joseph Galaskiewicz/ Peter V. Marsden, 1978: Community Structure as Interorganizational Linkages. In: *Annual Review of Sociology* 4, 455-484.

Lehmbruch, Gerhard/ Philippe C. Schmitter (eds.), 1982: *Patterns of corporatist policy-making.* London: Sage.

Luhmann, Niklas, 1968: Selbststeuerung der Wissenschaft. In: *Jahrbuch für Sozialwissenschaft* 19, 147-170.

Marsh, David/ R.A.W. Rhodes, 1991: New directions in the study of policy networks. In: A. Grant Jordan/ Klaus Schubert (eds.), *Institutions, Structures and Intermediation of Interest.* Special Issue of the European Journal of Political Research. Amsterdam: Elsevier (forthcoming).

Mayntz, Renate (ed.), 1980: *Implementation politischer Programme.* Königstein/Ts.: Hain.

Mayntz, Renate (ed.), 1982: *Implementation politischer Programme II.* Opladen: Westdeutscher Verlag.

Mennicken, Jan-Baldem, 1988: Spektrum der Forschungs- und Innovationsförderung in der Bundesrepublik Deutschland. In: *BDI-Handbuch der Forschung- und Innovationsförderung* 1, Erläuterungen 1, 1-21 (loose-leaf edition, February 1988).

Mersits, U./ H. Nowotny, 1989: *Striking Gold in the '90s: The Discovery of High Temperature Superconductivity and its Consequences.* Wien: Institute for Theory and Social Studies of Science.

Midtun, Atle, 1988: The Negotiated Political Economy of a Heavy Industrial Sector: The Norwegian Hydropower Complex in the 1970s and 1980s. In: *Scandinavian Political Studies* 11(2), 115-143.

Nakajima, Akira, 1988: Preparing for the Age of Superconductors: Experts Judge the Prospects. In: *Nikkei High Tech Report* 3(18), 1-4.

Nelson, Richard R., 1987: *Understanding Technical Change as an Evolutionary Process.* Amsterdam: North Holland.

Nöldechen, Arno, 1988: *Die Supraleitung. Nobelpreis für eine technische Revolution.* Düsseldorf: Econ.

Polanyi, M., 1951: *The Logic of Liberty. Reflections and Rejoinders.* London: Routledge.

Polanyi, M., 1968: The Republic of Science. In: E. Shils (ed.), *Criteria for Scientific Development.* Cambridge Mass.: MIT Press.

Politis, Constantin, 1987: Die Suche nach der Hochtemperatursupraleitung. In: *KfK-Nachrichten* 19, 119-129.

Rembser, Josef, 1987: *Das Forschungs- und Technologiesystem der Bundesrepublik Deutschland und ein Vergleich mit den Vereinigten Staaten, Japan und Großbritannien.* Paper presented at the international conference on "Die nationalen Forschungs- und Technologiesysteme westlicher Industrieländer - ein internationaler Vergleich" at the BMFT Bonn, 26-27 May 1987.

Rilling, Rainer, 1986: The Structure of the "Gesellschaft Deutscher Chemiker" (Society of German Chemists). In: *Social Studies of Science* 16, 235-260.

Rip, Arie/ Nederhof, Anton J., 1986: Between dirigism and laissez-faire: Effects of implementing the science policy priority for biotechnology in the Netherlands. In: *Research Policy* 15, 253-268.

Robyn, D. et al., 1988: Bringing Superconductivity to Market. In: *Issues in Science and Technology* 5(2), 38-45.

Schauer, F. et al., 1987: *Assessment of Potential Advantages of High T$_c$-Superconductors for Technical Application of Superconductivity.* Karlsruhe: KfK 4308.

Schimank, Uwe, 1988: *Institutionelle Differenzierung und Verselbständigung der deutschen Großforschungseinrichtungen.* MPIFG Discussion Paper 88/7. Köln: Max-Planck-Institut für Gesellschaftsforschung.

Schmitter, Philippe C./ Gerhard Lehmbruch (eds.), 1979: *Trends Toward Corporatist Intermediation.* London: Sage.

Schuh, Lothar, 1988: *Keramische Supraleiter.* Haar bei München: Markt und Technik.

Schulte, Peter/ Heinz Rüschenschmidt, 1987-1988: *Technologie- und Wissenstransfer an den deutschen Fachhochschulen.* 2 Vols. Ed. by the Bundesminister für Bildung und Wissenschaft. Bad Honnef: Bock.

Shrum, Wesley, 1984: Scientific Specialities and Technical Systems. In: *Social Studies of Science* 14, 63-90.

Shrum, Wesley, 1985: *Organized Technology. Networks and Innovation in Technical Systems.* West Lafayette, IN.: Purdue University Press.

Shrum, Wesley/ Robert Wuthnow/ James Beniger, 1985: The Organization of Technology in Advanced Industrial Society: A Hypothesis on Technical Systems. In: *Social Forces* 64, 46-63.

Simon, Arndt, 1987: Supraleitung - ein chemisches Phänomen? In: *Angewandte Chemie* 99, 602.

Slivka, Donald C. et al., 1988: *Ceramic Superconductors: Status and Opportunities.* Frankfurt a.M.: Battelle.

Smith, G.J. et al., 1989: High Temperature Superconductivity. Prospects and Politics. In: *Futures* 21, 235-248.

Smith, T. Fred, 1987: The Superconductivity Revolution? In: *Impact of Science on Society* 149, 15-24.

Streeck, Wolfgang/ Philippe C. Schmitter (eds.), 1985: *Private Interest Government. Beyond Market and State.* London: Sage.

U.S. Congress, Office of Technology Assessment, 1988: *Commerzializing High-Temperature Superconductivity.* OTA-ITE-388. Washington, DC: U.S. Government Printing Office.

Verie, Christian, 1988: The Technological and Economic Impacts of the New Superconductors. In: *STI-Review 1988,* 99-134.

Waarden, Frans van, 1985: Varieties of collective self-regulation of business: the example of the Dutch dairy industry. In: Wolfgang Streeck/ Philippe Schmitter (eds.), *Private Interest Government. Beyond Market and State.* London: Sage, 197-220.

Waarden, Frans van, 1990: *The genesis and institutionalization of national types of policy networks between the state and societal interests. A model for analysis and some historical comparisons between the USA and the Netherlands.* Paper presented at the ECPR Workshop "Institutions, Structures and Intermediation of Interests", Ruhr-Universität Bochum, 2-7 April 1990.

Wigand, R.T./ G.L. Frankwick, 1989: Inter-organizational Communication and Technology Transfer. In: *International Journal of Technology Management* 4, 63 ff.

Wilks, Stephen/ Maurice Wright (eds.), 1987: *Comparative Government-Industry Relations.* Oxford: Clarendon Press.

Williamson, Oliver E., 1975: *Markets and Hierarchies.* New York: The Free Press.

Williamson, Peter J., 1989: *Corporatism in Perspective.* London: Sage.

Windhoff-Héritier, Adrienne, 1980: *Politikimplementation. Ziel und Wirklichkeit politischer Entscheidungen.* Königstein/Ts.: Hain.

Wittrock, Björn/ Stefan Lindström/ Kent Zetterberg 1982: Implementation Beyond Hierarchy: Swedish Energy Research Policy. In: *European Journal of Political Research* 10, 131-143.

Part Three

Cross-National Variations In Policy Domains

Chapter 6
Political Exchange in the German and American Labor Policy Domains

Franz Urban Pappi and David Knoke

Introduction

Labor policy is concerned with collective decisions at the national level of a political system that regulate relations between capital and labor and which affect the resource distribution between these factors of production. The decisions we are interested in are bills, government regulations, and decisions of federal courts as, for instance, the Bundesarbeitsgericht in Germany. The actors interested in certain decision outcomes are conceived as corporate actors such as interest groups, parliamentary parties, federal agencies, and departments or ministries. These same actors partially control the decision outcomes, but the control they possess does not necessarily fit their interest profile. Organization A may be interested in bill 1 which is partially controlled by organization B. When B is interested in government regulation 2 which is controlled by A, an exchange of control would guarantee higher satisfaction or interest realization for both actors.

This concept of political exchange is more than a metaphor. The practice of log-rolling in parliaments is a realistic example showing the meaningfulness of the concept. But there exists a wide gap between single, meaningful examples of political or social exchange and the type of generalized exchange postulated by models which are available for economic exchange on a perfect market.

Research for this paper was supported in Germany by a grant from the Volkswagen Stiftung and in the United States by a grant from the National Science Foundation (SES - 8615909), by a grant-in-aid from the University of Minnesota, and by a Fulbright Senior Research Fellowship. The research assistance of Thomas König is gratefully acknowledged.

What we shall do in this paper is to use an exchange model as a baseline from which supply and effective demand for control can be derived and possibilities of profitable exchange can be identified. Whether the actors will indeed get involved in profitable exchange is a second question about which we shall speculate in the concluding section.

In the following, we shall first explicate the exchange model and justify its use as a baseline. In the second section, we shall describe our comparative study of decision making in the German and American labor policy domain. Then, we apply the model, not to the concrete decision process itself, but at the more abstract level of interest in and control of the different subdomains of labor policy. The derived measures of value or price of the subdomains and power or income of the actors will be discussed. In a fourth section the exchange potential of the two systems will be derived in the sense of the minimum exchange volume necessary for the optimal interest realization of the actors, given their interest profile and initial control.

1   A Model of Political Exchange

The exchange model developed by James Coleman (1986, 1990) which we are using was successfully applied to political influence systems, the basic idea being that actors gain generalized power by exchanging their influence resources (Pappi/ Kappelhoff 1984; Marsden/ Laumann 1977). We shall first outline the basic logic of this model and then show that this model has a minimum interpretation in which the interest dependencies among the actors are taken into account, but not necessarily exchange processes.

The basic elements of the model are the interest of actors j in events i which are controlled by the same actors. A first assumption is that we deal with a closed system in which all relevant actors and events are included. Formally the interest matrix X is standardized rowwise with the amount of interest of actor j in all events treated as a fixed sum of 1.

(1) $\Sigma_i x_{ji} = 1.0$

In the same way the total amount of control over event i across all actors is fixed, too.

(2) $\Sigma_j c_{ij} = 1.0$

These two input matrices X and C are given. We are thus able to derive a matrix Z which tells us how dependent the row actors are on the column actors.

(3) $Z = X \, C$ or $z_{jk} = \Sigma_i \, x_{ji} \, c_{ik}$

Z is a matrix of inter-actor-dependency and since X and C sum to 1 rowwise, Z is row stochastic, too. Thus, z_{jk} is a measure of the dependency of j on k, which results from the fact that j is interested in some events which are controlled by k. Using the logic of sociometric status measures we could already compute a power measure for which we take into account only direct and indirect dependencies without any exchange processes.

(4) $p = pZ$ or $p_k = \Sigma_j \, p_j \, z_{jk}$

Thus actor k is powerful to the extent that other powerful actors depend on him or her. In our case we interpret the power of j as j's share of generalized control in the system with the constraint:

(5) $\Sigma_j \, p_j = 1.0$

For the exchange process, we need a decision rule according to which the actors are supposed to exchange the control for power in their possession. Coleman assumes that the actors will allocate their resources or power proportional to their interests such that the effective demand of actor j for control over event i is $p_j \, x_{ji}$.

In equilibrium, effective demand equals the valued supply of control, now c_{ij}^* indicating the control which actor j has after exchange has reached an equilibrium and v_i being the value or price of control over event i.

(6) $x_{ji} \, p_j = v_i c_{ij}^*$

The value concept is directly related to power because value is an expression of the effective demand for control over event i under equilibrium conditions.

(7) $v_i = \Sigma_j \, p_j \, x_{ji}$

The reverse equation for power is:

(8) $p_j = \Sigma_i \, v_i \, c_{ij}$

Going back to the interpretation of power as a status measure, we are now able to distinguish between a minimal and a full interpretation of the Coleman model. The minimal interpretation is not based on the exchange logic. It is enough to assume that the actors know their dependencies from other actors and are thus able to estimate the power of actors from their mutual interdependencies. Only if the concept of control after exchange is to be treated as meaningful, we need the behavioral assumption of proportional resource allocation as the decision rule for actual exchange processes (Kappelhoff 1988: 250).

Value and power are meaningful concepts under the equilibrium condition, but these do not imply exchange. On the other side, exchange on a perfect market does imply an equilibrium (Kappelhoff 1988: 172).

In this paper, we leave the question open whether the actors do indeed get involved in exchanges. We assume that the actors use their perception of power and of the value of events as orienting devices for the actual exchange performed by them. Then we are able to recover exchange possibilities between actors as an important information about our system.

Formally, we have effective demand on the one side and valued initial control of actors on the other side. The difference between the two signals opportunities of profitable exchange.

(9) $P_{diag} \, X - (V_{diag} \, C)^T = D$

D is the matrix of disaggregated demand for and supply of valued control. A positive d_{ji} indicates how much excess demand actor j has for control over event i, a negative d_{ji} is the excess supply, respectively. Excess demand and supply are weighted with the equilibrium prices of control and the income or power of the actors with the consequence that the amounts of demand and supply of a given actor are equal. The sum of the absolute values of demand or supply amounts are a measure of minimal exchange necessary for optimal interest realization. The upper limit of this measure is the power or resources of actor j. Seen from the perspective of the event, the upper limit of supply of control available for exchange is the value of the event. In our closed system the arbitrary scales of the sums of value and power are standardized to 1.0.

As an example let us assume that an actor is interested only in one event for which he has no initial control. What is our measure of minimal exchange necessary for interest realization?

$$(10) \quad d_{ji} = p_j x_{ji} - v_i c_{ij}$$

In this extreme case, $x_{ji} = 1$ and $c_{ij} = 0$, thus $d_{ji} = p_j$. This actor reaches the upper limit of our measure, he is totally dependent on exchange because he does not possess any initial control for that event in which he is interested.

We could define the following relative measure of dependency on exchange (g) for an actor:

$$(11) \quad g_j = \Sigma_i |d_{ji}| / 2p_j$$

Summed over the actors, this measure indicates the dependency on exchange for the total system.

$$(12) \quad g = \Sigma_j (\Sigma_i |d_{ji}|) / 2p_j$$

The closer g is to 0, the more the system is already in equilibrium without exchange. The closer g is to 1.0, the higher the dependency on exchange for an optimal interest satisfaction.

The parallel concept of g_j for the events is a measure of how much valued control is already possessed by actors interested in that event and how much is available as excess supply.

$$(13) \quad e_i = \Sigma_j |d_{ji}| / 2v_i$$

The upper limit of supply made available by an actor is v_i if he is not interested in event i but does control it totally as a single actor. This will normally be an extreme situation and the more probable case is that the upper limit is reached if the control is distributed among a set of actors but none of them is interested in that control. The closer e_i is to 0, the more the control of event i is already possessed by the actors interested in i.

For the labor policy domain we would expect that the older, classical subdomains are more in equilibrium than the more recent ones.

2   The German and American Labor Policy Domains: An Overview of a Comparative Project

A policy domain is a basic policy making subsystem within a larger polity. Sociologically speaking, we interpret a policy domain as a social system, that is as a plurality of actors interacting on the basis of a shared symbol system (Parsons 1951: 19). For a comparative study we could not rely on concrete institutional delineations of a policy domain because the institutions are different in the United States and the Federal Republic of Germany. Our more concrete analytical definition of a policy domain follows Knoke and Laumann (1982: 256), who define it as a subsystem "identified by specifying a substantively defined criterion of mutual relevance or common orientation among a set of consequential actors concerned with formulating, advocating, and selecting courses of actions (i.e., policy options) that are intended to resolve the delimited substantive problems in question". For a delineation of such a system, two tasks have to be performed: First, the theoretically guided definition of the substantive concerns of the policy domain, and second the identification of the relevant domain actors.

As already mentioned, we understand a "labor policy domain" to involve collective decisions at the national level of a political system that regulate relations between capital and labor and which affect the resource distributions between these factors of production. For Americans, the concept "labor policy" has somewhat the same meaning, but in Germany the concept of "Arbeitspolitik" involves different connotations. Thus, the next step was to make the concept more meaningful by enumerating the subdomains which belong to labor policy. These subdomains are treated as elements of the labor policy not because we as experts think that they should belong to the policy domain. This would give us a completely analytical system which may not be used as a frame of reference by political actors. We had to pay attention to the major laws and institutions organizing the labor policy domain in the two countries, using the concepts of labor law and not our own. Table 1 gives an overview of the subdomains we thought are relevant together with the major laws for the subdomains in Germany and the United States.

In a market economy, workers exchange their labor power for monetary compensation from employers. All governmental policies that shape the conditions under which these labor-capital-relations occur are encompassed by our analytical definition of the labor policy domain. The regulatory policies of the domain are identical to those codified in labor law statutes, including collective bargaining rights, union election procedures, codetermination, and workplace regulations. The domain also includes those aspects of social policies that are directly tied to workers' wages and employers' contributions and not only indirectly to general taxes. And, it embraces some aspects of macroeconomic policies that attempt to regulate the labor market. For both nations, we classified these various dimensions as labor policy subdomains. In most instances identical subdomains were identified in each country, but three differences occurred. The German institution of codetermination at the enterprise level does not exist in the US and the formal representation of workers at the plant level (work council in Germany, union elections in the US) is quite different. Secondly, no equivalent exists in the US for the subdomain of labor law courts (Arbeitsgerichtsbarkeit) although some aspects of the National Labor Relations Board suggest a parallel. Thirdly, the single American subdomain of employment conditions was broken into two categories for Germany, one dealing with labor contracts (Arbeitsvertragsrecht) and another with labor hour standards (Arbeitszeitschutz).

The subdomains listed in table 1 structure the substantive content of labor policy over longer periods of time. In Germany, the first laws of this domain go back to the 19th century, especially in the regulation of working conditions, another part was first formulated in the early years of the Weimar Republic when the ministry of labor was founded. This period can be compared to the New Deal-period in the United States, when the first important US laws of the labor policy domain were enacted.

Table 1: The Subdomain of Labor Policy: The Most Important Laws in the FRG and the USA

	FRG	USA
I Tarifvertragsrecht[a] 1. Collective Bargaining Regulations	Collective Bargaining Agreement Act 1949	National Labor Relations (Wagner) Act 1935, Labor Management Relations (Taft-Hartley) Act 1947, Civil Service Reform Act 1978
II Unternehmensmitbestimmung 2. Participation of Labor in Management	Codetermination Act 1976, Iron Codetermination Act 1951, Par. 76, 77, 77a, 81, 85, 87 Works Constitutions Law 1952	-
III Betriebsverfassung (Works Constitution)	Works Constitutions Law 1972 Federal Staff Representation Law 1974	National Labor Relations Act 1935
IV Innere Organisation von Gewerkschaften und Arbeitgeberverbänden 3. Internal Organization and Governance of Labor Unions and Employer Associations	Art. 9 (3) Basic Law	Labor Management Reporting and Disclosure (Landrum-Griffin) Act 1959
V Arbeitsvertragsrecht 5. Employment Conditions	Civil Legal Code, Basic Business Law, Notice of Termination Law	Fair Labor Standards Act 1938
VII Arbeitszeitschutz (Working Time Regulations)	Working Time Regulations, Shop Closing Hours Law 1956	Fair Labor Standards Act 1938

continued on following page

Table 1: *continued*

	FRG	USA
VI Technischer Arbeitsschutz 4.Working Conditions	Basic Business Law, Reich-Social-Insurance-Regulation, Chemical Act 1980	Occupational Safety and Health Act 1970
VIII Sozialpolitik für Arbeitnehmer 6.Social Policies	Reich-Social-Insurance-Regulation, Law for the Improvement of Enterprise Old-Age Pensions, Workmen's Compensation Act	Social Security Act 1935, Employee Retirement Income Security Act 1974
IX Schutz besonderer Personengruppen 7.Disadvantaged Populations	Handicapped Protection Law, Maternity Leave Law, Youth Working Conditions Law	Fair Labor Standards Act 1938
X Diskriminierung im Beschäftigungssystem 8.Discrimination in Employment	Implementation of EC-Regulations	Civil Rights Act (Title VII) 1964, Fair Labor Standards Act 1938
XI Arbeitsmarktpolitik 9.Labor Market Policy	Work Promotion Law 1969, Employment Promotion Law 1985	
XII Arbeitsgerichtsbarkeit (Labor Courts)	Labor Court Law 1953	-

a German concepts of subdomains (I to XII) and equivalent American concepts (1 to 9). For non-existent American subdomains, the English translation of the German concept is listed in parentheses. The sequence numbers indicate the sequence of subdomains in the questionnaire, not in this table.

Sources: For FRG: Halbach et al. (1984); for USA: Aaron (1986).

The purpose of our comparative project is not to study labor law historically. We aim at explaining the decision process in this policy domain over the last several years, in Germany for the 10th and 11th legislature of the Bundestag and in the United States for the period of the Reagan administration. Thus, as a second step, we identified the most important issues for these periods and then, as a third step, all important political decisions of the policy domain for the same periods were collected in a data bank.

This last step was important for the performance of our second task, that is the identification of the policy actors. In Germany, we collected all the available information of the participants in parliamentary hearings for the bills in our data bank. All interest groups participating in at least two hearings in the period from 1983 to 1988 are supposed to be actors of this policy domain. At the level of the political system itself, we treat all organizations as relevant actors which have a direct or indirect authority over problems of this policy domain.

The actors of a policy domain of a modern national state are supposed to be corporate actors, and normally not individual persons. For our comparative project, we thought it useful to apply the concept of the organizational state developed by Laumann and Knoke (1987). This concept was developed to grasp the following crucial aspects of policy making in the American polity: (1) The acting units are organizations, or corporate actors; (2) both private and public actors compete for influence on the final decision outcome, and (3) the state is not participating as a single actor, but as a loosely coupled system of agencies, each of which has its own interest profile.

All these characteristics apply to the German polity, which can also be conceptualized as a loosely coupled system of agencies (Behörden), and political actors as the parties, and politically oriented organizations (Interessenverbände). Thus, the overall concept was the same for the two polities, but the details of the operationalization differed a little bit.

In the American project, four methods were used to compile the list of labor policy organizations whose agents were to be interviewed:

(1) Organizations that testified before the Senate Committee on Labor and Human Resources and the House Committee on Education and Labor in the 1980s through the 100th congress, as abstracted by the Congressional Information Service. Only the 297 hearings dealing with labor or vocational education matters were tabulated.

(2) Organizations mentioned in New York Times' Annual Index Labor Abstracts from 1981 to mid 1987.

(3) Organizations registered as congressional labor lobbyists, reported annually from 1981 to 1986 by the Congressional Quarterly.

(4) Organizations filing Supreme Court amicus curiae briefs in 16 major labor cases, indexed in the LEXIS computerized database.

A total of 112 organizations were mentioned five or more times during the seven years. Because of criterion (2) federal agencies and the two congressional labor committees were also on this list. Since we only used criterion (1) for the German case, we had to add the members of the political system itself using strictly authority criteria. This same criterion was used in the American case, too, by adding five major units within the Department of Labor and by separately listing the Republican and Democratic "members and staff" of the House and Senate full labor committees.

An overview of the most important corporate actors of the policy domain in the two polities will be given when we present the power measure and list those actors separately which possess more than the mean power in the next section.

The fieldwork for the American study was in the spring and summer of 1988 and the fieldwork of the German study in the fall and winter of the same year and the first two months of 1989. The following analysis is based on those 124 German actors and 111 American actors for which we have complete information on interest and control. For Germany we had to omit two actors and for the US eight actors due to missing data.

3   The Power of Actors and the Value of Control for Subdomains

We apply the model at the relatively abstract level of interest in and control of the subdomains. We first asked the respondents as agents of their organizations how strongly their organization was interested in each subdomain. In Table 2 the mean interests and the variances are listed for the two polities. We see that social policy is the one subdomain in both polities in which the actors are interested most. Interest in the problems of disadvantaged populations in the labor market and

Table 2: The Interests [a] of Actors in the Subdomains in the USA and the FRG: Means and Variance Compared [b]

Subdomains USA	Mean	Variance	Mean	Variance	Subdomains FRG [c]
1. Collective Bargaining Regulations	2.51	3.63	3.39	2.44	I. Tarifvertragsrecht
2. Participation of Labor in Management and Control of Enterprises, Employee Stock Ownership Plans	1.90	2.78	3.07	3.07	II. Unternehmensmitbestimmung
			3.27	3.08	III. Betriebsverfassung
3. Internal Organization and Governance of Labor Unions and Employer Organizations	1.96	3.13	2.84	2.90	IV. Innere Organisation von Gewerkschaften und Arbeitgeberverbänden
4. Working Conditions: Safety and Physical Conditions	3.48	2.72	2.84	2.49	VI. Technischer Arbeitsschutz
5. Employment Conditions: Hiring, Promotion, Firing, Layoff, Retirement, Time and Wages	3.94	2.06	3.65	1.62	V. Arbeitsvertragsrecht (einschl. Vermögensbildung und Arbeitnehmerüberlassung
			3.31	2.53	VII. Arbeitszeitschutz (einschließlich Ladenschluß)
6. Social Policies: Pensions, Insurance, Maternity Leave, Job Rights	4.07	1.69	4.28	1.18	VIII. Sozialpolitik für Arbeitnehmer
7. Disadvantaged Populations in the Labor Market: Women, Minorities, Handicaped, Youth, Elderly, Veterans, Welfare, Vocational Education and Retraining	3.98	2.07	3.84	1.61	IX. Schutz besonderer Personengruppen (Schwerbehinderte, Mutterschutz, Jugendarbeitsschutz)
8. Discrimination in Employment	3.95	1.71	3.33	2.29	X. Diskriminierung im Beschäftigungssystem (z.B. nach Geschlecht)
9. Labor Market Policies: Job Creation, Immigration, Underground Economy, Plant Closings	3.75	2.25	3.85	1.86	XI. Arbeitsmarktpolitik
-	-	-	2.62	2.34	XII. Arbeitsgerichtsbarkeit

a Interests are measured on a scale running from 5 = very strong to 0 = almost none. b Means and variance based on n = 111 in the US and n = 122 actors in the FRG. c Translations see Table 1.

in labor market policy is strong, too, in both polities, whereas American actors are more interested in employment conditions and discrimination problems and German actors in collective bargaining regulations and codetermination both at the enterprise and the plant level.

To construct the interest matrix X we had to compute the relative interest of an actor in each subdomain.

The control matrix C should tell us the share of control of the actors for each subdomain. To recover this information we first asked the respondents which subfield they know the most about, and then they were asked to name those organizations that are especially influential within this subfield. We had prepared a list of all participants in the labor policy domain so that the relevant organizations had just to be checked. Apart from a question on the general influence reputation which is not used for our model we have therefore gathered data on the subdomain specific influence reputation. The number of mentions an organization received for a subdomain is used as a proxy for the control distribution. When a respondent saw himself as an expert in several subfields his mentions were counted for each one.

The power measure of the model is a summary indicator of the control the actors have in the different subdomains, weighted by the different demands for subdomain specific control. The mean power is $1/n$, that is $1/124 = 0.008$ in the German case and $1/109 = 0.009$ in the American case. Actors who possess more power than this mean are listed individually in Table 3 or 4. For the less powerful actors we just sum their power and include this information in that actor category to which the organizations belong. The organizational typology differentiates crudely between interest groups and political actors in the strict sense of the term. The more detailed categories had to take into account the institutional peculiarities of the two polities.

The first important information on the power distribution is its inequality which we measure with the Gini index. What we expect is that power is distributed more equally in the American pluralistic system than in Germany whose system of interest groups is characterized by few peak organizations. A Gini index of 0.439 for the Federal Republic and of 0.405 for the US seems to verify the hypothesis, even if the difference is quite small. This difference becomes larger when we include only the non-political actors. Then the Gini index for Germany is 0.479

Table 3: The Power of Actors in the American Labor Policy Domain by Organization Type

	n	Σ p_j x 10,000	Σ	mean p_j x 10,000
1. Labor Unions		19	2,253	118
AFL/CIO	1	284		
United Auto Workers	1	182		
Communications Workers	1	150		
United Steelworkers	1	147		
Int. Brotherhood of Teamsters	1	140		
Int. Ladies' Garment Workers	1	137		
Am Fed. State, County, Mun. Empl.	1	136		
United Mine Workers	1	130		
Amal. Clothing & Textiles	1	120		
Service Empl. Int. Union	1	117		
Am. Fed. of Teachers	1	115		
Int. Assn. of Machinists	1	103		
United Food & Commercial Workers	1	100		
Σp_j others	6	392		
2. Employers Assn. and Corporations		27	1,559	57
Business Roundtable	1	157		
Am. Trucking Assns.	1	156		
Assoc. Builders and Contractors	1	145		
Natl. Assn. of Home Builders	1	145		
Blue Cross & Blue Shield Assn.	1	137		
Σp_j others	22	816		
3. Professionals		11	571	51
Am. Vocational Assn.	1	151		
Natl. Academy of Sciences	1	118		
Natl. Education Assn.	1	97		
Σp_j others	8	204		

continued on following page

Table 3: *continued*

	n	Σ	p_j x 10,000	Σ	mean p_j x 10,000
4. Public Interest Groups	32		1,593	49	
Natl. League of Cities	1		116		
Am. Legion	1		99		
Σp_j others	30		1,377		
5. Federal Government		16		1,504	94
Off. of the Secretary of Labor	1		183		
Assistant Secretary for Policy	1		164		
Equal Employment Opportunity Comm.	1		154		
Natl. Labor Relations Bd.	1		151		
Occupational Safety and Health	1		123		
Employment and Training Administr.	1		118		
Natl. Inst. of Occ. Safety & Health	1		96		
Σp_j others	9		513		
6. Congress		4		2,517	629
House Democrats	1		880		
House Republicans	1		612		
Senate Democrats	1		584		
Senate Republicans	1		439		

and for the United States 0.397. This result does better fit the overall hypothesis.

Differences for all actors may be partially influenced by our different procedures to identify political actors. For the Federal Republic we included more political actors in the system out of theoretical considerations than were included in the American polity. Originally, subcommittees of both the House and Senate Committee were also included in the list of participants, but the party groups within subcommittees were not interviewed due to practical considerations. Thus the subcommittees could be mentioned as influential without the main committees being mentioned. We solved this problem in the following way: The mentions received by the subcommittees were counted as mentions of the respective full committee. With these corrections, the control data are better to compare between the two systems.

Comparing first the power sums of the different types of organizations, the congressional actors in the US and the parliamentary actors and political parties in Germany rank first, followed by the unions at rank two. Since the number of organizations within the broad categories is different, we get a better insight of the top of the power pyramid if we focus on individual organizations. In Germany, the two peak organizations of labor and business, the Bundesvereinigung Deutscher Arbeitgeberverbände (BDA) and the Deutscher Gewerkschaftsbund (DGB) rank first, followed by the Ministry of Labor (BMA) at rank three and a group of parliamentary actors at rank four. Within the latter group, the CDU/CSU members of the labor committee are ahead of the SPD members of the same committee, followed by the FDP members and the CDU/CSU Bundestagsfraktion.

In the United States, the legislative actors are far ahead everybody else. This may be partially an artefact of the procedure to include only four actors within this category in the American case.

If we would sum up the power measures of the different political actors in Germany which are of the same party, the majority party in parliament would have a position very similar to the House Democrats in the US. Thus, even if the top three organizations in Germany seem to confirm the corporatist notion of a tripartite system consisting of labor, business and government, the parliamentary actors are not less important if we conceptualize them as collective actors organized along party lines.

The biggest difference between the two countries concerns the position of employers' associations in the power pyramid. In Germany, the BDA ranks first among all organizations, followed closely by the DGB. In the US, the Business Roundtable and some more specialized business organisations are not on par with the more powerful unions, especially the AFL/CIO. And, for example, the two peak business associations with the highest *general* influence reputations (the Chamber of Commerce of the United States and the National Association of Manufacturers) have generalized control below the mean. This result may reflect the majority situation in both House and Senate. Since 1986, the Democrats were the majority party, not only in the House, but in the Senate, too; the unions may therefore have had better access to Congress, being affiliated to the

Table 4: The Power of Actors in the German Labor Policy Domain by
Organization Type

	n	Σ p_j x 10,000	Σ	mean p_j x 10,000
1. Union and Work Council	18		1,696	94
German Trade Union Federation (DGB)	1	459		
Metal Workers' Union	1	223		
Public Services and Transport Workers' Union (ÖTV)	1	160		
German White Collar Workers' Union (DAG)	1	159		
Chemical Workers' Union	1	147		
Σp$_j$ others	13	548		
2. Employers' Assn. and Corporations	22		1,379	63
Federal Confederation of German Employers' Associations (BDA)	1	487		
Federal Association of German Industry (BDI)	1	242		
Metal Industry Empolyers' Assn.	1	92		
Σp$_j$ others	19	557		
3. Peak Org.s of States and Communes	6		421	70
Confederation of Communal Employers	1	150		
Collective Bargaining Assn. of German States	1	106		
Federal Confederation of Communal Peak Associations	1	81		
Σp$_j$ others	3	83		
4. Health System	7		342	49
Federal Chamber of Physicians	1	117		
Σp$_j$ others	6	225		
5. Other Professional Associations	5		62	12
Σp$_j$ others	5	62		

continued on following page

Table 4: *continued*

	n	Σ	p_j x 10,000	Σ	mean p_j x 10,000
6. Mandatory Social Insurance Institutions		13		619	48
Federal Labor Office	1		187		
Confederation of German Pension Insurance Institutions	1		111		
Σp_j others	11		321		
7. Churches and Welfare Assn.		8		460	58
Protestant Church in Germany (EKD)	1		93		
Office of German Catholic Bishops	1		89		
Σp_j others	11		321		
8. Assn. of Disadvantaged Groups		5		267	53
German Womens' Council	1		85		
Σp_j others	4		182		
9. Parliament and Parties		17		2,637	155
Christian Democratic Members of Bundestag Committee on Labor and Social Policy	1		293		
Social Democratic Members of Bundestag Committee on Labor and Social Policy	1		271		
Free Democratic Members of Bundestag Committee on Labor and Social Policy	1		258		
Christian Democratic Parliamentary Party	1		243		
Christian Democratic Association of Employees (CDA)	1		241		
Social Democratic Association of Employees (AfA)	1		221		
Free Democratic Parliamentary Party	1		213		

continued on following page

Table 4: *continued*

	n	Σ p$_j$ x 10,000	Σ mean p$_j$ x 10,000
Social Democratic Parliamentary Party	1	171	
Economic Council of Christian Democratic Party	1	155	
Executive Committee of Free Democratic Party	1	113	
Executive Committee of Christian Democratic Party	1	103	
Green Party Members of Bundestag Committee on Labor and Social Policy	1	92	
Christian Democratic Small Business Association	1	88	
Σpj others	4	175	
10. Federal Government	13	1,609	124
Federal Ministry of Labor and Social Affairs (BMA)	1	349	
Section III of BMA: Labor Law	1	245	
Federal Ministry of the Interior (BMI)	1	240	
Section II of BMA: Labor Market Policy	1	155	
Section I of BMA: Internal Organization	1	137	
Federal Ministry of Economics (BMWi)	1	92	
Section IV of BMA: Social Insurance	1	91	
Σpj others	6	301	
11. German Länder	10	475	48
Bavarian State	1	84	
Σpj others	9	391	
Σ	124	10,000	

Democratic party. And on the other side, President Reagan had decided quite consciously that labor policy should not be one of the areas in which he was eager to perform a proactive role of leadership. A similar decision was made by business associations which concentrated their efforts on issues in other policy domains, for instance tax reform.

The values of the subdomains can be compared more easily between the two countries than the power of actors (cf. Table 5). Here the number of categories is almost the same, 9 subdomains for the United States and 12 for the Federal Republic. The values of the domains can be interpreted as the prices of control for a specific subdomain. This is a generalization of the demand factors weighted by the generalized resources backing the single demands. Within the American polity, the value of control of the following subdomains is almost alike and higher than the value of control of a second group. To the first belong working conditions, social policies, disadvantaged populations, discrimination in employment, and labor market policies, and with a small difference, employment conditions. To a second group of less important domains belong collective bargaining, participation of labor in management, and internal organization of union and employers' organizations. Within this second group the collective bargaining regulations are a little bit more important than the other two.

Within the German polity, the values are all a little bit smaller because we have 12 instead of 9 categories. When we compare the values only within the German polity, we see that social policies, disadvantaged populations, labor market policies, and "Arbeitsvertragsrecht" are within a first group for which control is relatively expensive. "Tarifvertragsrecht", "Betriebsverfassung", "Arbeitszeitschutz", and discrimination in employment are within a middle group and codetermination at the enterprise level, internal organization of union and employers' organizations, working conditions, and labor law courts all have in common that the value of control is relatively cheap. This is especially astonishing for "Technischer Arbeitsschutz", for which control is much cheaper than for the equivalent working conditions in the United States. Interpreting this result we have to consider that working conditions are in Germany mainly regulated by government regulations and less by bills passed by Parliament.

Table 5: The Value of Control for American and German Labor Policy Subdomain

American Subdomains	Values	Values	German Subdomains [a]
1. Collective Bargaining Regulations	.091	.082	I. Tarifvertragsrecht
2. Participation of Labor in Management	.063	.077	II. Unternehmensmitbestimmung
		.082	III. Betriebsverfassung
3. Internal Organization of Union and Employers' Organizations	.066	.072	IV. Innere Organisation von Gewerkschaften und Arbeitgeberverbänden
5. Employment Conditions	.122	.092	V. Arbeitvertragsrecht
		.082	VII. Arbeitszeitschutz
4. Working Conditions	.129	.069	VI. Technischer Arbeitsschutz
6. Social Policies	.128	.105	VIII. Sozialpolitik für Arbeitnehmer
7. Disadvantaged Populations	.133	.094	IX. Schutz besonderer Personengruppen
8. Discrimination in Employment	.133	.085	X. Diskriminierung im Beschäftigungssystem
9. Labor Market Policies	.131	.094	XI. Arbeitsmarktpolitik
-	-	.065	XII. Arbeitsgerichtsbarkeit

a Translations see Table 1.

4   Demand for and Supply of Subdomain-Specific Control

We are using power of actors and value of events as reference points
for use by participants in resource exchange systems. Therefore, we are
able to derive the volume of exchange which would be at least necessary
to realize one's interests. A first important comparative information on
the two polities are the dependencies on exchange (g).

When we correlate the x_{ji} and the c_{ij} across actors for a given event,
we get a first impression of the need for profitable exchange. The
higher these correlations, the more subdomain specific control is already
possessed by those actors most interested in that event. These correlations
are generally lower in the US than in the German labor policy domain.
Computing the percent of necessary exchange for an optimal realization
of interests results in a figure of 58 percent for the US and 39 for the
Federal Republic. Thus, the initial control distribution in Germany is
already closer to the equilibrium distribution C* than in the US. When
we aggregate the d_{ji}'s across actors for each subdomain and standardize
this sum as a percentage of the event value, the resulting figures are
indicators of excess supply of control for this event. The closer the percentage is to 0, the more supply and demand are already in equilibrium
before exchange. One would hypothesize that the more settled a subdomain is the more it should be in equilibrium. For Germany one could
argue that collective bargaining regulations, codetermination, protection
of disadvantaged groups, and labor law court regulations are more settled
subdomains than the others which raised controversies more recently,
especially labor hours standards and labor market policies. But the results
of Table 6 do not support this hypothesis. The simple result is, both for
the US and for Germany, that the lower the value of control for a subdomain, the higher the percentage of control which is offered for exchange.

The original matrix D, at the level of individual organisations, is
much too detailed for an interpretation. But we can aggregate the d_{ji}'s
for the organization types and interpret the different supply and demand
volumes at this level of analysis. Due to the aggregation, we are losing
about half of the exchange volumes of the disaggregated matrix. Interpreting the results one has to remember that p_j or v_i are the upper
limits of the demand of actor j and the supply of control over event i.

Among the American actors the unions would profit most if they
could "buy" control of subdomain 3, internal organization of employers'

Table 6: The Excess Supply of Control over Events as Percentages of the Value of Events (Upper Limit of d_{ji})

American Subdomains	e_i 100	e_i 100	German Subdomains [a]
1. Collective Bargaining Regulations	27.2	17.6	I. Tarifvertragsrecht
		17.2	II. Unternehmensmit-bestimmung
2. Participation of Labor in Management	35.7		
		12.8	III. Betriebsverfassung
3. Internal Organization of Union and Employers' Organizations	54.5	23.8	IV. Innere Organisation von Gewerkschaften und Arbeitgeberverbänden
		21.5	V. Arbeitvertragsrecht
5. Employment Conditions	28.1		
		14.6	VII. Arbeitszeitschutz
4. Working Conditions	22.5	29.1	VI. Technischer Arbeitsschutz
6. Social Policies	24.8	17.6	VIII. Sozialpolitik für Arbeitnehmer
7. Disadvantaged Populations	22.7	13.4	IX. Schutz besonderer Personengruppen
8. Discrimination in Employment	28.1	20.0	X. Diskriminierung im Beschäftigungssystem
9. Labor Market Policies	23.5	15.2	XI. Arbeitsmarktpolitik
-	-	36.7	XII. Arbeitsgerichtsbarkeit

a Translations see Table 1.

associations and unions, and, with some distance, of subdomains 7 and 8 dealing with disadvantaged population groups and discrimination in employment. The greatest suppliers of control for these latter domains are the public interest groups which are most dependent on control of the subfields of working and employment conditions for their interest realization. The Federal government is above all demanding control of labor market policy which could be supplied by the legislative committees. These latter actors are mainly demanding control of collective bargaining regulations and participation of labor in management. In general, the governmental and legislative actors demand and supply less control than the public interest groups, unions or employers' associations. With the exception of discrimination and disadvantaged populations, it is astonishing how much unions and business could gain from exchange between their respective organisations. Their demand and supply vectors are almost complementary to each other indicating very good exchange potentials. But since we already know that the cleavage between labor and business is deeper in the US than in Germany (Knoke/ Pappi 1990), one may doubt whether profitable deals are made across this cleavage line.

For the German system the mean entries of Table 8 are smaller compared to the ones in Table 7, indicating less dependency on exchange. Concentrating on the most expensive subdomain, that is social policies for employees, the unions have the highest demand, followed by the employers' association and the Federal government. They could receive the subdomain-specific control mainly from mandatory social insurance institutions and from the associations of the health system. The power of these latter two types of organizations is based to a large part on their control of the most valued German subdomain. One is reminded that at the time of the fieldwork of our study the reform of the mandatory health insurance system was hotly debated.

Table 8 contains many interesting details which we cannot comment on due to space restrictions. Let us only focus on the two governmental actors, the Federal government mainly represented by the Ministry of Labor and its departments and the German states' representatives at the Bundesrat in Bonn. The German states (*Länder*) rank in the power hierarchy in a middle position due to their role in implementing laws. An important part of the implementation process is the formulation of government regulations (Verordnungen). Even in the labor policy domain where many regulations are enacted by the Federal Ministry of Labor or the Federal government, the Bundesrat has often to give its permission. Thus, it is not surprising that the *Länder* have an excess demand for control of that subdomain for which this type of decision making

Table 7: Derived Demand for Control over Events by Organization Type (d_{ji} 10,000) in the USA

Organization Type	Subdomains								
	1. Collective bargaining	2. Participation	3. Internal Org.	5. Employment Cond.	4. Working Cond.	6. Social Policies	7. Disadv. Population	8. Discrimination	9. Labor Market Policy
1. Unions	-91	-62	193	-73	-231	56	82	84	42
2. Employers' Organizations, Corporations	2	5	-114	-18	57	-16	41	63	-20
3. Professional Societies	-1	-2	-13	37	33	-51	-2	14	-15
4. Public Interest Groups	67	42	46	81	100	-3	-122	-193	-17
5. Federal Government; Departments and Agencies	-18	-29	-47	-26	35	23	-18	8	71
6. Legislative Committees	41	46	-64	-2	5	-8	20	22	-60

is most important: working conditions with respect to health and security standards. The *Länder* could pay for this control mainly from their stock of labor court resources.

Demand and supply is more evenly distributed across the subdomains for the Federal government than for the *Länder* or the parliamentary groups and parties. This is mainly due to the division of labor between governmental institutions. Overall, the demand for control over discrimination in employment and social policies is the highest with an excess supply of control for labor court influence and employment conditions with the exception of labor hours' standards.

Since we have already learned that the higher the value of a subdomain the lower its share offered at the open market it is no surprise to find out that the more resourceful actors are less dependent on exchange than the ones with fewer resources. The correlation between power and dependency on exchange (g_j) is -.67 in the US and -.65 in Germany; and as one would expect the volume offered or supplied for exchange correlates positively with power, in Germany a little bit more (r=0.68) than in the US (r = 0,59).

Assuming for a moment that the actors do indeed exchange their influence resources on a perfect market the control distribution C* after exchange can be derived. As one would expect, the correlations between power and the c^*_{ij} for each subdomain are very high. In Germany none of 12 correlations is smaller than .81, in the US none of the 9 correlations is smaller than .69. Besides power, the other important factor for satisfying exchange results is interest concentration. The more one's interests are concentrated on a few subdomains the better, ceteris paribus, the chances of interest realization. Only two correlations are positive between interest concentration of actors and their final control. In the US, the positive example is discrimination in employment, a subfield where many public interest groups are active, and in Germany it is the law of labor contracts (Arbeitsvertragsrecht). In this field, in which for instance hiring and firing rules are included, we observe the activities of business organizations which have concentrated their interests in this subfield. These two results may give some hope to intensive minorities without a lot of power in the labor policy domain.

Table 8: Derived Demand for Control over Events by Organization Type (d_{ji} 10,000) in the FRG

Organization Type	I. TVR	II. UMB	III. BV	IV. IOGA	V. AVR	VII. AZS	VI. TAS	VIII. SP	IX. SbP	X. DiB	XI. AMP	XII. AGB
1. Unions, Work Councils	-18	-2	2	-33	-48	24	11	45	0	-28	31	16
2. Employers' Org.s	-35	12	-9	-14	-7	18	-9	24	-9	-25	11	44
3. Peak Org.s of States and Communes	-4	-21	5	14	16	2	0	5	2	-6	-13	6
4. Health System	-2	-2	-2	-4	11	-1	12	-32	7	-8	4	17
5. Other Professional Organizations	-2	-1	-1	-5	-2	0	3	4	2	7	1	-6
6. Mandatory Social Insurance Institutions	33	-8	0	35	39	-33	-6	-48	-6	-30	-24	49
7. Churches, Welfare Organizations	18	-2	2	-6	28	-13	-4	2	-7	-19	8	-6
8. Assn. of Disadvantaged Groups	-3	-1	0	-10	8	-7	4	-17	5	8	4	9
9. Parliament, Parties	11	21	-6	28	-27	-4	-51	-13	28	54	-12	-29
10. Federal Government	8	-1	10	-9	-14	10	-5	22	-13	29	-9	-27
11. German Länder	-6	5	1	5	-4	5	45	8	-4	19	-1	-72

a See Table 1 for English translation of German subdomains.

5 Conclusion

Up to now, with the exception of the last paragraph, we did not assume that the actors do indeed exchange their influence resources. Following a minimal interpretation of the Coleman model we just assumed that the actors are familiar with their interdependencies so that they know, at least vaguely, which exchanges would be profitable. But which type of political exchange makes sense in a situation in which no generalized medium of exchange is available and in which mutual trust may be an important precondition?

Exchange on a perfect market is a theoretical concept for which transaction costs such as mutual trust do not count. In addition, the concept is silent concerning concrete dyadic interaction. The idea of a central clearing house which clears the market at equilibrium prices does fit the concept better than a sequence of dyadic exchanges. All exchange has to go on at once, when the system is at equilibrium.

These strong assumptions can not be made for political exchange. If we can expect exchange of influence resources at all, then we should start with the simple idea of barter. A and B will be able to exchange their influence resources only when there exists a double coincidence of wants, that is when A demands what B can supply and B demands what A can supply. This is exactly the type of information contained in the D matrix. A comparison of the demand and supply vectors of two actors informs these two actors about the possible amount of barter between them. Such measures derived from D would be plausible predictors of actual exchange processes.

But there exist competing predictors. If trust is a precondition of political exchange, a social network of amicable cooperation would be a second plausible predictor, provided that exchange is at all possible because of a double coincidence of wants.

Since we are dealing with collective decisions, the actors having the right to make these final binding decisions are the plausible targets for influence attempts. Part of this information should be contained in the control matrix. But it is plausible to assume that an interest group having the alternative of barter with another interest group or a political actor with authority, will choose the latter one. Such a behavior would be contrary to the exchange logic of the organizational state according to which all consequential actors of a policy domain are treated as equal. Some of these actors may be more equal than others, and in a parliamentary system these actors could well be the government and the parliamentary parties. Or, to give another example, in a corporatist system, these actors could be the peak organizations of labor, of the business community, and the Ministry of Labor. We are exploring these possibilities as our analysis continues.

References

Aaron, Benjamin, 1986: Fifty years of labor law and social security: Main developments and prospects in the United States. In: Max G. Rood (ed.), *Fifty Years of Labor Law and Social Security.* Deventer, Nl.: Kluwer, 15-50.

Coleman, James S., 1986: *Individual Interests and Collective Action. Selected Essays.* Cambridge: Cambridge University Press.

Coleman, James S., 1990: *Foundations of Social Theory.* Cambridge, Mass.: The Belknap Press of Harvard University Press.

Halbach, Günter/ Alfred Mertens/ Rolf Schwedes/ Otfried Wlotzke, 1987: *Übersicht über das Recht der Arbeit.* Bonn: Der Bundesminister für Arbeit und Sozialordnung.

Kappelhoff, Peter, 1988: *Soziale Tauschsysteme.* Habilitation thesis. Wirtschafts- und Sozialwissenschaftliche Fakultät der Universität Kiel.

Knoke, David/ Edward O. Laumann, 1982: The social organization of national policy domains: An exploration of some structural hypotheses. In: Peter V. Marsden/ Nan Lin (eds.), *Social Structure and Network Analysis.* Beverly Hills and London: Sage Publications, 255-270.

Knoke, David/ Franz Urban Pappi, 1990: *Fighting Collectively: Collective Actors, Action Sets, and Opposition Networks in the U.S. and German Labor Policy Domain.* University of Minnesota and Universität Mannheim. Unpublished manuscript.

Laumann, Edward O./ David Knoke, 1987: *The Organizational State. Social Choice in National Policy Domains.* Madison: University of Wisconsin Press.

Marsden, Peter/ Edward O. Laumann, 1977: Collective action in a community elite: Exchange, influence resources and issue resolution.

In: R.J. Liebert/ A.W. Imersheim (eds.), *Power, Paradigms, and Community Research.* London: Sage, 199-250.

Pappi, Franz Urban/ Peter Kappelhoff, 1984: Abhängigkeit, Tausch und kollektive Entscheidung in einer Gemeindeelite. In: *Zeitschrift für Soziologie* 13, 87-117.

Söllner, Alfred, 1987: *Grundriß des Arbeitsrechts.* Ninth ed. München: Vahlen.

Chapter 7
Fencing Off: Central Banks and Networks in Canada and the United States

William D. Coleman

This chapter examines the extent to which macropolitical institutions shape both the formal structural relationships and informal networks in a policy arena. By focussing on monetary policy, a policy domain where the state seeks to constrain sharply the avenues for networks between central banks and other institutions, the role of macropolitical variables is brought into clear relief. In this respect, this chapter seeks to redress somewhat the balance between macropolitical and sectoral variables in the study of public policy. Recent analysis both of formal relationships and of informal networks linking actors in a policy domain has tended to focus on sector-specific variables for explaining particular policy outcomes. Thus scholars have stressed the importance of assessing the relative capacity and autonomy of various sector-specific state agencies, the degree of co-ordination or conflict among them, the interdependence between these agencies and societal actors, whether these be large firms or interest associations, and the policy capacity of these societal actors. In many instances, these assessments have yielded results that diverge from expectations: strong sectoral state actors and anticipatory policies have been found in polities normally considered to possess a weak and reactive state and reactive policies have been identified in polities usually understood to have strong, interventionist states. Some scholars have responded to these findings by calling for a new "disaggregated" approach to the study of the state (Cawson et al. 1987; Skocpol 1985),

The author would like to thank the following persons for comments on an earlier draft of this chapter: Michael M. Atkinson, Charles Freedman, Henry J. Jacek, Louis Pauly, Grace Skogstad and participants at the conference on "Policy Networks". Research for the chapter has been supported by the Social Sciences and Humanities Research Council of Canada, grant 410-88-0629.

a study that would distance itself considerably from the holistic state theories developed in radical political economy or in international relations studies.

Although it is evident that studies of sectoral policy have raised serious doubts about existing holistic state theories, it would be a mistake to take this criticism to the point where policy studies focussed on sectoral variables alone. Broad institutional factors implicit to such concepts as a state tradition (Dyson 1980), policy styles (Richardson et al. 1982), or national paths (Grant 1989) do have effects both on the formal structures linking state and society and on the relative importance of informal networks. These effects can be sufficiently important that the relationship between macro-level institutions and the organization of communication in policy arenas should be treated as a *variable* in its own right. Thus we can expect that the capacity, autonomy and policy decisions of sectoral state actors will be more or less constrained by macropolitical institutions. In some policy arenas, the specific properties of the firms or individuals in a sector, of their interest associations, and of the sector-specific state agencies will determine largely the nature of policy outcomes. But in other policy arenas, a national policy style or state tradition may be an important factor in shaping formal structures and informal networks, and thus the character of policy outcomes.

The introduction of this order of variable into policy analysis presents a major challenge. As Hayward (1982: 112; 1986: 19) has noted, a policy style does not itself determine patterns of conduct in any given instance. Rather it affects the capacity of the state to act and its propensity to impose its will in a given situation. Hence the analyst must identify carefully the principal characteristics of a policy style or state tradition and then trace how these characteristics encourage networks among some actors and discourage them among others. Perhaps the most systematic attempt at this kind of analysis is found in Dyson's (1980) work on state traditions in Western Europe. He suggests (1980: 5) the concept of "'political world pictures', in terms of which political conduct is defined, and attitudes towards the accommodation of interests typical of different polities are closely related to an experience of authority ... exercised through both public institutions and a particular set of social relations." Hancher and Moran (1989: 280) second this emphasis on an experience of authority and add that such national traditions may condition which societal actors participate in a given policy arena. In these perspectives, then, an experience of authority as determined by broader macropolitical institutions will enter the political world pictures of sectoral actors, shape to some degree both who participates and the patterns of networks among participants in a policy arena, and thereby affect ultimately the decisions reached.

One can hypothesize further that the importance of this experience of authority in structuring a given policy domain will vary depending on the relative strength of state actors. Thus in policy arenas where state actors have a pre-eminent role, macropolitical influences will be greater than those where state actors have a weaker position. If this hypothesis is credible, then we might expect to find some considerable evidence of macropolitical influences in policy arenas where state actors assume a dominant role. State-directed policy arenas are those where highly capable and autonomous state agencies are faced with weakly developed associational systems representing societal actors (Atkinson/ Coleman 1989). Consequently, organized interests play neither an important advocacy nor a participant role in the policy process. Networking should thus be more pronounced *within* the state itself than between state and societal actors. In other arrangements such as corporatism or clientele pluralism where societal actors are stronger, the influence of macropolitical institutions should be weaker. Here the organizational characteristics of the sector being represented and of the associational systems themselves may become more important in shaping paths of communication. Informal networks between state and societal actors are given freer rein.

In an attempt, then, to trace the effects of state traditions or broader experiences of authority on the organization of a sectoral policy arena, this chapter focusses on arrangements for formulating and implementing monetary policy in Canada and the United States. Quite consciously, the chapter utilizes what Przeworski and Teune (1970) identify as a "most similar systems" design. In both countries not only are state actors dominant in the policy arena, but also the rules of the game loosely fit Dyson's "adversary" model. In addition, the shape of the monetary policy community in the two countries assumed its present configuration at about the same time, viz. during the Great Depression. As Hancher and Moran (1989: 284) stress, the historical timing of the crystallization of a policy "space" is crucial to understanding its subsequent development. Finally, both policy communities developed in tandem with a capital-markets based financial system (Zysman 1983). Despite several idiosyncrasies of their respective banking systems, monetary policy in both countries came to rely relatively quickly on market-oriented policy instruments rather than on moral suasion, exchange controls and informal credit controls. These similarities are all useful because they make it easier to isolate the effects of broader experiences of authority in determining which actors become involved in informal networks and in formal structural ties in a policy arena.

The analysis is carried out in two steps. First, the chapter reviews Dyson's definition of an adversary polity and then seeks to delineate differences within this broad type relevant to Canada and the United States. Specifically, it outlines the different experiences of authority associated with a Westminster model parliamentary system as opposed to a congressional system. Second, with these differences in mind, it analyzes the organization of the monetary policy communities in the two countries focussing on three properties: the "independence" of the central bank, the internal structure of the central bank and the relative transparency of the policy process, and the patterns of consultation with private sector actors. The chapter shows that broader macropolitical institutions in Canada facilitate a more significant limitation of informal networks and formal linkages involving the central bank than occurs in the United States.

1   Defining Experiences of Authority

In his study of state traditions and experiences of authority, Dyson devises a nine-fold typology of different types of polity which he applies to the study of Western Europe. One of these nine types, the "adversary" polity which he associates with the United Kingdom, provides a useful starting point for the analysis of national traditions in the United States and Canada. A competitive, accusatory style of politics dominates in this "adversary" polity. This system stresses the role of public debate, is hostile to inter-party coalitions and power sharing, and discourages the effective functioning of investigative machinery within Parliament. Consistent with the absence of an abstract conception of the state, power is diffused away from the center to a host of independent decision making agencies. Accompanying political world views are "not informed by a deep institutional consciousness or constitutional awareness but rather by the notion of politics as a game in which the rules, which are often vague and subject to various interpretations, are mainly the result of mutual understandings between contestants who compete for the favor of the spectators" (Dyson 1980: 67).

Interest groups give precedence to the advocacy of policy rather than to participation in the making of policy. Relations among groups are fluid and pluralistic, alliances short-term, and networking extensive but informal. With the executive perceived as a broker among contending interests, groups compete with one another both for the ear of the state and for members. Establishing stable, tripartite arrangements with the government at the peak level proves an elusive quest (Dyson 1980: 66). Rather, informal networking among elites becomes an essential tool for policy change. In such circumstances, permanent integrating mechanisms across sector and territory in the interest intermediation system are not encouraged. Peak associations either will not emerge at all or, if they do, will be mixed associations that give equal precedence to the concerns of individual and associational members.

This conception of an adversary polity fits broadly patterns of politics in Canada and the US. Yet within this general type, distinct experiences of authority emerge in the two countries consistent with differences in their basic constitutional principles.[1] Canada possesses what has been termed a Westminster model of parliamentary government. Central to this model is the principle that "the Cabinet is in charge of, and responsible for, the conduct of parliamentary business" (Atkinson 1990: 337). Accordingly, in the Westminster model, authority and responsibility are *concentrated* in the hands of a ministry drawn from a party that enjoys the support of the electorate. The concentration of authority is assumed to be essential to good government. In contrast, in the United States, authority and responsibility are *divided* among the executive, the Congress, and the judiciary. Behind this separation of powers lies the notion that authority must be dispersed in order to produce good government and to avoid the abuse of power.

Translated into institutional forms, these principles provide somewhat distinctive experiences of authority in the two polities. In Canada, the norm of ministerial responsibility prevails; there is strong pressure not

---

1   The following discussion focusses primarily on executive-legislature relations. Other constitutional principles such as federalism and charters of rights also affect experiences of authority in the two polities. But when it comes to monetary policy, neither of these principles is particularly relevant. Monetary policy is the responsibility of the central government in both countries with the states/provinces having virtually no systematic involvement. Nor has monetary policy to date raised questions of human rights.

only to trace policy responsibilities back to one person who is in the Cabinet but also to hold that person accountable for the exercise of those responsibilities. Hence there is a decided reluctance to grant any bureaucratic agency "independence" because such a conferral of authority would weaken the accountability and the authority of the government. Although power might be diffused away from the center, at least the formalities of ministerial responsibility will be retained. In the US, members of Cabinet are accountable to the President who, in turn, shares power with the legislature. The notion of an "independent" agency fits better in such a system because it is broadly consistent with the idea of dividing rather than concentrating power. If there are lines of accountability, they will flow both to the President and the Congress; having two, often competing, superiors often reinforces independence rather than weakening it.

Consistent with the US experience is a determination that the civil service not be an independent power base in its own right. The civil service exists to serve the President and accordingly a large number of its senior and middle-level officials change with the election of the President. These officials often participate in partisan debates with the Congress on behalf of the President and possess relatively less discretion over policy (Vogel 1986: 280). In the Canadian Westminster model by contrast, the civil service is cast as an apolitical reservoir of policy expertise and advice for the Cabinet. Its relations with ministers are conducted in secret as are its own internal deliberations. Officials normally enjoy considerable discretion in formulating policy to be submitted for ministerial consideration.

These several norms governing relationships among the chief executive, members of Cabinet, the legislature, and the civil service affect, in turn, modes of consultation between state and societal actors. The US system, with its aversion to any concentration of power, frowns upon any mode of consultation that privileges one group over another or that smacks of collusion. The preference is for "open, unstructured competition among interest groups" (Vogel 1986: 279). Relations between government agencies and groups tend to be more formal, with disputes often resolved in the courts rather than in private negotiations. In contrast, the Canadian system is biased toward conciliatory, collaborative networks between groups and state actors (Grant 1989: 81). Consultation tends to be frequent, routinized and discrete; unlike the US example, there is a strong preference for resolving disputes in private discussions, with public debates being reserved for politicians only who conduct themselves in the more stylized and less significant forum of the House of Commons.

This admittedly sketchy summary of different national policy styles or traditions in Canada and the United States provides us with several key norms for comparing monetary policy arrangements in the two countries. These arrangements lead to somewhat distinct patterns of communication within the respective policy communities. Such differences become evident in an examination of three sets of relationships: the central bank and the political executive, the internal structure of the central bank, and the central bank and private sector actors.

2   Comparing Monetary Policy Communities

John Woolley (1984: 4) describes monetary policy as being concerned with maintaining large economic variables - interest rates, exchange rates, bank credit and so on - in some appropriate relationship to broad economic goals related to inflation, employment, economic growth and international payments flows. More specifically, monetary policy involves the regulation of the stock of money in the pursuit of these goals. Although the specifics of implementation vary somewhat across states and the instruments involved are very complex, the approach may be roughly summarized as follows. Monetary policy involves the use of a set of instruments that affects bank reserves or balances held on deposit at the central bank that, in turn, are aimed at a "proximate" target (short-term interest rates) which trigger movements in "intermediate" targets (exchange rates, monetary aggregates) that, finally, assist in reaching ultimate targets or goals (price stability, employment, economic growth).[2]

In Canada and the US, expert, highly centralized and autonomous state agencies design and implement monetary policy with minimal input from societal interests. Interest associations and large financial firms may be consulted for their impressions of the development of the economy, but possess neither the expertise nor the capacity to act as strong

---

2   For a discussion along these lines, see Freedman and Dingle (1986).

advocates or participants in the policy process. Nonetheless, different kinds of networks have developed within the state in the two countries, particularly as they involve the Finance Ministry and the legislature, and between the central bank and private sector actors. In the United States, contacts tend to be more prolific, taking place informally and through formal representative arrangements. Some of this variation appears to be related to different national policy styles.

2.1 Central Bank Independence: Networking within the State

Assigning responsibility for the conduct of monetary policy has long been a controversial issue in liberal democracies. On the one side are ranged those who argue that monetary policy is sufficiently crucial to a capitalist economy that it merits special constitutional arrangements. A recent editorial in the *Financial Times* (1990) summarizes this position: "Painful experience with the modern manipulation of monetary policy suggests that money is more appropriately an element of the constitutional framework of democracy than an object of political struggle. Monetary stability is a necessary condition for a working market economy, which is itself a basis for a stable democracy." On the other side can be found those who argue that monetary policy is not special nor any more susceptible to political mismanagement than any other policy area. In the words of the late Harry Johnson (1972: 173), any other assumption "involves the establishment of a special position in Government for the owners of one form of property - owners of money and of assets fixed in terms of money - a position which is inconsistent with the principles of democratic equality and the presumption of democracy that the purpose of government is to serve the social good."

Central to this debate is the relationship between the central bank, the agency responsible for the implementation of monetary policy, and the finance ministry. The more political leaders favor the position that monetary policy is a special policy area, the more they will want to assign the central bank responsibility for policy formulation as well as implementation and to keep it independent from this ministry. Practically speaking then, independence involves an attempt by the state to constrain sharply both formal relationships between central banks and finance ministries and the content of communications in informal networks.

Political leaders in both Canada and the US have tended to favor this independence position. Yet the institutionalization of this idea has varied in the two countries and this variation appears to be related closely to their different experiences of authority. The Canadian central bank is formally accountable but informally independent. A direct structural link exists between the Governor of the central bank and the Finance Minister creating a personalized policy network. But other ties tend to be underdeveloped and less relevant to policy formulation. The US counterpart is formally independent in the sense that no formal accountability exists between the Federal Reserve and the Department of the Treasury or the President. But this absence of a formal tie with the executive branch is counterbalanced by extensive informal networking with Treasury officials and Congress.

Central to the monetary policy arena in Canada is the relationship between the Bank of Canada and the Minister of Finance. The ties between the two institutions are complex because they seek to balance the perceived need for an autonomous institution, one removed from short-term political concerns, and the parliamentary principle of ministerial responsibility, the idea that the government of the day must be accountable to Parliament for policy. Canada attempts to achieve this balance in the following way: the Bank of Canada has ongoing responsibility for formulating monetary policy, but the Minister of Finance has ultimate responsibility.

J.F. Ilsey, Minister of Finance during the early 1940s, articulated the spirit of this relationship in the following way: "Conflict between Bank policy and government policy cannot arise for these are the same. The only conflict possible is that management of the bank may disagree with the basic policy desired by the government. Should this happen, the procedure is clear - management would at some stage be expected to resign" (Neufeld 1958: 13). This spirit was not given legal form until the 1960s following a series of disputes between the Governor of the Bank of Canada and the Minister of Finance. In 1967, a legislative change institutionalized a procedure already adopted informally in 1961: in the event of a disagreement between the Governor and the government, the Minister, with the approval of cabinet, may issue a directive to the Bank as to the monetary policy to follow. If such a directive were to be issued (none has been to date), it is most likely that the Governor would resign. The law takes the additional step of creating a network by requiring regular meetings between the Minister and the Governor.

The directive power plus the legislated network symbolize that the government retains ultimate responsibility.

But the implication is that, in the absence of a directive, the Bank of Canada is responsible for monetary policy. Asked what this meant, a close observer replied:

> Full responsibility. It's not like being an agent where the Bank says, 'Well, they told us to do this.' The Governor cannot appear before the House of Commons Finance Committee and say Michael Wilson [the Minister] made me do it. Not on monetary policy ... The Bank of Canada would not take that way out. As long as there is no directive, it has responsibility for monetary policy. That is why I use the term 'co-responsibility'. In practice, of course, the way that works out is that the Governor and the Minister talk over the issues. The Minister can have his views and they will discuss it, but ultimately the Bank feels that it has responsibility for monetary policy.[3]

In short, given that no directive has been issued over the 22 years that this instrument has been available, the Bank of Canada has been pre-eminent in the formulation and conduct of monetary policy in Canada.

This pre-eminence is reinforced by several properties of the Governor's position, properties, in turn, that discourage extensive informal networks with other agencies of the state. First, the nature of the Bank of Canada's Board of Directors places the management of the Bank at arms length from the Minister. Responsibility for the affairs of the Bank is vested in the Board which is composed of 12 persons appointed for three year terms by the Minister of Finance with the approval of the Governor in Council. They oversee the expenditures of the bank and have the occasional, but important, task of selecting the Governor and Senior Deputy Governor.[4] But the responsibility for the formulation and implementation of monetary policy lies with the Governor. Second, the Governor is appointed for a seven-year term and holds office during good behavior. In this respect, the office enjoys similar legal protection to that afforded to the judiciary, the Chief Electoral Officer and the Auditor General. Third, the Bank is financially independent of the government, drawing its revenues from profits on its own operations.

This arrangement between the Bank and the Minister, in turn, creates a very tenuous tie between the central bank and the legislature. The few relationships that exist are highly formalized; informal networks are virtually non-existent. Major policy changes are announced by the Governor

---

3   Confidential interview, April 1989.
4   Their choice is then approved by Governor-in-Council, that is, by the Cabinet.

and not by the Minister in the House of Commons. The Minister will defend the Bank's policy when questioned in the House and the Governor appears before Commons committees to present his Annual Report. But the House cannot hold the Governor accountable directly; the Westminster model dictates that accountability be routed through the Minister. Yet, as we have seen, the Minister does not have primary responsibility. As a consequence, the formalities of the Westminster model create considerable ambiguity when it comes to accountability for monetary policy. Furthermore, they facilitate greatly the limitation of networks between the central bank and members of Parliament.

In the United States, arrangements for monetary policy take a different form. The national policy style, as we have argued, leaves more room for the creation of agencies that are "independent" from the executive branch. It also favors a larger role for the legislature in policy making. Both of these properties shape the conduct of monetary policy which is the responsibility of the Federal Reserve.

The Federal Reserve System, which embraces central banking as one of its principal functions, was established in 1913. Although the original structure of a central board based in Washington and 12 regional reserve banks dispersed throughout the country, each with its own governor and board of directors, remains, criticism of the System following the 1929 Crash led to major amendments in 1935 that established the modern structure. At this time, members of the central board were given the title of "governor" while the heads of the regional banks were downgraded to "president", signifying a shift in power to Washington (Melton 1985: 9). An informal committee to oversee open market operations, originally created at the urging of Benjamin Strong, the first head of the Federal Reserve Bank of New York (FRBNY) (Greider 1988: 293), was recognized in legislation, given the name of the Federal Open Market Committee (FOMC), and assigned functions that have allowed it to become the pre-eminent organization responsible for the formulation of monetary policy. The committee is composed of the seven members of the Board of Governors, the President of the FRBNY, and four other reserve bank presidents who serve on a rotating basis. All 12 presidents attend and speak at FOMC meetings.

Unlike the Governor of the Bank of Canada who is ultimately subject to the Minister of Finance, the FOMC is described as "independent within government" (FRB 1985: 2). Neither the Canadian minister's analogue, the Secretary of the Treasury, nor the President have any direct responsibility for monetary policy. The basis for independence was laid in 1935 when the Secretary of the Treasury and the Comptroller of the Currency were removed from the FRS Board. Autonomy was reaffirmed following a protracted dispute with the Treasury in the late 1940s and early 1950s that led to an agreement that Treasury would not interfere or presume to tell the FOMC how to conduct monetary policy.[5] Since that time, the FRB has guarded its independence zealously. As late as the fall of 1989, the Congress was proposing that the Secretary of the Treasury be made a member of the FOMC. Current Chairman Alan Greenspan reiterated the by now traditional line in testimony before Congress:

> ... expanding the Secretary's responsibilities in that manner could have significant adverse effects on monetary policy ... As the Administration official responsible for funding the federal government, the Secretary might face conflicting goals - on the one hand, the immediate need to finance the deficit at the lowest possible interest rates, and, on the other, the obligation to support a monetary policy consistent with a stable economic environment over time (Greenspan 1989: 9).

In short, as Beck (1987: 198) emphasizes, the President through the Secretary is in no position to command the FOMC to do anything.[6]

Various institutional arrangements reinforce the independence of FOMC members. Members of the Board of Governors serve long 14 year terms. Reserve bank presidents are appointed by the respective bank's board of directors and not by the President. The law provides that the boards of reserve banks consist of nine persons: three Class A directors, who represent member commercial banks and three Class B directors, who represent the public (A and B directors are elected by member banks in the Federal Reserve district); and three Class C directors, who also represent the public, but who are appointed by the Board of Governors. Nonetheless, the Board of Governors must approve the appointment of regional bank presidents. In practice, the Governors, particularly the Chairman of the Board of Governors, play an active role in the selection of presidents. The Fed does not submit its budget to the Office of Management and Budget, and key staff persons are appointed by the Board and not the Administration.

---

5   For an analysis of this dispute, see Clifford (1965).
6   This fact is illustrated very well by Greider (1989: 378) when he describes the extraordinary meeting between Chairman Paul Volcker and Ronald Reagan at the height of the challenge by monetarists in 1981.

In view of the paucity of formal ties between the Fed and the Executive branch, informal networks become the only means for communication. Chairmen of the Board of Governors serve four-year terms, are appointed by the President, and are approved by the Senate. Given that the Chairman enjoys considerable influence within the FOMC, sometime during her or his term a President has an indirect opportunity to influence monetary policy through making this one key appointment. The Chairman meets once a week with the Treasury Secretary and Treasury officials lunch weekly at the Fed with FRB staffers. Informal networks link economists at the Fed, the Treasury, and the President's Council of Economic Advisers; these are buttressed by regular exchanges of personnel at the highest levels (Woolley 1984).[7] The so-called Quadriad (the FRB Chairman, the Treasury Secretary, the Director of Office of Management and Budget, and the Chairman of Council of Economic Advisers) also meets frequently.[8] In short, the Administration and the FOMC keep well-informed about each other's concerns through informal networks. Yet even here there are clear limits on what can be transmitted in these channels. In the words of a Fed official, "There's no reason why they [the Administration] can't tell us what they think. But it's very, very clear that they could tell us what they think all they want, but they can't tell us what to do."[9]

Reliance on informal networks and indirect communication creates a more public style of monetary politics in the US. In Canada, the directive power of the Minister of Finance, coupled with the legally required meetings between the Minister and the Governor, leave little room for protracted disagreements. The Canadian Governor never criticizes or offers opinions in public fora on fiscal policy. In contrast, public disputes do occur in the US; the Administration often uses the press to increase

---

7   For example, Paul Volcker was former Treasury Undersecretary for Monetary Affairs, Alan Greenspan the former Chairman of the Council of Economic Advisers, and Manuel Johnson, the former Vice-Chairman, the former Assistant Treasury Secretary for Economic Policy. David Mullins, the latest appointee, was formerly the Deputy Treasury Secretary for Domestic Finance.

8   Nonetheless Alan Greenspan has rejected publicly the idea that the Quadriad be required to meet prior to each FOMC meeting. In his congressional testimony, he said: "Although intended only to improve the coordination of economic policy making, the proposal, by subjecting the FOMC to a more intensely political perspective, could risk bending monetary policy away from long-term strategic goals" (Greenspan 1989: 11).

9   Confidential interview, 30 October 1989.

the political heat on the FOMC and members of the Board of Governors may criticize publicly both the executive branch or Congress.

If there is any analogue in the US system to the directive power of the Canadian minister, it lies with the Congress. Congress, if it wished, could not only end the independent status of the Federal Reserve, but also could issue very explicit instructions on how monetary policy should be conducted. But having this directive power rest in the hands of a legislature rather than a government minister reduces significantly the likelihood of its ever being exercised. Woolley (1984) notes that the distributive consequences of monetary policy, the consequences that might prompt a political response from legislators, do not flow from one or two discrete decisions but from a series of decisions made over a period of time. Monetary policy is established incrementally on close to a monthly basis with small adjustments being made daily. The nature of these decisions is not always obvious from a reading of policy reports of the FOMC, and these reports are not released until after the next FOMC meeting in any event. Hence effective oversight by the legislature would require sustained attention to the policy area, considerable expertise, and much more frequent information. The Senate and House Banking Committees concern themselves with too many other issues to give this sustained attention to monetary policy and have little political motivation to provide it in any event (Woolley 1984: chap. 7).

Yet, in contrast to Canada, the presence in the US of a legislature with independent law-making ability has produced stronger formal ties and much more extensive networking between the legislature and the central bank. The Congress has increased its oversight by requiring semi-annual reports on progress on monetary targets. These reports allow for regular interchange between the Fed and the Congress. In addition, the Chairman and other governors keep a set of informal contacts on Capitol Hill to help ensure that there are no legislative surprises. The Fed has an office responsible for Congressional affairs that tracks legislative activity and that cultivates relationships with crucial individual members. The Federal Reserve can never take its independence for granted politically. Woolley writes:

> ... congressional interest is quite real. Congress possesses the capacity to force great changes on the Federal Reserve and on the way it conducts monetary policy. The Federal Reserve obviously respects this capacity and fears that Congress might, in the heat of the moment, take action largely for symbolic reasons that would later, again for symbolic reasons, be very difficult to reverse. Fear and respect seem to lead to Federal Reserve efforts to defuse congressional ire ... (Woolley 1984: 152).

2.2   Central Bank Structure: Creating Opportunities for Networks

The two central banks at the heart of monetary policy formulation in Canada and the US also differ substantially in the way in which they are organized internally. These differences, in turn, reflect the varying experiences of authority found in the two countries. They also yield rather different styles of monetary politics: policy making in Canada is more hierarchical, secretive and discouraging of networks that might provide societal input; the US system creates more opportunities for networks and thus appears better able to incorporate a greater diversity of views on policy issues.

Primary responsibility for monetary policy in Canada is concentrated in the hands of one person, the Governor of the Bank of Canada. The Bank of Canada Act confers on this person the power to chair the Board and to act as chief executive officer. Only the Governor and the Senior Deputy Governor are both directors and full-time officers of the Bank. As the Bank states: "Since other directors are expected to devote only a small part of their time to the affairs of the Bank and are not required to be expert in the field of monetary policy, it would not, as a practical matter, be reasonable to look to them to formulate monetary policy ..." (BOC 1987: 6). In no way then is a directorship of the Bank of Canada analogous to being a member of the Board of Governors of the Federal Reserve System.

The Governor oversees the day-to-day conduct of monetary policy utilizing a Management Committee composed of senior Bank staff and reports on the Bank's activities once a week to an Executive Committee of the Board composed of the Governor, the Senior Deputy Governor, two to four directors, and the Deputy Minister of Finance (without a vote). The Executive Committee does not act as a decision making body on monetary policy; decisions are taken by the Governor following consultation with the Management Committee. Rather, the Executive Committee acts as a conduit to keep both the Board and the Department of Finance informed of policy developments.

Such a hierarchical structure is perfectly consistent with the Westminster model - one person, the Governor, reports to the Minister who is responsible to Parliament. And it produces a style of politics also to be expected with such a model. Policy discussions within the Management Committee are confidential as are briefings to the Executive Committee. The Bank does publish the remarks of the Governor given to the approximately eight meetings per year of the Board of Directors, but these remarks simply convey the Governor's point of view on the current economic situation. They give little, if any, indication of various policy options being considered or of the subjects of debates internal to the Bank. The Management Committee works on the model's conception of the civil service; Bank staff provide the Governor with impartial advice in secret. Hence it is not an arrangement that encourages the expression of diverse views in formulating policy. The Management Committee exists to serve the Governor who oversees the staff of the Bank and hence chooses its members.

The US system, as should already be clear, differs significantly. Whereas the Canadian system concentrates power in the hands of one person, the American system devolves power onto a council of persons. Members of the FOMC share the responsibilities that the Canadian governor controls. The formation of this council virtually ensures that it will reflect a greater diversity of views than is found in the Management Committee of the Bank of Canada. In fact, when appointing members of the Board of Governors, the President is required by the Federal Reserve Act to "have due regard to a fair representation of the financial, agricultural, industrial, and commercial interests, and geographical divisions of the country." Reserve bank presidents, who also sit on the FOMC, are not chosen by the President but by the boards of directors of the regional reserve banks. Although the Chairman of the Federal Reserve Board normally has considerable influence over these appointments, again the chances are greater for a diversity of viewpoints. Consequently, even though the heterogeneity of the US policy making group should not be exaggerated,[10] there is a greater likelihood of diversity of views at the policy center in the US. The Reserve Bank presidents and boards of directors have their own networks that allow them to keep in relatively close contact with developments in their regions and serve as a conduit of information on regional conditions to the FOMC (Melton 1985; Reagan 1963). Woolley's (1984) close study of FOMC minutes prior to 1975 and a casual reading of FOMC records of policy actions

---

10 For example, Woolley (1984: 56) notes that 45 per cent of the governors between 1955-1982 had been economists; 26 per cent of them had had a previous career in private finance. At the time of writing, 8 of the presidents had a Ph.D. in economics, 2 were lawyers, and 2 had a financial/business background. Similarly, four of the six governors had economics doctorates and two had a business/finance background. One seat on the Board was vacant.

since 1975 indicates that dissent occurs frequently within the FOMC. Governors and reserve bank presidents seek out their own personal sources of information as a supplement to analysis by the Fed staff. In short, the council structure at the center of US monetary policy affords more opportunities for networking, and provides a better forum for the voicing of dissent and for a dialogue between competing policy paradigms than the hierarchical Canadian arrangement.

Similarly, although the US network has been criticized for its secrecy (Goodfriend 1986), it is still more open than its Canadian counterpart. The FOMC does publish, after the fact, a summary of the minutes of its meetings. These summaries suggest where there have been disagreements and make it possible to divine who the dissident governors or presidents might be. The FOMC also publishes a record of its policy decisions which again can be decoded yielding a useful assessment of the direction of monetary policy. There are no public records of these kinds in Canada. Consistent with the national policy style, the US arrangement seeks to avoid concentrating authority while favoring networks that encourage more public debate and interchange over policy.

2.3   Private Sector Consultation

Our analysis of national policy styles suggests that consultation with private sector actors should be somewhat more informal in Canada than in the US. The US national style should demand a somewhat more formalized and more competitive interest group process. Some differences consistent with these hypotheses do exist but it would be a mistake to overemphasize them. In order to identify these differences, it is useful to distinguish between the formulation and the implementation of monetary policy.

When it comes to the *formulation* of monetary policy in the two countries, the two countries have similar approaches: systematic consultation does not take place. In both Canada and the US, increased reliance on market-based instruments in the 1980s at the expense of moral suasion, exchange controls and selective credit controls which had been more common previously, makes the policy process more distant to policy advocates. Decisions on intervention are made on a day-to-day, incremental basis and are not discussed publicly for fear of distorting market responses. In interviews in both countries, interest associations and financial firms indicated that they did not really "lobby" on monetary policy.

If the central banks have any constituency in civil society that is relevant to policy formulation, it would be academic economists. Participation in monetary policy formulation more and more requires professional economics credentials. Here some one-way networks exist in the sense that central bank economists participate in academic economics circles and may even invite certain specialists to serve as "scholars-in-residence." Still academic economists do not have a direct influence on the formulation of monetary policy.

When it comes to *policy implementation*, there are again important similarities between the two countries. Both central banks rely on close, reciprocal working networks with major financial institutions. Through offices in major financial centers, the Securities Department of the Bank of Canada and the Open Market desk at the Federal Reserve Bank of New York (which assume respectively primary responsibility for implementing day-to-day monetary policy) maintain daily contact with money market participants. These contacts help the central banks to understand the psychology of market players and to gauge the reception these players are likely to give to their actions. When it comes to broader policy issues relating to the functioning of money and capital markets, the Bank of Canada meets regularly with the Investment Dealers Association of Canada and the New York Fed with the Securities Industry Association, the Public Securities Association, and the National Security Traders Association which represent dealers and traders.

It is when one moves beyond the discussion of the technicalities of monetary policy implementation to gaining assessments of the impacts of monetary policy that some differences between the two systems emerge. Such assessments, in turn, are used by policy-makers in subsequent attempts to formulate policy. Central to understanding the differences between the two countries is the fact that the Federal Reserve functions in a congressional system and must pay close attention to influencing the legislature. The Bank of Canada needs to be far less concerned with the Canadian House of Commons. Influencing a Congress requires a different kind of politics than influencing a single minister. In a political battle, the central bank has to be able to draw on the ready support of its own political constituency, what Woolley (1985: 338-339) has termed the sound finance community.[11] Hence, we hypothesize that the linkages between the central bank and the sound finance community will need to be more institutionalized and extensive in the US with its stronger legislature than in Canada where the legislature is largely irrelevant. In noting these links, we by no means imply that the sound finance community participates in the making of monetary policy. Rather, we suggest that institutions will function such that the members of the FOMC are more likely to be aware of this community's concerns than those of any other community. The FOMC will also be better placed to communicate its own policy objectives and to highlight its political worries to this constituency than to any other. If that community needs to be mobilized politically to fight attacks from the Congress, the FOMC has the linkages to make this need known.

Four structures provide a framework for networking with the sound finance community. First, as we have noted, in appointing members of the Board of Governors, the President is required by the Federal Reserve Act to have "due regard" to a broad representation of economic interests. Practically, this provision has meant that at least one member of the Board, if not more, has a banking background. Second, the Act provides for a Federal Advisory Council composed of twelve persons, one appointed by each reserve bank district. Invariably, the members of this Council are chief executive officers of commercial banks. It is required by law to meet four times per year in Washington with the Board and it may discuss any or all aspects of the Board's responsibilities, including monetary policy.[12] Third, as we have noted, commercial banks elect three of their own as Class A directors of reserve banks, and three others as Class B directors. Normally, the Class B directors are chief executives of non-banking corporations. A cursory survey of Class B and Class C directors (appointed by the Board of Governors) indicates that 1 in 6 is not from a business background; academia provides most of the non-

---

11   Woolley understands this community to consist of those who wish to protect the currency against inflation, to sustain moderate, stable economic growth, to dampen sharp market fluctuations, to promote profitable strong financial institutions, and to protect the financial system from panics.

12   Two other advisory councils exist, the Thrift Advisory Council and the Consumer Advisory Council. Neither has relevance to monetary policy. The Thrifts council helps keep the FRB informed of development in the savings and loan sub-sector while the Consumer council arises out of the FRB's responsibilities for consumer protection in the financial services area.

business directors. In short, the commercial banking community has a decisive say on the composition of the boards of directors of the regional reserve banks. These directors, in turn, play mediating roles in networks joining the Board of Governors and the sound finance constituency in each of the regions of the US.

Finally, distinct from the Bank of Canada, the Federal Reserve has a direct role in the regulation and supervision of commercial banks. The Board of Governors is the primary federal regulator for bank holding companies and for state chartered banks that belong to the Reserve System. The FRB also plays a direct role in running the payments system and has been assigned responsibility for enforcing consumer protection laws in the financial services area. In its own words the Fed argues:

> Experience gained in the process of supervision and regulation also enables monetary policy decisions to be made against the background of a more practical and knowledge-able assessment of how such decisions will flow through and interact with the banking and depository system and financial markets generally (FRB 1985: 87).

Virtually to a person, interviewees at the FRB echoed this sentiment; the formal ties and informal networks that develop between the regulator and the regulated foster a certain mutuality and again attune the FRB more closely to commercial banks than to any other constituency.

Relationships between the Bank of Canada and the sound finance constituency do not have the formal framework found in the US and thus tend to take the form of informal networks only. Whereas it is normal for a banker to be a governor of the Federal Reserve, such ties are es-chewed in Canada. Except for the first governor of the Bank of Canada, all governors have been chosen from within the Bank following a long central banking career. Similarly, formal ties with the banking sector are not allowed in forming the Bank's Board of Directors.[13] No structure similar to the FAC exists in Canada. Rather, regular consultations take place in informal private networks with the chartered (commercial) banks, who are both the largest direct clearers and most important players in money markets. The Governor meets two to three times a year with the chief executive officers of the domestically-owned chartered banks. To-

---

13 Members cannot be a director, officer or shareholder of a chartered bank or any other member of the Canadian Payments Association that maintains a deposit with the Bank, or an investment dealer that acts as a primary distributor for new Government of Canada securities (BOC 1987: 9). Generally, they are lay persons in the sense that they are normally neither economists nor persons with any specific expertise in monetary policy.

gether with senior staff, he also meets twice a year with the Executive Council of the Canadian Bankers' Association (CBA) which is composed of the chief operating officers of the domestically-owned chartered banks plus two representatives of foreign-controlled banks. Finally, the research staff of the Bank has ongoing contact on policy issues related to payments and money market matters with expert committees of the CBA. Contacts also take place with representatives of other financial institutions (trust companies, financial co-operatives, insurance firms), but these networks are less well-established and viewed as less important by the Bank.

Nor are there analogous institutions to the other linkages found in the US. The Bank of Canada has no regional reserve banks or even regional committees that provide a direct tie to sound finance communities in various parts of the country. The Bank does not have any direct responsibilities for the supervision of banks. In short, in contrast to the US monetary policy arrangements, a restricted amount of informal consultation is the only avenue available to the Bank when seeking information on the impact of monetary policy. That said, macropolitical structures do not require the Bank of Canada to broaden its networks. Its US counterpart must keep a close watching brief over Congress and be prepared to play congressional political games. The Fed's more structured relationship with the sound finance community is an asset in this process.

3 Conclusion

This chapter has sought to examine how patterns of consultation in a specialized sectoral policy arena are shaped by broader macropolitical institutions. It took as its starting point monetary policy communities in Canada and the US, both dominated by state actors, and hence both particularly susceptible to macropolitical constraints. It argued that within the broad outlines of Dyson's adversary polity, important institutional differences exist between the central governing institutions of Canada and the United States. Canada inherited from the United Kingdom a Westminster model of parliamentary government. This model tends to concentrate power in the hands of the Cabinet and to balance this concentration by drawing clear lines of responsibility between ministers and the parliament. Parliament itself acts as a deliberative assembly and functions primarily as an organization exercising surveillance over the government/cabinet. The civil service is non-partisan and prefers closed collaborative consultation in informal networks with private sector groups as it offers advice and prepares policy proposals for the consideration of ministers. The United States departed consciously from this Westminster model stressing, in particular, the avoidance of the concentration of power. Accordingly, the US constitution provides for the division of power between the legislature and the executive. Congress is a law-making body in its own right and not simply an institution exercising surveillance over the President. In dispersing power, the US system attenuates lines of responsibility and creates a setting that indulges willingly the creation of "independent" agencies. The fear of a concentration of power also favors supplementing closed, collaborative relationships with more open, competitive relationships and with formalized interest representation on advisory councils.

The question then became whether these contrasting experiences of authority had any impact on the organization of the monetary policy space. The analysis reveals differences that clearly correspond to these macropolitical constraints. The Canadian central bank was formally tied and subject to the Minister of Finance with the Minister possessing a legal directive power. In practice, this formal tie was not supplemented by extensive informal networks. The US central bank prided itself on its "independence" from both the Secretary of the Treasury and the Congress, with the President through the Secretary having no direct control over the actions of the Federal Open Market Committee. But in the absence of a formal tie, a wider range of informal networking between the Federal Reserve and the executive branch has developed. In addition, whereas the Bank of Canada spoke primarily to parliament through the Minister of Finance, the Federal Reserve had a direct relationship with Congress, reporting on its activities twice a year. Managing this formal tie required extensive informal politicking between the Fed and individual members of Congress.

Consistent with the US bias in favor of dividing power, the conduct of monetary policy was left in the hands of a council of appointed governors and reserve bank presidents. This structure leaves the way more open again to a variety of networks and thus encourages a certain diversity of viewpoints and the introduction of competing policy paradigms. In contrast, the Canadian system concentrated authority in one person, the Governor, and gave this person complete control over the choice of advisers. These arrangements significantly dampen networking with other actors, whether within the state or outside, and thus decrease the likelihood of diverse viewpoints and the introduction of competing policy paradigms. If diversity of opinion and a broader range of ideas help improve the efficacy of policy making, then the Canadian system suffers in comparison with that of the US.

Finally, when it came to relationships between central banks and private sector actors, differences were less pronounced but still related to macropolitical institutions. In both countries, little lobbying or advocacy politics was evident when it came to the formulation of monetary policy. But active networks were maintained with private sector firms and associations for managing the implementation of monetary policy. Differences arose only when it came to the methods used by the respective banks for collecting information on the impact of policies. The US system formally incorporated banking interests into the policy process through the appointment of members of the Board of Governors, the use of the Federal Advisory Council, the selection of reserve bank presidents, and through contacts developed in the supervision and regulation of banks. None of these mechanisms occurred in Canada. Rather, again consistent with the Westminster model, relations with private sector groups tended to be limited to informal, private and collaborative networks.

When all of these findings are reviewed, they provide considerable support for treating relationships between macropolitical institutions and the patterns of communication in a policy arena as a variable. Yet it must also be cautioned that the analysis may be more straightforward when policy arenas are state-directed. If a policy arena is structured in another way, whether it be corporatist, clientelist, or pressure pluralist, the analysis is bound to become more complex. In each of these types, the organizational development of intermediary associational systems becomes a more central variable. And their level of organizational development will be affected by the autonomy and capacity of sector-specific state agencies, the specific characteristics of the sector being represented (banking, coal-mining, dairy farming, consumers), the labor relations system, as well as macropolitical institutions. Despite these added complexities, careful comparative analysis of public policy must include basic macropolitical institutions in its assessment of communication patterns and its evaluation of policy outcomes.

References

Atkinson, Michael M., 1990: Parliamentary Government in Canada. In: Michael Whittington/ Glen Williams (eds.), *Canadian Politics in the 1990s*. Toronto: Nelson Canada.

Atkinson, Michael M./ William D. Coleman, 1989: Strong States and Weak States: Sectoral Policy Networks in Advanced Capitalist Economies. In: *British Journal of Political Science* 19, 47-67.

Beck, Nathaniel, 1987: Elections and the Fed: Is There a Political Monetary Cycle? In: *American Journal of Political Science* 31, 194-216.

BOC, Bank of Canada, 1987: *Bank of Canada: Management and Accountability*. Ottawa: Bank of Canada.

Cawson, Alan/ Peter Holmes/ Anne Stevens, 1987: The Interaction between Firms and the State in France: The Telecommunications and Consumer Electronics Sectors. In: Stephen Wilks/ Maurice Wright (eds.), *Comparative Government-Industry Relations*. Oxford: Oxford University Press, 10-34.

Clifford, A. Jerome, 1965: *The Independence of the Federal Reserve System*. Philadelphia: University of Pennsylvania Press.

Dyson, Kenneth, 1980: *The State Tradition in Western Europe*. Oxford: Martin Robertson.

Financial Times, 1990: Editorial: *Pöhl throws a gauntlet*. 23 January 1990.

FRB, Federal Reserve Board, 1985: *The Federal Reserve System: Purposes and Functions*. Washington: FRB.

Freedman, Charles/ J.F. Dingle, 1986: Monetary Policy Implementation in Canada: Traditional Structure and Recent Developments. In: Bank for International Settlements (BIS), *Changes in Money-Market Instruments and Procedures: Objectives and Implications*. Basel: BIS.

Goodfriend, Marvin, 1986: Monetary Mystique: Secrecy and Central Banking. In: *Journal of Monetary Economics* 17, 63-92.

Grant, Wyn, 1989: *Government and Industry: A Comparative Analysis of the US, Canada and the UK*. Aldershot: Edward Elgar.

Greenspan, Alan, 1989: *Statement before the Subcommittee on Domestic Monetary Policy of the Committee on Banking, Finance and Urban Affairs*. U.S. House of Representatives, 25 October.

Greider, William, 1988: *Secrets of the Temple: How the Federal Reserve Runs the Country*. New York: Simon and Schuster.

Hancher, Leigh/ Michael Moran, 1989: Organizing Regulatory Space. In: L. Hancher/ M. Moran (eds.), *Capitalism, Culture and Economic Regulation*. Oxford: Clarendon Press, 271-299.

Hayward, Jack, 1982: Mobilising Private Interests in the Service of Public Ambitions: The Salient Element in the Dual French Policy Style? In: J.J. Richardson (ed.), *Policy Styles in Western Europe*. London: George Allen & Unwin.

Hayward, Jack, 1986: *The State and the Market Economy: Industrial Patriotism and Economic Intervention in France*. Brighton: Wheatsheaf.

Johnson, Harry, 1972: Should There Be an Independent Monetary Authority? Testimony before the US Congress, 1964. Reprinted in J.P. Cairns/ H.H. Binhammer/ R.W. Boadway (eds.), *Canadian Banking and Monetary Policy*. Second Edition. Toronto: McGraw-Hill.

Melton, William C., 1985: *Inside the Fed: Making Monetary Policy*. Homewood, Ill.: Dow-Jones Irwin.

Neufeld, E.P., 1958: *Bank of Canada Operations and Policy*. Toronto: University of Toronto Press.

Przeworski, Adam/ Henry Teune, 1970: *The Logic of Comparative Social Inquiry*. New York: Wiley.

Reagan, Michael D., 1963: The Political Structure of the Federal Reserve System. In: *American Political Science Review* 55, 64-76.

Richardson, J.J./ G. Gustafsson/ A.G. Jordan, 1982: The Concept of Policy Style. In: J.J. Richardson (ed.), *Policy Styles in Western Europe*. London: George Allen & Unwin, 1-16.

Skocpol, Theda, 1985: Bringing the State Back In: Strategies of Analysis in Current Research. In: Peter B. Evans/ Dietrich Rueschmeyer/ Theda Skocpol (eds.), *Bringing the State Back In*. New York: Cambridge University Press, 3-37.

Vogel, David, 1986: *National Styles of Regulation: Environmental Policy in Great Britain and the United States*. Ithaca: Cornell University Press.

Woolley, John T., 1984: *Monetary Politics: The Federal Reserve and the Politics of Monetary Policy*. Cambridge: Cambridge University Press.

Woolley, John T., 1985: Central Banks and Inflation. In: Leon N. Lindberg/ C.S. Maier (eds.), *The Politics of Inflation and Economic Stagnation*. Washington: Brookings, 318-348.

Zysman, John, 1983: *Governments, Markets and Growth*. Ithaca: Cornell University Press.

Chapter 8
Policy Networks, Opportunity Structures and Neo-Conservative Reform Strategies in Health Policy

Marian Döhler

1   Introduction

This chapter is about structures and strategies, or to be more precise: it deals with the "goodness of fit", i.e. the functional matching, between a new political strategy aimed at expanding market forces and the established institutional configurations in health care. Starting with the election victory of the British Conservative Party in 1979, several changes in government took place in the early 1980s which were perceived as going beyond the normal routine of alternating party governments. The leadership takeover by Margaret Thatcher, Ronald Reagan and the Christian-Liberal coalition in the Federal Republic of Germany appeared to mark a watershed between the Keynesian interventionist strategy of the post-war period and a "neo-conservative" strategy which intended to replace governmental regulations and interventions, if not completely then perceptibly, by virtue of the free market. The novelty of neo-conservatism consisted in the explicit revocation of the post-war consensus regarding the active role of the state for counterbalancing the business cycle and smoothing out social inequalities. The scope of this strategic reorientation seemed to be more than a national extravagance since the general aim of the three governments coincided to a remarkable extent: the goal was "more market and less state".

After roughly a decade of neo-conservative reform efforts, it became increasingly certain that the extent to which the rhetoric of the political

I would like to thank Jens Alber, Christa Altenstetter, Henry A. Landsberger, Bernd Marin and Renate Mayntz for their helpful comments on an earlier version of this paper which was presented at the International Sociological Association XIIth World Congress of Sociology, 9-13 July 1990, in Madrid, Spain.

"turn-around" - in Germany it was called *Wende* - had been translated into reality differed from country to country. In principle, it is fair to maintain that compared with the Christian-Liberal government in the FRG, the Reagan and Thatcher governments were more successful in enforcing a market-oriented strategy. This leads one to question what the conditions for changing the political course are and how variances in the government's enforcement capacities can be explained. In the following, this problem is examined by analyzing first, how successful the three governments have been in broadening the sphere of market governance in health care and second, which variables have guided the course of policy.

2 Reconciling Institutional and Network Approaches

In recent years a number of researchers have stressed the potential contribution of a "neo-institutional" approach (March/ Olson 1984) to the analysis of public policy (most notably Zysman 1983; Evans/ Rueschemeyer/ Skocpol 1985; Scharpf 1987). The main difference between the traditional understanding of political institutions which has centered around formal organizations such as parties, parliaments and interest groups and the neo-institutional way of thinking consists of the range of what is subsumed under the term institution. In the modern version, patterns of behavior, structures of economic distribution and non-political organization are also defined as institutions. One of the outstanding innovations of neo-institutional thinking was to take into consideration the organization of markets as an important independent variable (Zysman 1983; Hollingsworth/ Lindberg 1985; Hall 1986), which shapes actors' incentives through different forms of economic coordination, i.e. markets or hierarchies.

A common denominator of these scholarly works has been the observation that governments' performance in economic problem solving has differed, even in cases when the same strategy was employed. Having found that the outcomes of governmental policy differ even when the economic problems are similar, the neo-institutionalists have rejected explanatory models in which economic pressure is assumed to be the major determinant for public policy. Instead, political institutions are being reconsidered as independent variables. One of the important conclusions is the thesis that the state capacity for successful intervention in the industrial or welfare spheres depends on the congruence between the interventionist strategy and the institutional structure of the policy field.

Another train of thought running through the neo-institutional literature is the emphasis on prior choices for future decisions (Weir/ Skocpol 1985: 120-125; Krasner 1988). This consideration has far-reaching implications for the understanding of the political process. By pointing out that the current institutional structure of a policy field has to be regarded as the result of historical course setting, it is no longer sufficient to look at policy outcomes simply from the perspective of pressure group activities or to expect that "socially rooted demands" (Weir/ Skocpol 1985: 117) have an immediate and undiluted impact on public policies. If there is anything novel in the institutional perspective then it is the notion of institutional resistance to change. Following Stephen Krasner, an institutional perspective has to ask two basic questions. First, "how institutions persist over time, even though their environment may change", and second, "how preexisting structures delimit the range of possible options" (Krasner 1988: 91). The impact of institutions on political life was nicely summarized by Johan Olson:

> Institutions regulate the use of authority and power and provide actors with resources, legitimacy, standards of evaluation, perceptions, identities and a set of meaning. They provide a set of rules, compliance procedures, and moral and ethical behavioral norms which buffer environmental influence, modify individual motives, regulate self-interested behavior and create order and meaning (Olson 1988: 13).

The conditioning impact of political and economic institutions on the strategies of corporate actors, the feasibility of political options and the contents of public policy has been convincingly demonstrated. However, what is usually referred to as "institutional arrangement" not always contributes to conceptual clarity. In order to avoid the often used mere enumeration of institutions with relevance for the political process, in this chapter the institutional argument is merged with parts from interorganizational and network theory. Since Hugh Heclo (1978) and Peter Katzenstein (1977) first introduced the network metaphor into political science, the idea of analyzing policies in terms of sectoral systems of patterned interrelations between public and private actors has gained increasing recognition. The concept of the policy network, as it is applied in the following sections, denotes a sectoral system of interaction which links public and private actors through resource dependencies (Benson

1982: 148) around a certain policy subject such as energy, environment or health. Those segments of the political system which are relevant for health policy are treated as a part of the network.

The integration of institutional and network perspectives aims at bypassing the weak points of each approach and combining the advantages. In simplified terms it can be said that the strength of institutionalists was to elucidate the political impact of institutions, while they often lack an integrative perspective which allows one to grasp the single components of an institutional arrangement as interrelated and not as a more or less arbitrary set of institutions. Network analysts, on the other hand, have been strong in the detailed description of interaction systems but often are not able to link mappings of relations to underlying institutional frameworks. By stressing the institutional foundation of policy networks, this chapter tries to combine the strength of both analytical concepts.

Aside from the heuristic value of the term policy network which forces the analyst to think in terms of an interrelated set of structures and actors and thereby could help to avoid the traditional "dialogous" construction of politics, as is reflected in political science idioms like "government-industry relations", there are several conceptual ideas, derived from interorganizational and network theory, which could be used to the benefit of policy analysis. First, the application of the network perspective provides a joint framework for the comprehension and classification of structural characteristics of a policy field in different countries. Second, analytical dimensions like the cohesion of a network, the interlacing between actors and between institutions, or the separation from other networks create instructive points of reference for comparative research. Finally, the idea that interactions inside a network are fused into a set of standard operating procedures points to an important source of "structural inertia" (Hannan/ Freeman 1978). Policy networks achieve stability through interactive routines which cannot be overturned straight away because often they form the basis for cooperative relations between the actors and already the problem perception is taking place under the influence of belief systems and cognitive maps structured by the network.

The argument of this chapter is based on the notions of *network structure*, *stability* and *goodness of fit/selectivity*. The basic idea is that policy networks, as a result of previous political decisions, produce certain interactive routines, modes of interest intermediation and decision making. This "sedimentation" (Lehmbruch 1990: 223) of preceding policies, which is likely to suit particular political strategies, is a process that closely resembles the notion of "lock-in" (Arthur 1989) used by economists to explain the persistence of certain technologies despite a competitive environment. In other words, the "old" political strategy has left its imprint on the institutions and patterns of collective behavior of a policy network, so that the successful enforcement of a "new" strategy depends on the *opportunities* embodied in the network.

Political opportunities emanate, inter alia, from the goodness of fit between new strategy and old structure. This implies thinking of policy networks in terms of constraints *and* opportunities which both together form a particular strategic adaptability, i.e. selectivity. An important assumption in support of this consideration is the idea of a "contingent" relationship between network structure and policy (Scharpf 1978: 362). This assumption refers to the fact that each policy has a distinct set of "interaction requirements" (Scharpf 1978: 363). Whereas the political strategy "more market" may be confronted with serious resistance in one country, it may be facilitated by the network structure of another. Thus the feasibility or the incompatibility between an established network structure and a new policy is inferred only from the practical confrontation of both.

For the problem at hand, it is justified to expect a certain degree of misfit since the formative influence of regulations and other forms of public control and guidance, inherited from the interventionist postwar era, will most probably be at odds with a strategy based on competition and market transactions. This suggests that a change in the operating structure of the network is an important precondition for the enforcement of a new political strategy (Olson 1988: 10). Such a "window of opportunity" which provides a reform-minded government with a starting-point for introducing a new strategy is most likely to appear if the network structure is modified, for example, by the occurrence of a new actor or the break-up of coalitions, or runs into a state of instability caused by economic troubles or technological innovations (Aldrich/ Whetten 1981: 381f.). As opposed to the standard type of analysis, where policy networks are treated as steady state structures, in the following a *dynamic* research strategy is employed in which network structures are analyzed at *three points in time*.

In a first step the policy network is analyzed at the point of change in government (t_0). Then, in a second step (t_1), the confrontation between old structure and new strategy over a period of time is described. This

Figure 1: The Structure of the Argument

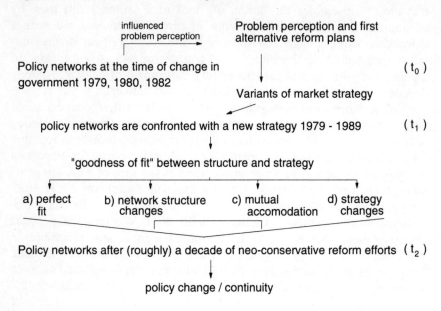

confrontation is expected to result in goodness-of-fit outcomes ranging from a to d. Finally, the impact of the new strategy on the old structure, and vice versa, are described (t_2) by detecting the alterations in the network structure and the degree to which the new strategy has been successfully implemented.

3   The Characteristics of Health Policy Networks

In the following sections, health policy networks in Britain, the US and the FRG are described through five characteristics each of which is divided into a more fine-grained set of variables: (1) the structure of the network, (2) the actors and their coalitions, (3) the governance structure, (4) patterns of interaction, and (5) the strategic selectivity of the network.

Figure 2: The Structure of Health Policy Networks

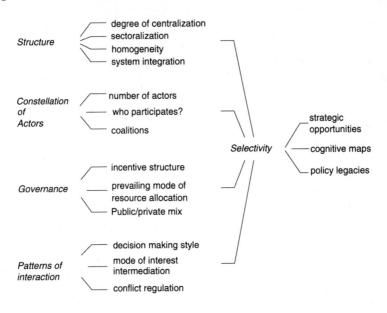

(1) *Structure*: The structure of a policy network encompasses the organization of medical care administration and those parts of the political systems which are relevant for health policy. In this conception of policy networks, the state appears not only as part of the structure but also as an actor with a distinct strategic orientation (see infra). An analysis of the network structure has to take into account the four different features of centralization, system integration, sectoralization, and homogeneity.

With respect to their degree of centralization, the health policy networks of the three countries represent a maximum of variety. Certainly, the most centralized system is Britain's National Health Service (NHS). At first sight, the NHS, founded in 1948, appears as a hierarchically ordered and governed system of service delivery where political responsibility and control is concentrated at the top, i.e. in the Department of Health and Social Services (DHSS) which is empowered with considerable authority to guide the subordinated administrative entities. However, it also true that the center-periphery relations were never unambiguously in favor of the central government (Haywood/ Alaszewski 1980; Hunter 1983). The Health Authorities, which are mainly responsible for hospital care, and the Family Practitioner Committees (FPCs), the Health Authorities' equivalent for ambulatory care, traditionally had an impervious life of their own. This was caused by the collegial administration of NHS agencies recruited from the ranks of physicians, nurses, technicians, local government officials, including union representatives, and finance officers (Levitt/ Wall 1984: 47ff.). The result was a strong orientation of the NHS periphery towards professional and local needs. The professional point of view was additionally reinforced by an extensive system of advisory boards reaching from the bottom to the top of the DHSS. Even though the NHS administrative machinery was never simply in the weak position of being a recipient of central orders, the control of the DHSS over NHS finances and manpower planning has placed the central government in a more powerful position than the German or American federal governments.

The United States shows quite an opposite picture. According to an influential analysis, US health care is a "non-system" (Alford 1975: 257). This is as true for the organization of health services as it is for the structure of decision making in health policy. Aside from the two dominating programs Medicare and Medicaid, through which the basic health needs of the elderly and the poor are financed, there is a large variety of governmental health activities scattered among a vast universe of programs such as the Black Lung Program, the Children Mental Health Services Program, the Indian Health Service etc. (Altman/ Sapolsky 1981: Appendix A). There is no clear focus of state involvement in health care. Governmental activities range from financing, to regulation and the direct provision of medical services, for example through the medical care system of the Veterans Administration. This fragmented pattern is continued in the administrative structure of the federal government (Rosenthal 1983). The Department of Health and Human Services (DHHS) is divided into four principal units and a large number of highly autonomous "bureaus", each of which is entangled in its own idiosyncratic operating ideology based on different clientelist linkages and administrative traditions (Starr 1982: 283-289). A first step towards an internal homogenization was achieved, however, through the creation of the Health Care Financing Administration (HCFA) which became responsible for both Medicare and Medicaid in 1978 (Balutis 1984). Yet compared to Britain and the FRG, the structure of the US network has to be characterized as highly fragmented and decentralized.

In between the two extremes stands the German case with a decentralized but fairly clear cut structure. The core of the German health policy network is formed by the statutory health insurance (Gesetzliche Krankenversicherung, GKV), comprising roughly 1,200 individual health insurance funds, which are organized into seven peak associations and financed through equal contributions from employers and employees. This system is largely based on collective bargaining between the associations of health insurance funds and organized providers. On the provider side, physicians are organized into 18 regional associations of fund doctors empowered with quasi public legal status and bargaining rights on behalf of their member physicians. Hospitals are more loosely organized into 11 private peak associations. The federal government has mainly the function of providing statutes and guidelines for the self-administered associations. There are two federal ministries, the Department of Labour and Social Affairs and the Department of Youth, Women, Family, and Health, each of which is primarily concerned with preparing federal legislation. Due to German federalism, there are no subordinated administrative units charged with implementing policies. The main responsibility of carrying out federal policies is delegated to the associations which in fact gives a strong decentralized bias to the German health policy network.

System integration refers to the institutional as well as ideological affiliation of the health policy network with the welfare state. The consideration behind this variable is based on the expectation that the integration of health care into the broader sphere of the welfare state serves as a protective cover since a political assault on health care is perceived as threatening the whole system. Whereas in the German and British cases, health care has strong ties to welfare state structures and belief systems, the integration of the US network is almost non-existent (Laumann/ Knoke 1987: 391ff.). The reason is simple. The underdeveloped American welfare state provides neither a solid institutional nor an ideological fundament for lending stability to any other subsystem.

A somewhat different relation between a network and its environment can be described as *sectoralization*. This denotes the degree to which a network is protected by isolation from other policy domains. Sectoralization is important for regulating spill-overs of problems or strategies from other networks. The most well developed sectoralization is to be found in the German case, where the health policy network in many aspects is differentiated from the federal government and other branches of social security, both with respect to organization and financing. A less well developed sectoralization is encountered in Britain. Although the NHS is a separated administrative branch of its own, it remains part of the state apparatus which controls the money flow. Thus the central government does not have to bridge a gap between separate sectors. The US health policy network, finally, is too fragmented to maintain any solid boundary as is confirmed by the lack of an autonomous ideology of health care such as the notion of health as a "special commodity", which prevents it from being treated as just any other commodity in Britain and Germany.

An analysis of network structures would be incomplete without making reference to "networks of networks" (Heclo 1978: 106). Each policy network is likely to consist of several segments in which a number of actors and institutions are clustered around a special issue such as hospital policy, health research or drug safety (Laumann/ Knoke 1987). The number of distinguishable network segments is a good indicator of the internal *homogeneity* which in turn is a crucial measure for institutional and interactive stability. The most heterogeneous health policy network can be found in the US where virtually dozens of governmental health programs are distinguished from each other (Milward/ Francesco 1983) through special bureaus in the DHHS, often narrowly defined target groups, especially appropriated funds and political supporters located in different congressional (sub)committees. The German and British networks are characterized by a much stronger homogeneity. Although in both countries subsystems exist, in contrast to the US, they are interlocked by means of a common source of money, a joint institutional framework and an almost generalized entitlement by the whole population.

(2) *Constellation of Actors*: Actors are the dynamic element of every network. Not everything is a result of their intentional behavior, but nothing happens without the participation of corporate or individual actors. Of decisive importance for the stability and the strategic selectivity of a policy network are the questions of *who* participates, *how many* actors are involved, and *how* they are *linked* to each other and to the network.

It will not come as a surprise that in health policy, the state, the medical profession, hospital and insurance (third party) associations are involved in all three countries. But when it comes to the participation of employers associations and labor unions, some marked differences appear. Whereas in the FRG, labor unions and employers are firmly integrated into the decision making process of the self-government of the health insurance funds and a corporatist institution at the federal level, no such participation is institutionalized in the British NHS. Although labor unions are present as representatives of the NHS work force, British employers appear to have almost no interest in health policy. This finds a simple explanation: The NHS has socialized the costs of medical care via taxes and is a comparatively cheap arrangement so that there is no need for employers to change anything in the health domain. In the US network, up to the late 1970s, labor unions were much more involved in health policy than employers.

In all three countries the state appears not as a united but as a multiple actor. The "balkanized" structure of the US federal government has already been mentioned. But also in Britain, the state does not act as a single entity. The DHSS has to deal with a "syndicalist" NHS, in which Health Authorities, FPCs, and local governments all pursue their own agendas. This is also true for the FRG where the major rift is between the federal government and the 11 regional governments (Länder) which are powerfully represented through the Bundesrat, the second chamber of the German parliament.

In his classic essay on "The Semi-sovereign People", Schattschneider has argued that "the number of people involved in any conflict determines what happens" (Schattschneider 1960: 2). This assumption is particularly valid for the internal operations of a policy network. The greater the number of actors involved, the more difficult it becomes to achieve a cooperative or consensual solution. The number of relevant actors in the health policy network is much greater in the US than in Britain and the FRG. This is not simply based on the sheer size of the country, but is rather a result of the balkanized state structure and the lack of a European-like system of peak associations which effectively have monopolized interest representation. In short: "fragmented groups face a divided government" (Wilson 1982: 225). Additionally, the *entry* for new actors is almost unrestricted in the US system because of its multiple points of access. As early as the 1970s, the number of actors increased (Scott/ Lammers 1985), most notably through the establishment of subcommittees in Congress and the foundation of new influential interest groups such as the American Federation of Health Systems, a commercial hospital association, or the consumer group American Association of Retired Persons. In the British network, there is no such increase in the number of actors. In general, the ability for new actors to participate in health policy is more restricted since the NHS provides a dominant and fairly exclusive framework for interest representation. The corporatist network in Germany has not only a small number of participants but has also been most effective in containing the growth and entry of new actors.

The *linkage* or *interdependence* between the actors is also an important structural variable that has a strong impact on the mode of *coalition building*. The British and the US health policy networks are characterized by varying degrees of vertical linkage of the actors. In the British NHS, due to its hierarchical structure, there is no need for a horizontal coordination of actors. Therefore, only vertical interconnections between state and associations are of relevance. In the US, the vertical linkages also dominate mainly through policy subsystems, earlier often referred to as "iron triangles", which link parts of the Washington bureaucracy to a congressional committee and a number of affected interest groups. Vertical linkage is not only a measure for inter- but also for intra-organizational relations (Lehmbruch 1984: 68f.). In this respect, the German health policy network is characterized by a strong vertical integration of single associations which is complemented by an additional horizontal interdependence between peak associations at the regional and the federal level which is a result of corporatist concertation. This latter trait distinguishes the German case from Britain and the US where there is almost no horizontal linkage in health care and no indicator for corporatist policy processing.

A higher degree of convergence appears with respect to *coalitions* in health policy. In each of the three countries the providers of medical care could find powerful coalition partners. In the FRG physicians were in charge of close connections with the pharmaceutical industry and both actors in crucial decisions could count on the political support of the CDU/CSU (Christian Democratic Union/ Christian Social Union). Health insurance funds were highly fragmented and often divided in the face of physicians' associations. In Britain, the British Medical Association (BMA) was able to rely on a clientelist relationship with the DHSS (Eckstein 1960). However, there was also tension between center and periphery where the medical profession, nurses, local government representatives and administrators often joined forces against the DHSS. In the US, providers were in the strongest coalition. The medical profession, represented powerfully by the American Medical Association (AMA), was not only linked through interlocking directorates with the market leaders among the voluntary health insurers, i.e. Blue Cross and Blue Shield, but additionally formed a close coalition with the American Hospital Association (AHA). Consumers were classified only as a "repressed coalition" (Alford 1975: 15f.) with almost no influence.

For the problem at hand, the question which *policy instruments* are available for the government to intervene with in the health sector is of central concern. Governmental control of the resource flow in health care is most effectively developed in Britain. The DHSS, with approval by the House of Commons, determines the annual budget of the NHS, has the right to appoint administrative personnel at the regional level and is equipped with a fairly broad political leeway derived from so-called "delegated legislation" (Hayhurst/ Wallington 1988). The day-to-day instrument of governing the NHS are the so-called circulars which contain advice and guidance to the NHS administration (Parkin 1985). This form of executive orders is also available to the American president but his power to influence the health bureaucracy is more circumscribed. In addition, the president has to share the budget power with Congress which is eager to preserve its budgetary prerogative. In the German case, neither executive orders nor a direct parliamentary or executive control of the health budget are regularly available as policy instruments. The civil law system has a tradition of detailed legislative drafting and executive orders are a rather unusual instrument. Finally, the greatest part of the health budget is not included in the annual budget bill of the federal government but is administered by the para-fiscal health insurance funds or, in the case of hospital investment, is appropriated by the Länder. If the federal government wants to achieve a change in health expenditure, it has to enact a federal law which alters the range of services provided or population covered. This rule generally applies to health policy making so that in Germany there are no convenient political opportunities for intervening in the policy network.

(3) *Governance*: In recent years "governance" has become nearly a catch-all phrase running the risk of losing its analytic value. Therefore, the term is used here in a more restricted sense, namely as a description of the mode of *economic coordination* in the health sector. By taking into account the problem at hand, governance could be split into two components. First, the coordinating mechanism for resource allocation

in health care and second, the public/private mix which refers to the size and the vitality of the private health sector in relation to its public counterpart. Both components of governance help to shape the actors' incentives, i.e. their preferences for or against markets in health care and the opportunity for governments to deploy the private sector's impulse for expansion as a lever to strengthen market forces.

With respect to governance structures, the differences between the three countries are straightforward. In Britain, governmental *planning* is responsible for the predominant part of health resources, whereas in Germany, the flow of resources is controlled mainly by *collective bargaining* between physicians, health insurance funds and, increasingly, hospitals. Even though during the 1970s numerous regulatory laws were enacted for health care, the dominance of private, *market-oriented* transactions in the US has prevailed.

In Britain, the private medical sector has experienced a modest economic consolidation in the post-war decades but its size was almost negligible when Margaret Thatcher came to power. In 1980, only 5 percent of the British population had private health insurance and only 153 out of 1,560 non-psychiatric hospitals were private (DHSS 1987a: 55; IHA 1988). It is interesting to note that due to its existence in the shadow of the NHS, the private medical sector in Britain has adopted a subsidiary and non-expansive market strategy.

A similar attitude can be found in Germany, although the private sector in health care is much greater than in Britain. In 1980, roughly 10 percent of the population was covered by private health insurance and, at any rate, about two thirds of German hospitals were owned by voluntary associations or private owners. Additionally, office-based physicians, who worked as fund doctors, have the status of private, independent professionals. Despite the significant size of the private sector in health care, there has been no expansionist tendency or even a political demand for broadening the sphere of the free market to physicians, private hospitals or health insurers. As in Britain, private owners of health care facilities have flourished and thus had no cause to demand a change of the status quo. Neither the British nor the German government thus had the opportunity to build on an already existing demand for more market in health care.

The US differed in many respects from both other cases but most important was the *developmental timing* that determined the relation between the public and private sectors. As opposed to Britain and Germany where public or semi-public organization models were introduced early enough to lay down the "terms of trade" for the public/ private relationship, in the US the private sector was already well developed as the welfare state expansion started during the New Deal (Stevens 1988: 145-148). This applies primarily to the prevailing system of private insurance carriers and employment-based health insurance whose existence diluted public interventions. For example, as Medicare and Medicaid were enacted in 1965, this most important expansion of the government into the health sector was not linked to an expansion of governmental organizations. For the most part, the program administration and claims processing was delegated to private insurance firms which acted as "fiscal intermediaries" on behalf of the government. Thus, despite increasing state intervention since the mid-1960s, the private sector always played a powerful role in determining the incentives and operating ideology of health sector governance. The Reagan administration, therefore, faced a situation in the early 1980s in which the path for private sector solutions was already paved. Health care was undergoing a large scale commercial transformation (Relman 1980; Starr 1982: 420-449) and a stronger orientation towards competition and market transactions, liberated from restrictive governmental regulations, dominated the health policy agenda.

(4) *Patterns of Interaction*: This dimension refers to what is usually called "policy style", i.e. a standard operating procedure which is constantly used in a particular policy sector or on the national level. As far as possible, in this chapter patterns of interaction should describe *sectoral* rules of decision making, interest intermediation and conflict regulation because the possibility of sectoral variations has to be considered. Often, however, it will be very difficult to distinguish sectoral from national styles (Freeman 1986).

This is particularly true for the British case where the *consultation* principle has dominated in most policy sectors, including health (Page 1985: 103ff.; Haywood/ Hunter 1982). This consensual way of policy making was expressed, for example, by the use of Royal Commissions which based on a broadly representative membership had the function of preparing crucial political decisions. Another manifestation of the consensus-oriented decision making style was the extensive consultation between government and interest groups which preceded the passage of nearly every law (Haywood/ Hunter 1982: 154ff.).

At first sight, this pattern of interaction closely resembles the rules of the game in Germany. In the health policy network, *negotiations* between the federal government and peak associations have dominated the political decision making process. Because in corporatist bodies of interest intermediation, such as the Concerted Action in Health Care (Konzertierte Aktion im Gesundheitswesen, KAG), antagonistic interests like physicians and health insurance funds are integrated and urged by the federal government to coordinate their behavior according to general systemic needs, this arrangement can be called *corporatist concertation* (Lehmbruch 1984: 62). An important by-product is a close and institutionalized policy interpenetration between the federal government and the associations as well as between the associations. Aside from the KAG, this interpenetration takes place through the Bundesausschuß der Ärzte und Krankenkassen, a corporatist decision making body that has to issue obligatory guidelines about pharmaceutical prescriptions, maternity treatment, the regional distribution of physicians etc. (Thiemeyer 1984: 91). This self-government is extremely difficult for the federal government to bypass in policy formulation as well as in policy implementation. What makes the difference between German and British health policy making is the ability of the British central government to declare certain policy issues as "non-negotiable" (Page 1985: 94) which is tantamount to the government's exercising final decision making authority. In German health policy, the resource dependence of the federal government on the association network, resulting from the extensive delegation of regulative and allocative functions towards self-administration, almost excludes this kind of action. Thus collective bargaining is not only the dominating mode for structuring the economic relations between corporate actors but also applies to the process of making health policy.

Again, a different picture is presented in the US where health policy is dominated by a *pluralist* mode of decision making and interest intermediation. Although the federal government intervened during the 1970s by means of several regulatory initiatives in the health domain, the "demand for legislation" (Feldstein 1977) by interest groups and a competitive and controversial relationship, which also applies to the governmental system of "adversarial institutions" (Kelman 1981: 131), dominates the health policy network. As opposed to the more cooperative relations in the German and British health policy networks, the logic of decision making in the US is aptly described by one single question - "who wins?" (Feick/ Jann 1988: 215). For generations of political scientists, it was also clear that only in a few cases the US government would resist group pressure (Page 1985: 94). The non-cooperative and competition-oriented operating ideology is reflected in a 1975 decision by the Supreme Court in which collective agreements between the medical profession and third-party payers were classified as a "violation of the antitrust laws" (quoted in Glaser 1978: 182). This underlines the American aversion against negotiated prices and reflects the preference for market-governed relations even in health care. One implication of this mode of interaction is that the underdevelopment of cooperative structures of decision making, which enable the actors to ground their behavior on complementary expectations, supports ad-hoc interactions with few stable patterns and high insecurity.

(5) *Selectivity*: This network dimension is used as a summarizing category that results from the constraints and opportunities provided by the previously mentioned variables. The selectivity of a policy network determines the *range of available strategic options*. There are two dimensions of network selectivity: One coming from the "real world" of actual institutions, actors and legal regulations and a second dimension derived from the "world of ideas". The structure of the policy network is important for both dimensions. First, the real world dimension permits only a certain number of strategic options and second, the network serves as an object of reflection by the actors, as an "institutionalized thought structure" (Milward 1982: 472). If decision making elites are scanning for solutions to urgent problems, the existing structures are permanently retrieved and thereby form a cognitive map which structures the problem perception and the range of "thinkable" alternatives for the status quo. This effect will be amplified if current solutions are linked to successful political junctures and are stored as collective memories.

The selectivity of health policy networks at t_0 and their strategy profiles can now be summarized as follows. Both German and British health policy strategies during the 1960s and 1970s appeared to be continuous. In Britain, the health policy repertoire focused on central budgeting, organizational reform and an increase of managerial efficiency (Haywood/ Alasziewsky 1980: 26-43). The German health policy was characterized by an expansion of the realm of collective bargaining in the hospital sector (Thiemeyer 1984: 93ff.), the formalization of political negotiations through the introduction of the KAG and an increasing reliance on self-administration ("Vorrang der Selbstverwaltung") as the proper arena for problem solving. The American health policy strategy seemed to be more discontinuous during the two decades preceding the Reagan presidency. Despite the apparent predominance towards expanding the realm of governmental responsibility for health care financing, strategic orientations teetered between competition and regulation. Aside from the already mentioned regulatory and interventionist programs, there were also legislative steps aimed at more competition since the early 1970s. Most important in this respect was the HMO Act of 1973 which provided federal funds for qualified Health Maintenance Organizations (HMOs) (Brown 1983). The intention behind this law was to spur the growth of competitive HMOs as a means of restraining health care expenditures. Although of limited success, the Nixon administration enacted a pro-competition law when this strategy was nearly unthinkable in most Western countries. Even under Jimmy Carter, some competitive elements were included in the health planning program (Havighurst 1981). The following table provides a summary of the network conditions at the time of the change of governments.

Table 1: Health Policy Networks in the Early 1980s

	Great Britain	United States	FRG
Structure	centralized and hierarchical; strong vertical interconnections; moderate sectoralization; strong system integration	strong fragmentation; numerous subsystems through vertical linkages; almost no system integration	decentralized structure with strong vertical and horizontal interconnections; strong sectoralization and system integration
Constellation of Actors	medium-sized number of important actors; number slowly growing; fairly stable coalitions; mainly vertical linkages	large number of important actors; number rapidly growing; fairly stable coalitions	few important actors with almost no increase in numbers; stable coalitions
Governance	dominance of state planning; almost no market transactions; very small private sector	dominance of market transactions, but also various governmental regulations; large private sector	dominance of associational self-government and collective bargaining; medium-sized private sector
Patterns of Interaction	preponderance of consultation between government and organized interests; despite some conflicts, consensus orientation	pluralist lobbying with conflict orientation; only rarely long-term cooperation	corporatist concertation; proportional representation and strong emphasis on negotiating and compromising
Selectivity	central budgeting; organizational reforms; emphasis on management	mixture between regulatory interventions and competitive policies	limited state intervention; strong reliance on self-regulation by self-government

4   The Process of Policy Formation

As the majority of industrialized nations had to face the end of the post-war growth period in the aftermath of the first oil price shock in 1973, health care expenditures, as a substantial portion of welfare service provision, became increasingly scrutinized and marginal costs were questioned. However, the perception of health care cost increases, the strategic response and the radicalism of changes in health policy strategies from regulation to competition have not been simply determined by

economic pressure but rather influenced by the selectivity of health policy networks. Because conservative parties functioned as upholders and,
once in office, as executors of the pro-market strategy, their role in the
formation of the neo-conservative strategy is emphasized.

One important point of departure is the programmatic commitment
of the conservative parties to the existing structures and principles of
the welfare state in general and health care in particular. In Britain as
well as in the FRG, a neo-conservative approach was confronted with
a well elaborated set of fairly binding principles in favor of the status
quo in health care. The dominating policy legacy in Britain was the
"welfare consensus" which included the government's commitment to
full-employment policy, an active economic policy and the pronounced
belief in the British welfare state model (Kavanagh 1987: 26-60). This
comprised the basic construction principles of the NHS: public ownership
of health facilities, the responsibility to guarantee free access to health
care for everybody without financial barriers and the method of tax financing. Similarly, in Germany a set of "Strukturprinzipien" guided the
CDU's philosophy in health policy: self-government, a plurality of statutory health insurance funds, the solidarity principle and the idea of subsi-
diarity (Wittkämper 1982: 256-269).

The different degrees to which both parties embraced a neo-conservative approach to welfare is determined, inter alia, by the structure of
party organization and the interpenetration with external interests. Whereas the Conservative Party in Britain is strongly centralized and hierarchical, the German CDU is a "polycentric" party with a complex and highly
decentralized structure which inhibits the central formulation of policies
(Schmid 1984, 1988). In the Conservative Party, the "Tories", with a
commitment to preserve the essentials of the welfare consensus, were
superseded by the "dries". This group, led by Margaret Thatcher, obviously had abandoned the consensus principle. Thus, around 1979, several
prominent conservatives entertained the idea of replacing NHS tax funding with insurance contributions (Krieger 1986: 91; Howe 1981) and
supported a massive roll back of social service provisions. This radicalization became possible due to a lack of institutional barriers which could
have restricted programmatic changes in the Conservative Party.

In the German CDU, it was not possible to overcome the resistance
of supporters of the status quo. Neo-conservatives, although in a strong
position in the late 1970s and early 1980s, never dominated the process
of policy formulation. As opposed to the British Conservatives, the Ger-

man CDU has a well developed division of labor which allows internal party organizations to occupy "their" policy domains (Schmid 1988: 228f.). Neo-conservatives, mainly recruited from the party's auxiliary organization of industry and business middle classes, have been thus unable to intrude in the social and health policy area which is the domain of the Christian Democratic trade unionists. Another institutional variable that had a dampening effect on the radicalization of the CDU's health policy was the existence of a system of special committees (Bundesfachausschüsse) which were highly important for the formulation of policies during the 1970s. The special committee for health is an excellent example for the party's consociational pattern of decision making and its close interpenetration with the health policy network since almost every special interest group was represented (Döhler/ Schmid 1988: 21-30). Due to the principle of unanimity, the committee's recommendations for a health policy program, which was adopted by the CDU in 1978, were biased in favor of status quo-oriented interests.

The process of formulating a neo-conservative health policy was affected by quite a different set of factors in the US. Due to the lack of a well-organized and disciplined party apparatus, institutional factors linked to the party organization played no important role. Instead, the following three events deserve mentioning. A first intrusion into the established structure of governance resulted from the emergence of the Federal Trade Commission (FTC) as a *new actor* in the health policy network. During the second half of the 1970s, the FTC actively challenged several anticompetitive practices by the American Medical Association and private health insurance carriers (Döhler 1990: 205ff.). The file of antitrust suits against health providers had a two-fold impact. On the one hand, several strategic positions of providers, based on the ability to restrict competition, were destabilized, for example, by prohibiting interlocking directorates between insurers such as Blue Cross and Blue Shield, and the AMA. On the other hand, it was demonstrated that health care could be treated as any other branch of the economy. Closely connected to the antitrust debate was a second development that contributed to the penetration of pro-market doctrines: the spill-over of the deregulation debate into the health domain. Already under President Carter, the successful deregulation of fixed prices in civil air traffic created a momentous precedent that invited being taken over in other policy areas. The *weak sectoralization* of the health policy network facilitated the new strategy's full adoption in health care. Third, the congressional defeat of Jimmy Carter's Hospital Cost Containment Act in 1979, which stipulated public controls on hospital rate setting, was perceived as a vital signal that the period of regulation in health policy had come to an end. Concomitantly, health economists like Alain Enthoven developed a flood of pro-competition plans (Enthoven 1980; Sigelman 1982). As opposed to Britain's scientific expertise, which was dominated by the social administration school with strong preferences for the NHS and against the market strategy and to Germany, where pro-market proposals were filtered and diluted by a complex party organization, no such selectivities slowed down the victory of the market strategy in the US.

5   Bringing the Market Back In

5.1   Great Britain

The Thatcher government did not immediately launch radical changes in health policy. During the *first phase* of Conservative health policy between 1979 to mid-1982, the strategy of the Thatcher government aimed at budget austerity and a strengthening of the private medical sector. In the 1979 Conservative Manifesto, there was no announcement of a cut-back in public health expenditures. Although there was repeated conjecture that the Thatcher government might cause a funding crisis of the NHS in order to justify a radical reform, the government's health expenditure does not support this suspicion. Compared to other sectors of the British welfare state such as housing or education, in which there was a real decline in public expenditure, the NHS fared comparatively well, although the small increases are no more than a "stand-still budget" (Klein 1985: 44; Social Services Committee 1986, 1988).

Similarly moderate was the increase of co-payments as a means of financing the NHS. Although the Conservatives extended prescription, dental and optical charges perceptively, the share of charges as percentage of total NHS expenditures only increased from 0.3 percent in 1979 to 0.9 percent in 1988 (Social Services Committee 1988: 77). With respect to privatizing the costs of the NHS via charges, the Conservatives were entangled in an inherited policy. Traditionally, low income groups are exempted from paying charges because otherwise free access, one of the basic philosophies of the NHS, would be no longer secured. Even the Thatcher government shied away from breaking with this principle (Birch 1986: 165-169). Thus, the means test has to be employed as an instrument to ascertain claims for being exempted from charges. Because of the high administrative costs of the means test, an increase in charges may raise rather than cut costs (Klein 1985: 46).

The most popular argument for explaining the moderate health spending approach and the lack of other reform measures refers to a culturally rooted, nearly sentimental public support for the NHS. However, the overwhelming public support is based rather on an encompassing coverage so that the whole population is a beneficiary of NHS services. In addition, among the actors in the British health policy network there was almost no supporter for a market-oriented strategy. Even from the perspective of the government, except for ideological reasons, there was no plausible explanation for a strategic change since the NHS is not only a really cheap system but also allows almost complete control of health spending. These traits served as an institutional cover against extensive reform plans.

This is not to say that the Thatcher government had completely abandoned the idea of implementing radical reforms. The most notable move during the first period in office was a ministerial working group on alternative methods of NHS financing which was appointed in 1980 by then DHSS secretary Patrick Jenkin. The report, leaked to the press in late 1981, caused a furor because it entertained the idea of switching NHS financing from taxes to insurance contributions. The Thatcher government strove to calm matters down with the famous slogan "the NHS is safe with us" (New Statesman 1982) which was to become part of the successful election campaign of 1983. This, however, should not lead to the conclusion that the Thatcher government was very receptive to public opinion.

An indicator for the restricted role of public preferences as a deterrent to unpopular political measures is the "contracting-out" initiative (Asher 1987; Key 1988). Since June 1980, the DHSS issued several circulars in which the Health Authorities were requested to invite tenders from private firms for ancillary services such as cleaning, laundry or maintenance. This initiative has met not only resistance from the affected NHS work force, but also from NHS administrators, who had misgivings concerning quality of the work performed by private firms which employed both badly-paid and -educated workers. In 1987, roughly 20 percent of the service contracts were assigned to private competitors; this percentage, however, stagnated (Sheaff 1988: 97). NHS employees, with the support of their administrators, had successfully resisted a more extensive privatization through "in-house tendering", i.e. NHS workers made concessions which allowed them to undercut private competitors.

Contracting-out, however, did not affect the core of medical service provisions in the same way as did the reversal of the Labour Party's policy towards the private medical sector (Higgins 1988: 84-90). In their 1979 manifesto, the Conservatives had announced to end the "vendetta" (Conservative Party 1979: 26) of the Labour Party against the private medical sector. In May 1980, the government abolished the Health Services Board (HSB), a kind of regulatory agency which was introduced in 1976 to reduce private "pay beds" in NHS hospitals. The Health Services Board's right to approve private hospitals was transferred to the DHSS, which had an obvious interest in the expansion of private facilities. Additionally, Health Authorities were allowed, for the first time, to contract with commercial providers (Mohan/ Woods 1985: 207), thus enabling hospital physicians to devote a larger percentage of their working capacities to the private sector, and for persons with an annual income up to 8,500 pounds private, health insurance contributions were made tax deductible (Forsyth 1982: 62).

Interestingly, the private medical market was not very receptive to Conservative policies. After a short boom period in the early 1980s, when provident societies experienced a growth rate in subscribers of 25.9 percent (1980) and 13.9 percent (1981), the annual growth declined to 1.9 percent in 1983. Obviously, the infusion of "bad risks" through the expansion of occupational insurance schemes for blue collar workers has distorted the fragile risk structure of private health insurers (Higgins 1988: 98-99) which were forced to dramatically increase their premiums. This, in turn, has reduced the attractivity of private health insurance. Private hospitals were entangled in a similar chain of events. The deregulation of the HSB, at first sight, appeared to be an effective measure for unchaining market forces. Between 1980 and 1988, the number of private hospitals increased from 153 to 204 (IHA 1988). But a second look reveals that the boom period ended as early as 1984 when already 199 private hospitals were in operation. Ironically, the unleashed private hospital growth itself produced obstacles to a further expansion. Due to a high spatial concentration in wealthy south-east England and the Thames region and the declining supply of privately insured patients, private hospitals have experienced fierce competition resulting in occupancy rates as low as 50-60% in general and even down to 40% in London (Economist 1988: 35).

The fact that the private medical sector proved not to be an effective strategic lever for the Thatcher government has to be explained by making reference to the governance structure and the ensuing incentives for private market actors. This is not so much a question of *size*, but rather a question of the *interrelations* between public and private sectors and the ensuing strategic opportunities. Of crucial importance for understanding the restricted growth capacity is the assumption that private health insurers and hospitals in Britain have accommodated their market operations to the existence of the NHS as the dominant health-care provider. Private providers are thus not equipped to compete with the NHS, rather they have been forced to occupy subsidiary "niches" resulting in high specialization, a selective market strategy and an overall restricted capacity for expansion.

The first period of Conservative health policy ended with an almost undisputed NHS administrative reorganization in April 1982, the basic outlines of which originated from a report of a Royal Commission already appointed by the Labour government. The 1982 reorganization reduced one tier of the NHS administration by merging 90 Area Health Authorities and roughly 220 District Management Teams into 192 District Health Authorities (DHAs) (Ham 1985: 28-32). Although in the public perception this administrative reform was largely a technical measure, the accompanying DHSS circulars indicate a strategic direction consistent with the Conservative's overall philosophy. The DHAs were provided with greater leeway to cooperate with the private sector and were thus cautiously pushed into "an almost entrepreneurial role" (Davies 1987: 306). This suggests that the selectivity of the health policy network is far more receptive to a strategy in which already existing structures are slowly transformed into a business-like direction, as opposed to a blunt promotion of the private health sector or using the budget as an instrument of reforming the NHS.

As was demonstrated at the beginning of the *second period* of conservative health policy, the Thatcher government passed through a process of policy learning. Especially the new DHSS secretary Norman Fowler appeared to have learned the lessons of the previously mentioned events. Fowler replaced the Conservative's rhetoric of decentralization, local autonomy and the virtues of the private sector with the language of a centralist *new managerialism* which was dominated by strategic orientations like "value for money", "managerial efficiency" and "upwards accountability".

The new managerialism started as a transfer of efficiency strategies, such as the Treasury's Financial Management Initiative, from the Civil Service into the NHS (Pollitt 1986: 156-158). The first step was the introduction in January 1982 of so-called "annual reviews", in which the chairmen of Regional Health Authorities (RHAs) have to defend the financial and service performance of their RHA before the DHSS. Since September 1983, a set of "performance indicators" has upgraded the review process into "a tighter system of control and accountability than had ever existed in the previous history of the NHS" (Klein 1989: 204). Thus the balance in the center-periphery relation has shifted increasingly in favor of the center, i.e. the DHSS.

The single most important step in the government's managerial offensive was to become the "Griffiths Reform", named after the chairman of the NHS Management Inquiry Team, Roy Griffiths, formerly managing director of a large supermarket chain. Appointed by Norman Fowler in early 1983 and charged with looking for a more efficient use of resources within the NHS administration, the group presented its inquiry report in October of same year (DHSS 1983). The Griffiths team, dominated by managers from private business firms, offered a blunt diagnosis and a no less clear-cut therapy. The lack of "leadership" and clear responsibilities caused by consensus management was identified as the single most important flaw in managerial efficiency. To take remedial action, the Griffiths team proposed the introduction of a new administrative elite, the *general management*, on every level of the NHS with the exception of FPCs. General managers, preferably recruited from the ranks of private business firms, should function as "final decision takers". This new hierarchy, equipped with broad and exclusive decision-making rights, was to be led by a NHS Management Board and a Health Services Supervisory Board inside the DHSS, both of which should provide central guidance and thus overcome bureaucratic inertia. After an unusually short period of public consultation, the DHSS started implementing the Griffiths reform in June 1984 and completed it during 1986.

The Griffiths reform did not represent a complete break with the past but rather an upgrading of an already existing drive towards managerialism. However, without altering the public/private mix, the Griffiths reform has changed the *governance* structure of the NHS by linking the incentives of managers to an increasingly tight efficiency regime.

Although the clear majority (62%) of roughly 800 newly created positions were filled with former NHS administrators, with only 12% recruited from outside (Harrison 1988: 66), it is justified to regard the general management as a *new actor* in the network. The new elite very rapidly adopted an independent attitude towards other occupational groups and local interest representatives by adhering to the three "Es", efficiency, economy, and effectiveness, as a *new operating ideology*. Their expanded rights to overrule consensus management furthermore challenged the established balance of power, particularly with regard to nurses and, to a lesser extent, the medical profession (Pollitt et al. 1988). In addition, the integration of general managers into a complete new hierarchy has further strengthened central control capacities, although it has not affected the network *stability*.

Although the Griffiths reform remained within the range of the established health policy repertoire, its successful implementation was far from being self-evident. Ever since its inception the NHS has been fairly robust in preserving a particular organizational culture (Bourn/ Ezzamel 1986) based on the predominance of the medical profession, a consensus-oriented and representative decision-making style and the prerogative of the "curing and caring" philosophy over efficiency. That the Thatcher government successfully challenged this entrenched operating ideology was due to the characteristics of the British health policy network. First, the opportunity of a spill-over of the managerialist attitude from the civil service in the NHS was due to an *incomplete sectoralization* of the health policy network. Second, and probably even more important was the activation of governmental authority reserves by utilizing *policy instruments* such as delegated legislation and the central government's ability to declare a policy issue as non-negotiable. Not only the completely unusual appointment of private businessmen as advisors and the concomitant renunciation of the use of a Royal Commission was a breach of the standard operating procedures, but furthermore, the governments' declaration of the essentials of the Griffiths recommendation as non-negotiable degraded the "consultation" phase into a mere acclamation event. Finally, the Griffiths Report was implemented via delegated legislation so that parliamentary hurdles were bypassed. All in all, the Griffiths Report has marked the beginning of a *new policy style*. Consulting interest groups is no longer regarded as a "must" of a proper decision making process, but rather as an annoying procedure, as confirmed by the vigorous conflict with the pharmaceutical industry in 1985 over a "limited list" of reimbursement for drugs (Hogwood 1987: 57f.) that proved the ability of the government to violate the interests of even powerful actors.

In the following two years, the conservatives' health policy was consistent with the managerialist orientation. The contracting out initiative was vitalized throughout 1983 and was extended to the "buying in" of medical services. DHAs were asked to reduce waiting lists for non-emergency operations, such as hip-replacement, by having them performed in private hospitals (Birch 1985) in contract with private firms for the purpose of "income generation" or to engage in joint ventures with the private sector (West 1986). All these initiatives contributed to a *blurring* of the formerly clear *boundaries* between the NHS and the private sector, a goal explicitly formulated in the 1983 Conservative Manifesto: "We shall promote closer partnership between the state and the private sector ..." (Conservative Party 1983: 296). However, the NHS was not endangered, rather a new kind of symbiotic relationship emerged which helped both sectors to supplement each other and strengthened the weight of efficiency concepts within the organizational culture of the NHS (Haywood/ Renade 1988: 24).

A clear example for the upgrading of a centralist managerialism was the new administrative arrangement for the FPCs which became effective in April 1985. By making the FPCs directly responsible to the DHSS, the ministry not only improved its interventionist capacity in face of the NHS periphery, i.e. by influencing the appointment of FPC members and the introduction of performance reviews but also contributed to a newly acquired managerialist self consciousness of FPC administrators (Ellis 1985: 610f.) who hitherto had a reputation for having servants' attitudes towards the medical profession.

The Thatcher government entered a *third phase* of their health policy strategy during 1985. The crucial innovation was the increasing reliance on the idea of *internal markets*, first introduced to a greater public by the already mentioned American health economist Alain Enthoven (1985). This renewed twist of the Thatcher governments' health policy could be described as variant c (see Figure 1) of the goodness-of-fit relationship. The mutual accommodation between strategy and network structure in the British case stands for a partial success of governmental reform efforts and an intelligent accommodation of the pro-market strategy to the opportunity structure of the British health policy network.

By focussing on the primary care sector, comprising the FPCs and their contractors, i.e. general practitioners, dentists, pharmacists, opticians, the Thatcher government discovered another object for their strategy: the economic cartel of medical providers which restricts the range of choice for a sovereign consumer. Presumably, both British antitrust authorities, the Office of Fair Trading and the Monopolies and Merger Commission, acted on behalf of the Thatcher government when they launched a series of inquiries into restrictive trade practices among medical providers. Their critical reports caused the government to implement several deregulation measures. In 1984, opticians lost their dispensing monopoly and the market for spectacles was radically liberalized. One year later, the government urged the General Dental Council to ease the restrictive regulations for dentist's advertising and in early 1989, even the medical profession came under pressure to ease their advertising rules (Harvard 1989). When the Thatcher government issued a green paper on "Primary Health Care" in 1986, even the opportunity of introducing competitive HMO-like "health shops" was discussed. However, the white paper "Promoting Better Health", issued in November 1987 (DHSS 1987) and implemented in 1989, included several concessions to the BMA. Whereas the idea of introducing competitive units of physicians was dropped, the governments' strategy swung back to managerialism by broadening the monitoring authority of FPCs vis-à-vis general practitioners. The decisive nuance of this policy episode was to focus on competition *within existing structures* of the NHS rather than looking for a private sector alternative.

On the verge of its third period in office, the Thatcher government appeared to have an ambiguous attitude towards the NHS. On the one hand, with John Moore, nick-named "Mr. Privatization", an outspoken dry had been appointed as new DHSS secretary. On the other hand, no radical policy proposal emerged on the agenda. The familiar managerialist ideology was presented once again in a different rhetorical guise: "The NHS ... is not a business, but it must be run in business-like way" (Conservative Party 1987: 50). Then, unexpectedly, conventional wisdom about the unlikeliness of radical reforms (Klein 1985) seemed to lose its relevance.

During the 1987 election campaign, the Labour Party succeeded to mobilize public doubts about the conservative's "safe in our hands" promise and thus triggered a heated debate about the shortcomings of Conservative health policy (Withney 1988: 5ff.). The public diagnosis of a dramatic NHS underfunding, resulting in urgent problems such as nursing shortages, hospital and operating theatre closures, and delayed or even cancelled operations forced the Thatcher government to an unprecedented extent into the political defense. In this critical situation Margaret Thatcher decided to take the offensive. In late 1987, the government announced for the first time a radical reform of NHS funding which was to be prepared by a "NHS review group" set up in January 1988.

This review process, which lasted a year, was a vivid confirmation of the earlier mentioned ability of the British central government to employ a powerful set of policy instruments. By setting up a small group of ministers and advisors, working isolated from the political battlefield, the government constructed a barrier between "insiders" and "outsiders" (Grant 1984: 132ff.). Otherwise influential actors such as the BMA were effectively cut off from the decision making process and even the bureaucratic apparatus of the DHSS was bypassed. Instead of established interest groups, the three neo-conservative think tanks, Center for Policy Studies, Institute of Economic Affairs and Adam Smith Institute, became for the first time "insiders" to the health policy network. Under their influence, the review group considered a number of radical reform options and finally ended with the white paper "Working for Patients", published in February 1989 (DoH 1989). In the following highly critical discussion, the Thatcher government once again declared a policy issue as non-negotiable and violated the consensus principle.

"Working for Patients" was halfway radical and halfway moderate. The moderate side of the review consisted in its affirmation of the basic principles of the NHS, tax financing, equal access, public ownership and responsibility for service provisions. As opposed to the original purpose of the review, no reform of NHS funding was planned and the managerial strategy was continued. By decreasing the number of non-management members of the Health Authorities and FPCs, the power of general managers was enhanced vis-à-vis physicians, nurses and local government nominees. This also means that a *new coalition* between center, i.e. DoH, and periphery, i.e. general management, is likely to emerge.

The radical side comprised the introduction of internal markets in the NHS. Hospitals with over 250 beds have the opportunity to become self-governing "NHS Hospital Trusts". These hospitals will be no longer subject to DHA supervision and are free to decide their budget, payment of personnel, and to negotiate service contracts with public or private customers. They may retain operating surpluses but also have to finance deficits. Similarly, general practitioners with more than 11,000 patients on their list may opt to act as "budget holders". As opposed to the existing system of capitation payment, budget holders will receive a fixed sum out of which also hospital services have to be paid. The intention is that budget holders negotiate with hospitals for cheap services because similarly to independent hospitals, they are allowed to retain surpluses and have to balance deficits out of their budgets. Whereas it is still unclear to what extent these reforms will be enforced, it is justified to expect that internal operations of the post-review NHS will become more market-like.

5.2 United States of America

The Reagan administration entered office with an ambitious health policy program (Arras 1983). The four most important proposals where a reduction of federal health expenditures, a termination of several regulation programs, a decentralization of responsibilities to the state level, and the introduction of a pro-competitive law (Döhler 1990: 319ff.). What particularly fuelled the expectation that these programmatic aims would lead to a sweeping change was that they enjoyed a bipartisan support in both houses of Congress (Iglehart 1981: 179ff.).

However, as can be illustrated by the administration's successful budget strategy during the 97th Congress (1981-1982), the political compliance of an otherwise highly idiosyncratic Congress was decisively promoted by taking advantage of procedural rules as *policy instruments*. Medicare and Medicaid almost automatically became the focus of budget cut efforts. Since 1970, expenditures for both programs doubled every five years corresponding to an annual increase of 15 percent (Feder et al. 1982: 274ff.). Within the scope of the first two budget laws, the Omnibus Budget Reconciliation Act of 1981 (OBRA) and the Tax Equity and Fiscal Responsibility Act of 1982 (TEFRA), the Reagan administration succeeded in getting the most sweeping reductions through Congress ever since 1965 when both programs were launched (data in US General Accounting Office 1988). OBRA and TEFRA also included several pro-competition elements which aimed at promoting HMOs and other alternative insurance plans (Gornick et al. 1985: 17; Iglehart 1985). Despite the bipartisan popularity of the Reagan cut-back program of expenditure increases, congressional approval would not have been possible without resort to a set of "fast-track" legislative procedures such as "reconciliation" and "omnibus bills" (Ellwood 1985: 329ff.; Hoadley 1986). An important role was played by the new director of the Office of Management and Budget (OMB), David Stockman, who successfully exploited the streamlined budget procedures to the advantage of the Reagan administration. The executive's dominance over the congressional budgeting process, however, lasted only during the 97th Congress. Afterwards, the bipartisan cut-back coalition gave way again to the constituency oriented individualism embedded in the American party system.

Reagan's "New Federalism" initiative was less successful. Whereas the administration succeeded in consolidating 21 federal health programs earmarked for four block grants permitting the states greater freedom for allocating these funds for multiple purposes, the second and decisive step, a "turnback" of roughly 40 federal grant-in-aid programs to the states designed to restore full responsibility but also transferring large additional costs to the states was rejected by Congress without extensive deliberation. Although the block grant consolidation reduced the federal share by 16.4% (Bovbjerg/ Davis 1983: 530), "many programs have continued to operate largely as they did when Ronald Reagan was a presidential contender" (Peterson et al. 1986: 218).

The relevance of the network structure for political opportunities is well reflected in the case of deregulation. As already mentioned, deregulation in other policy sectors spilled over into health care. During the early Reagan presidency, deregulation ranked high on the political agenda and the health sector was a specific target. The first agency to be abolished was the National Center for Health Care Technology (NCHCT) which ceased to exist in October 1981. The Center had only been set up in 1978 to make recommendations to the HCFA as to whether newly-developed medical technologies and procedures should be reimbursed through the Medicare program. This quasi-regulatory mandate soon provoked strong criticism from the affected medical technology industry and the AMA, which rejected the NCHCT's assessment activities as an inroad in the medical professions' prerogative to judge medical technologies. However, the termination of the Center was not mainly a result of pressure group politics but rather reflected a lack of internal bureaucratic backing (Blumenthal 1983: 602). Because the activities of the NCHCT overlapped with those of three other agencies with a more powerful constituency inside the DHHS and Congress (Blumenthal 1983: 595), opponents easily mobilized congressional and executive support against a re-authorization of funds.

The deregulation of the Professional Standards Review Organization (PSRO) program came about under similar circumstances. Since 1972, roughly 200 PSROs had to monitor the quality of medical services reimbursed under Medicare and Medicaid. However, the program never developed a strong anchorage within the policy network and was hampered by operating obstacles throughout the 1970s (Smits 1981: 254-256). Through the Peer Review Improvement Act (a part of TEFRA), Congress drastically reduced federal funding and stipulated a transformation of PSROs into Professional Review Organizations (PROs). As opposed to their predecessors, PROs are no longer required to be managed chiefly by physicians and are allowed to obtain the status of private profit-oriented enterprises which may contract with a large variety of private customers (Jost 1989). Similarly, the Reagan administration also succeeded in dismantling the 200 health systems agencies (HSAs), the single most important regulatory program of the 1970s. As in the case of PSROs, the administration could build on the *weakened stability* of the network segment which had hitherto supported the program. One of the most important functions of HSAs was the implementation of the states certificate-of-need (CON) laws which imposed capital investment controls on the hospital industry. With the growing commercialization of the hospital sector since the early 1980s, however, CON regulations were increasingly perceived as threatening restrictions on capital investment as the hospitals' most vital instrument for dealing with an increasingly turbulent environment. Thus the hospital industry, which earlier was a moderate supporter, formed a new coalition together with the OMB and republican market advocates which were eager to kill another "liberal" health program (Mueller 1988: 722). Federal funding ended in 1986 and only 40 HSAs survived this financial cutback (Kinzer 1988: 116). Interestingly, some of the HSAs are now maintained and financed by private business firms who are interested in preserving some measures of regulatory control over the health care industry (Perrin 1988). The appearance of private firms as a new actor in the policy network was even more evident in the case of PSROs. The deregulation/ privatization of this program enabled employers to use the control capacities of PROs for the first time to scrutinize hospitals and physicians who provide medical care for employment-related private health insurance.

The successful deregulation efforts during the early Reagan presidency were based on three network-related variables. First, congressional budget rules provided the administration with several essential *policy instruments* such as reconciliation and fast track legislative instruments. Second, the enforcement of financial cutback and deregulation measures was strongly bolstered by the *heterogeneity* of the health policy network. What in the US is usually referred to as "subsystem politics" suggests that only a restricted number of actors and an equally restrained number of affected groups is linked to a program. This has counterbalanced the mobilization of broad opposing forces. To the same degree as centralization constituted an opportunity for the Thatcher government, the fragmentation of governmental institutions and organized interests has enabled the Reagan administration to pursue its strategy. Third, there was an overall *abatement of network stability* that fostered the erosion of established configurations.

If there is any proper term for describing the US health policy network since the mid-1980s then it must be *instability*. Two large-scale processes have reinforced this development to a considerable extent. First, the rise of a "new medical industrial complex" (Relman 1980). Discussions about the commercial character of health services originated the early 1970s, but the prefix "new" was not chosen arbitrarily. The new entrepreneurialism differs from its predecessor by the rapid transformation of formerly independent hospitals, HMOs, nursing homes etc. into large multi-institutional conglomerates. In 1987, already 42.9% of US hospitals were integrated into multi-unit systems (Bell 1987: 44). Although the transformation of voluntary and religious hospitals into commercial hospitals did not cover more than 13.1% of all US hospitals (Gray 1986: 28), their commercialization is more intense than this data suggests, because non-profitmaking hospitals and HMOs are increasingly involved in "contract management" relations or are forced to imitate the market behavior of their commercial competitors (Marmor et al. 1986). Thus the rise of large-scale entrepreneurialism had a two-fold impact on the health policy network. By pushing the actors' incentives even further into a market-dominated direction (Arnold 1986), the new medical industrial complex has spurred the competitive behavior of health care providers. The arrival of new associations representing profit-oriented health care enterprises has also contributed to the increase in the number of political actors in Washington and thus furthered the fragmentation of interest representation (Kosterlitz 1986; Tierney 1987).

An analogous effect emanated from a second development: the appearance of employers as a new actor in health policy. As late as in 1979, employers showed no particular interest in the issue of rising health care costs (Sapolsky et al. 1981). But this stance dramatically changed during the following years. Since 75 percent of US employees are covered through employment-related private health insurance (Staples 1989: 416), soaring health care costs also became a problem for *private* actors, particularly for large firms with generous fringe benefits. As an ever growing number of firms was exposed to double digit health premium increases, the business community reacted with a complete new repertoire of cost containment strategies (Bagby/ Sullivan 1986; Döhler 1990: 348ff.). Business firms tried to hold down their health bills by tightening the screws of utilization and peer review programs and negotiating with "preferred providers" about cheaper rates and organizing regional "Business Coalitions" which acted as a political arm in the struggle for state legislation (Bergtold 1988) and provided consulting and negotiating support against physicians, HMOs, hospitals and the like. Whereas these activities have intensified the competitive behavior among physicians, hospitals and other providers, business organizations such as the Washington Business Group on Health or regional Business Coalitions could not be regarded as outspoken advocates of a competitive health policy. Several legislative initiatives by the Reagan administration, such as the reform of tax treatment for employment-based health insurance premiums, were forestalled by the business community (Demkovich 1984: 1509).

The combined effect of the emergence of two new actors in the health policy network was to transform the governance of the health economy and to rearrange established coalitions. The "structural interests" identified by Robert Alford (1975: 190-217) during the early 1970s ceased to exist. The professional monopolist coalition is now fragmented into competing providers and large-scale corporate enterprises (Immersheim/ Pond 1989); the corporate rationalizers' coalition is divided into federal and state bureaucrats and health care managers in corporate headquarters; the consumers, finally, are no longer represented solely by the "repressed" coalition of "equal health advocates" but are supplemented by powerful business firms such as Chrysler and General Motors which have identified themselves as consumers within an overcharged health care market. The result of this reorganized coalition landscape is a *new distribution of power* which is no longer dominated by the medical profession or stable "structural" coalitions but rather by unstable "action-sets" in which organized interests "have formed a temporary alliance for a limited purpose" (Aldrich/ Whetten 1981: 387; Iglehart 1987: 640f.).

The US health policy network has thus moved from relative stability and policy stalemate into a state of fragmentation and instability with a novel opportunity structure.

As was pointed out earlier, network instability provides the most promising opportunities for enforcing a new strategy. If this state of the network did not lead to a complete victory of the market strategy envisaged by the Reagan administration, then it was because the window of opportunity for a pro-competition strategy proved to be unstable. Thus since the mid-1980s, regulatory health policy re-emerged in the guise of an alternative policy which was implemented amidst an almost hegemonic market discourse. After all, the Reagan administration was successful in *deregulation* and *cutback* of federal health expenditures but failed to get a *pro*-competition law through Congress (Fuchs 1987: 220-224.). The ambivalent character of the Reagan administration's health policy thus consists of two contradictory policy legacies. On the one hand, health services were embraced as a new field of commercial trade, on the other hand, it was the Reagan administration that introduced the most powerful regulatory instrument ever to be at the disposal of a federal government - the so-called "Diagnostic Related Groups" (DRGs).[1]

This new payment system for Medicare hospital patients was "passed through Congress at the legislative equivalent of the speed of light" (Morone/ Dunham 1985: 263). DRGs were announced by DHHS secretary Richard Schweiker in December 1982, the bill was introduced in January 1983, approved by Congress without much debate in March 1983, and signed into law by President Reagan in April 1983. Aside from the unusual velocity, this legislative process was remarkable because it emanated as a bureaucratic initiative which was orchestrated by the HCFA with pressure group politics only playing a minor role (Fuchs/ Hoadley 1984). As opposed to the conventional "interest-group liberalism" (Lowi 1979: 50-52) image of the American political process where the role of government is restricted on "ratifying the agreements" (Lowi 1979: 51) of organized interests, in the DRG case the federal government appeared as an autonomous actor (Morone/ Dunham 1985:

---

1   As opposed to "retrospective" payment by which the hospital is reimbursed after the event for all "usual, customary and reasonable" costs, DRGs categorize each hospital patient into one of 471 diagnostic cases, each of which has a fixed "prospective" price. The hospital receives exactly this sum of money and is allowed to retain surpluses but also has to bear additional costs.

288ff.) which successfully seized the opportunity to extend its regulatory power in health care. Since the full implementation of DRGs in 1987, it is a federal agency, the HFCA, which controls roughly 40% of total US hospital revenues through a system of "administered prices" (Sloan et al. 1988: 210).

By aiming at the income of health care providers, DRGs created an influential strategic precedent which was buttressed by the dwindling veto power of formerly influential health associations. Unlike in former years, when budget cuts were largely obtained by increasing patients' cost sharing or tightening eligibility criteria, since 1984 physicians' pay has become a major target for cost containment efforts (Ginsberg 1989: 7-9). In 1984, Congress included a two year "fee freeze" for physicians' Medicare reimbursement in the Deficit Reduction Act (DEFRA), a restriction on the medical profession's income unbelievable only a decade ago. As part of the 1985 budget law Congress created the Physician Payment Review Commission which is charged with developing a prospective payment system analogous to hospital DRGs for office-based physicians. Again, reconciliation and "omnibus bills" provided the vehicle for legislative proposals that were not supposed to occur under a neo-conservative administration.

These steps already signalled a departure from the market strategy of the early Reagan presidency. Furthermore, Congress increasingly seized the initiative and implemented its own health policy agenda (Brown 1990). But the Reagan administration also deviated from its own ideology as the formerly hegemonic market discourse was increasingly superseded by the discussion about the growing number of uninsured Americans. In his last year in office, President Reagan signed into law the Medicare Catastrophic Coverage Act which aimed at narrowing the so-called "medigap", i.e. the costs for long-term hospital stays and drug bills which are not covered by Medicare, by introducing a small additional premium that - almost revolutionary - was linked to individual income, a financing mechanism promoted by Democrats (Iglehart 1988). Although the law was repealed only one year later under the pressure of an influential faction of wealthy elderly persons opposed to income-related premium financing of Medicare (Financial Times 1989a), it was an important indicator for the end of the market strategy in US health policy.

This re-emergence of regulatory health policy was permitted by a network characteristic that previously contributed to the rise of the pro-competition strategy in the late 1970s: a policy network which does not allow a stable *strategy lock-in*. A good indicator for the deficient anchorage of health policy strategies is the revival of an issue of bygone days: the discussion about a comprehensive national health insurance which, ironically, was fuelled at the end of the Reagan presidency (Brown 1988; Kinzer 1989). Anthony King's characterization of American politics as "building coalitions in the sand" (King 1978) appears to be particularly true in the case of health. Employers, an almost traditional opponent of national health insurance and therein united with health providers, are currently reconsidering their stance because a national health program is more likely to relieve private firms from rising health care costs than the private market (Brown 1988: 608; Financial Times 1989; New York Times 1989). Therefore, it is no longer far-fetched to expect a new coalition in which labor and business are united in their support for a national health program (on unions cf. Jacobs 1987).

5.3   Federal Republic of Germany

When the three-party coalition of CDU/CSU and FDP replaced the Social-Liberal coalition in October 1982, the neo-conservative faction in the new government was at the zenith of its influence. But compared to Britain and the US, the range of realistic health policy alternatives was far more restricted. Despite a then dominant anti-welfare state rhetoric, which also applied to the health sector, only two concrete measures were announced: an increase of co-payments in the statutory health insurance, and a reform of hospital finances (Kohl 1984: 23, 127). The implementation of these programmatic intentions hardly amounted to the "significant structural changes" (Biedenkopf 1984: 499) as they were envisaged by leading neo-conservatives.

Contrary to a widespread expectation and despite a supportive public mood, the Christian-Liberal government did not manage to introduce a sweeping expansion of cost-sharing elements in the early period of government. Two elements of the network configuration turned out to be of particular importance for this policy outcome. First, the strong interconnection of the CDU with the associations in the health policy network through several subdivisions of the party organization. The social committee, a party sub-organization representing the faction of Christian Democratic union members and employees, was then an outspoken opponent of increased cost sharing. Second, the resistance of this moderately influential party faction was amplified by the fact that the major strategic aim of government, a reduction of federal deficit spending, could not be advanced by health care savings because the statutory health insurance is organized into a system of parafiscal health insurance funds, each of which is equipped with a *separate* budget and financial autonomy. Thus, increased cost sharing, contrary to Britain and the US, is not automatically converted into reductions of governmental spending and therefore was of limited worth for the coalition's budget consolidation strategy.

The next important move of Christian-Liberal health policy was an overhaul of the existing system of hospital financing. Out of the whole outlay of the GKV, the percentage that was devoted to hospital care had increased from 25.2% (= DM 6 billion) in 1970 to 32.1% (= DM 33.2 billion) in 1984. This increased share of hospital costs might lead to the expectation that any reform effort would focus on cost containment measures. However, hospital financing reform was in fact more strongly influenced by the logic of intergovernmental relations than by political pressure for cost containment.

Up to 1972, the majority of German hospitals were in a state of chronic underfunding. The user charges which were negotiated between individual hospitals and health insurance funds did not provide the capital needed for hospital construction, modernization and extension. Thus the sponsoring organizations, such as churches, local government, voluntary associations or private owners, had to balance hospital deficits. Because of their limited capacity for raising such funds and the unstable financial situation of the hospital sector, the Social-Liberal coalition, with the agreement of CDU/CSU, enacted the "Krankenhausfinanzierungs-Gesetz" (KHG) in 1972 which for the first time introduced a legal claim for public funding of hospital capital costs. The KHG created the so-called system of "dual financing" in which daily operating costs are covered by user charges whereas capital costs are financed jointly by the federal government and the Länder. The instrument for allocating money was the "hospital need plan". Adhering to federal guidelines, the Länder were empowered to decide which hospitals should be included in the plan and thereby entitled to public money for capital investments. Due to this focal positioning and their final right to ratify user charge negotiations between health insurance funds and hospitals, the Länder became the dominant actor in hospital policy. Although the KHG, praised as a "law of the century", significantly contributed to a consolidation of hospital finances, the broad consensus on which the law was based had eroded since the late 1970s (Altenstetter 1985).

Hospitals increasingly perceived themselves as being captured within political calculations reflecting not their priorities but rather those of the Länder. The health insurance funds objected to being forced to bear the financial burdens of political decisions by the Länder which culminated in a costly oversupply of beds ("Bettenberg") and pressed for more influence on hospital planning as well as in user charge negotiations. Most important, however, was the growing dissatisfaction of the Länder who perceived the federal guidelines surrounding the joint financing as a restriction on their domain of hospital policy, not least due to the fact that the federal share never reached 30%, as envisaged originally, but had declined to 18% in 1983 (Altenstetter 1985: 251). Interestingly, the system of hospital financing shielded the decision making process from becoming a pure exercise in cost containment with an enlarged opportunity for introducing more market because the Länder had strong political incentives against market and competitive solutions which would weaken their grip on the hospital segment of the German health policy network.

When the federal government introduced a first draft of the bill in April 1983, this particular network selectivity had already become visible. No radical measures were included. The federal government's retreat from the hospital sector by terminating joint financing was undisputed. However, the federal government's plan to strengthen the position of health insurance funds in the process of hospital planning caused considerable dispute. The passage of this bill was intended to introduce some competition in the hospital sector by enabling the health insurance funds to exert economic pressure on the hospitals (Bruckenberger 1988). This proposal met fierce resistance from the Länder which were not willing to share their rights with the health insurance funds and the bill was rejected even by the CDU/CSU-governed Länder. The *decentralized structure* of the health policy network enabled the Länder to reject the competition plans through their veto right in the Bundesrat, so that the final version of the "Krankenhaus-Neuordnungsgesetz", which was approved by the Bundestag in December 1984, contained only minor improvements of the health insurance funds' position in the hospital sector. Most important were alterations in federal-state relations towards hospital financing and the extension of the *collective bargaining* principle. The latter change can be interpreted as one facette of an "institutional isomorphism" (DiMaggio/ Powell 1983) according to which the procedure for allocating resources in the hospital sector is becoming increasingly similar to that in the ambulatory sector.

The health policy debate in the mid-1980s was characterized by a political stalemate. Health policy activists, particularly academic health economists, strongly urged a general overhaul of the German health care system in order to allow market forces to play a greater role in the distribution of services. However, the federal government's reluctance to pursue this strategic direction was no less strong. After three years in office, "more market" in health care was no longer on the agenda of the Christian-Liberal coalition. This suggests that the *sectoralization* of the network was well enough developed to prevent a spill-over of alternative strategies. A good illustration of how the network structure guided the health policy outcome is provided by looking at the cases of a) drug policy and b) large-scale medical equipment. In both decision making processes the federal committee of physicians and health insurance funds played an important role.

a) As opposed to physicians' fees and hospital user charges, no instrument to influence drug pricing and consumption was available for the health insurance funds, although drug prescription mounted to 15% of their overall budget (BMJFFG 1989: 230). In late 1984, after an effort by the health insurance funds to introduce the "tough" instrument of direct price negotiations was rejected by the pharmaceutical industry, the Concerted Action recommended the compilation of a "comparative drug price list" as a "soft" and rather indirect measure for getting a grip on drug expenditures. This additional information instrument should enable physicians to consider the price as one parameter of their drug prescriptions - which, it was hoped, would activate price competition in the pharmaceutical industry. In accordance with the strategic selectivity of the German health policy network, the federal government did not issue the price list as a law or governmental decree but instead charged the federal committee with this delicate job. After a controversial discussion, the price list was approved by the BMA in September 1986 (Döhler 1990: 447ff.). Although the pharmaceutical industry managed to dilute the original concept, the interesting question is not so much how the industry did this but rather why exactly this instrument and not, for example, a limited list which would have excluded a number of drugs from GKV reimbursement was chosen. First, it has to be considered that the network configuration virtually pushed the federal government into a distinct strategic direction. Delegating certain responsibilities into the area of self-administration not only relieved the federal government from a troublesome political decision but additionally allowed it to build an important alliance. Since any regulation of prescribing behavior is likely to be perceived as a threat to physicians' clinical autonomy, this hurdle was effectively bypassed by relying on a committee in which half of the members came from the ranks of physicians. Second, if the federal government refers the regulation of a problem back to self-administration, it has to approve the particular bargaining rules of this intermediate sphere. In a way, the federal committee is among the most important policy tools of the federal government but it is one which can only be employed at the price of diluting the state's law-making authority with the bargaining logic of self-government. It is justifiable, therefore, to expect that the construction principles of the federal committee thoroughly exclude market-oriented decisions or indeed any radical policy outcomes.

b) Another verification of the increasing relevance of the federal committee and its compromise-oriented policy output are the "guidelines for the efficient use of large-scale medical equipment" from December 1985. As was the case with the price list, the federal government preferred to replace a governmental law with a guideline negotiated between the actors of the federal committee. The original aim of these guidelines was to regulate the growth of the use of medical technology equipment by private practitioners which was phenomenal in the early 1980s (Kirchberger 1986). As is to be expected from the previous analysis, the guidelines did not include stringent regulations but left a number of loopholes for office-based physicians. Most important in this respect was that physicians unwilling to comply with a new set of guidelines concerning the distribution of such equipment were *not* automatically sanctioned. The design of an efficient enforcement tool was left to *negotiated* contracts at the regional level. This suggests that the choice for German health policy makers, even neo-conservatives, is not between state and market, but between state and self-government. The increasing reliance on the federal committee strongly supports the hypothesis that the opportunity structure of the German health policy network creates a nearby irresistible attraction to build on existing institutional arrangements and to stay away from alternatives not in accordance with the system ("systemfremd").

So far, the German case closely resembles the variant d in Figure 1, i.e. even the modest strategic aspirations of the Christian-Liberal government to bring some competition into the health care sector have been bent into a direction compliant with the network. There was a change neither in the structure of the network, nor in governance or the operating ideology. If there was any chance for the government to enforce a radical policy change then this opportunity may have emerged from the discussion about the so-called "structural reform" in 1987 and 1988.

This reform effort was not a result of long-term strategic planning, but was triggered by a renewed rise in health insurance expenditures in late 1984 (Döhler 1990: 466ff.). Immediate legislative action, however, was deliberately postponed so as to prevent this issue from arising in the 1987 federal election campaign. In April 1985, the Labour Ministry issued a vague health policy concept which made it clear that a potential reform bill would not entail a "comprehensive" overhaul of the statutory health insurance as announced by chancellor Helmut Kohl later but would be restricted to some moderate adjustments primarily aimed at stabilizing health insurance premiums. However, the "10 principles" stipulated the appointment of a "council of expert advisors" for the KAG. This body of experts was commissioned to publish an annual report containing proposals for increasing the quality and efficiency of health care. Although the council functioned as a new actor, the range of strategic opportunities was circumscribed by appointing the members according to the principle of *proportional representation*, i.e. political and sectoral interests were included in a fairly balanced way through advisers close to these actors. Thus once again, the durability of a corporatist policy style was evident.

The discussion about the structural reform itself, however, was among the most controversial policy issues of the whole Christian-Liberal government before ultimately, in December 1988, after a painfully drawn-out political battle, the "Gesundheits-Reformgesetz" was adopted. The Minister of Labor, Norbert Blüm, has fuelled the perception of the law in which the dominant role of pressure groups is stressed (Webber 1989) by characterizing the reform effort as a "trail of courage in a field mined by interest groups" (quoted in Döhler 1990: 497). From the policy network perspective, a more elaborate interpretation is inferred. Conflict and group pressure occurred largely over the *details* of the reform but the *main direction* was furnished by the opportunity structure of the network.

First, the political decision making process made it clear that the autonomy of the federal government is decisively restricted by its *re-*

source dependence upon the system of self-governing associations. As opposed to the British case, the German federal government is not able to disregard or even to exclude the interests of the network actors from the decision making process. The broad delegation of implementation functions forces the federal government into concessions which are already granted during the stage in which alternative policy solutions are being considered.

A second important influence results from the actors' institutional integration and representation. Due to the fact that health insurance funds do not effectively advocate the insured population since the decision making bodies are staffed with employee *and* employer representatives in equal numbers, the new interpretation of the meaning of "solidarity" was primarily achieved by shifting the burden to the insurers. Patients' cost sharing was perceptively raised and several benefits such as dental services or funeral grants were curtailed. This became possible because at the same time, the social committee's resistance to cost sharing was bought off by making the health insurance funds responsible for financing ambulatory long-term care even though this new benefit remained on a very low level. Physicians and hospitals were not completely left out but their contribution to the "new conception of solidarity", as cost-shifting was hailed by the federal government, remained more than moderate. The most interesting facet of the whole law became the introduction of a new reimbursement procedure for prescription drugs.

Amidst a heated debate about the adequacy of the proposals to cut back the expenditures of health insurance funds, a working group of the coalition parties which was charged with preparing the essentials of the bill adopted the idea of fixed prices for pharmaceuticals ("Festbeträge"). According to this concept, health insurance funds would no longer have to reimburse the market price of each prescribed drug but rather a fixed sum based on the price of cheaper drugs with comparable therapeutical effects. If the patient asks for the product from the original producer then he has to bear the price difference out of his own pocket. It was expected that this new scheme, hailed as the "central plank" of the law by the federal government, would save health insurance funds DM 2 billion a year at the expense of the pharmaceutical industry. Despite several objections about the efficiency of this new scheme, recent empirical findings suggest that the fixed prices in fact have resulted in a significant decrease in turnover for the pharmaceutical industry (Manow-Borgwardt 1990: 48ff.). Thus the question occurs as to how this clear violation of the fundamental interests of an ostensibly influential actor became possible.

As was pointed out earlier, such political solutions can be explained by referring to a health policy network which is based on corporatist concertation and collective bargaining. In the same way as the weak *representation* of consumers made them politically vulnerable, the weak *integration* of the pharmaceutical industry into the bargaining structure of the network contributed to its defeat. Since direct price negotiations were rejected by the pharmaceutical industry and their membership in the Concerted Action did not prove to be an effective way of slowing down increasing drug costs, it was logical to switch from a loosely-coupled encompassing corporatism to a tighter mode of selective corporatism (Manow-Borgwardt 1990: 65). This interpretation becomes clearer when the method by which the fixed prices are determined is considered.

The highly complex procedure of dividing pharmaceuticals into comparable groups was delegated to the Bundesausschuß and in a second step the peak associations of health insurance funds are empowered to decide the fixed price for those drugs included in the scheme. Thus, the federal government has not only seized the opportunity for shifting the implementation of a conflict-ridden policy solution into the sphere of self-government but furthermore, it has excluded the pharmaceutical industry from determining drug prices. Two changes in the structure of the policy network have facilitated this political decision. First, since the early 1980s, the structure of the pharmaceutical market has changed. The generic producers ability to capture an increasing market share has created the strategic opportunity to exert pressure on traditional producers. Second, the established coalition between the medical profession and the brand name producing pharmaceutical industry was decisively weakened as physicians tried to move out of the cost containment battle by prescribing more generic drugs.

A third explaining variable, also linked to the network, refers to the already introduced hypothesis of institutional isomorphism. According to this general trend, the forms of governance of the hospital and the pharmaceutical segments of the network are slowly being adjusted to correspond to the model of the ambulatory sector, i.e. price fixing by collective bargaining between associations. The fixed pricing scheme is a clear indicator of this development because it has not only introduced an element of *negotiation* into the pharmaceutical sector but also has enhanced the willingness within the pharmaceutical industry to become involved in direct price negotiations with the health insurance funds (Ärzte Zeitung 1990) because this procedure has become more attractive in the face of complete exclusion from price determination. Seen from this perspective, the new pricing scheme not only became possible because of the rearrangement of coalitions but also because the selectivity of the German health policy network favors a collective bargaining strategy and tends to preclude competition and market strategies.

6   Conclusions: Policy Networks as Facilitators and Impediments to Change

In the previous country-related analysis, several indicators for assessing success or failure of neo-conservative reform strategies have been presented which will be considered now in a comparative perspective. Obviously, the US represents the case in which the market solution has flourished most. The initial success in deregulating health care and the sweeping transformation of health services into a large-scale commercial market clearly points in this direction. However, the thesis that it was the Reagan administration that was most successful in enforcing this strategy deserves significant qualification. This judgement is only correct in a limited sense because the current shift in governance structures was largely an endogenous process and was only to a certain extent influenced by political decisions of the Reagan administration. The fact that the Reagan administration returned to a regulatory strategy while, at the same time, the commercial transformation of health care providers continued, demonstrates why it is not easy to fit the US case into a scale of "more or less market". In clear opposition to the US, it is justified without any qualification to argue that no strategic "turn-around" has taken place in the FRG. The realm of market and competition in the statutory health insurance has remained as restricted as it was at the point of change in government. Great Britain falls between both other cases. The Thatcher government's record has been mixed. Although the basic structures and principles have been preserved, there has also been a perceptible increase in market or quasi-market transactions within the NHS.

At the beginning of this chapter, it was assumed that neo-conservative governments intending to expand the role of markets in health care had to face a particular functional matching between the established health policy network and an alternative political strategy. If the strategic adaptability of the network proves to be inhospitable to market mechanisms and competition, then change or instability of the network becomes a crucial prerequisite for implementing a new policy strategy. Thus a comparison of the network structure at different points in time (cf. Figure 1) with a focus on those network characteristics that have changed will provide an explanation for success or failure of neo-conservative reform efforts.

Table 2: Changes in the Policy Networks in the Late 1980s

	Great Britain	United States	FRG
Structure	more centralization	more fragmentation	more policy interconnection
Constellation of Actors	general managers as new actors; emerging coalition between center and periphery	strong increase of actors, most notably employers and commercial providers; coalition instability	almost no increase of actors; moderate change in coalitions
Governance	stronger efficiency orientation via managerialism; internal markets as new system of incentives	sweeping transformation of governance through commercialization; rapid expansion of market forces	principle of collective bargaining extended; private sector growth restricted
Patterns of Interaction	new policy style; consultation principle abandoned; break-up of clientelism between BMA and DoH	pluralist policy preserved, but state and congressional activism; organized interests weakened	no change
Selectivity	new opportunities for introducing managerial efficiency and internal markets	changing opportunities, after competition policy swing back to regulation and intervention	no change

Before taking a closer look at Table 2, it is necessary to consider the multiplicity of *network change*. The modification of the network structure may be both a *precondition* or a *result* of a political strategy. In the latter case, it has to be taken into account that not every change is identical with more market but may also go into a different strategic direction. Aside from network instability and changes, also opportunities emanating from existing network structures have to be taken into account.

The variable network *structure* contains some of the most basic determinants of neo-conservative policy making. As has already been stressed by Krieger (1986: 34), institutional centralization in Britain and fragmentation in the US both had the effect of enabling the government to enforce strategic intentions. In Britain it was the centralist and hierarchical organization of the NHS that opened the window of opportunity for introducing a whole battery of control techniques all aiming at improving efficiency and thus contributing to a perceptible change of the organizational culture of the NHS. The fragmentation of the policy network in the US, which spans across both governmental institutions and organized interests, proved to be particularly helpful in the case of deregulation since it allowed the Reagan administration to exploit the heterogeneity of organizational interests including those of regulatory bureaucracies. In Germany, the comparatively close interconnections between federal ministries, self-government, organized interests and political parties have resulted in a mutual resource dependence "in which preferences and organizational structures are conditioned by long-standing relationships and shared political values" (Krasner 1988: 81).

Similarly, the structural characteristics of sectoralization and system integration protected the German health policy network from being invaded with a market-oriented strategy. In Britain, however, a spill-over of the managerialist ideology became possible because the NHS was not completely isolated from the Civil Service which has been strongly challenged by the Thatcher government. In the US, the sectoralization of the policy network was so weak that even the Federal Trade Commission was able to expose health care to an "ordinary" antitrust scrutiny. In Germany and to a lesser extent in Britain, the equation of health care with any other service would be almost unthinkable.

Some of the most interesting changes have occurred in the configuration of *actors*. As was the case with other network characteristics in Germany, with the exception of drug pricing, there have been no significant changes which have remodelled the opportunity structure. This contrasted with the American development where not only the number of relevant actors has strongly increased but also coalitions have been rebuilt to a considerable degree. Most important in this respect has been the loss of influence of formerly important interest groups, particularly the AMA and the AHA. Due to a growing heterogeneity of membership interests, these associations no longer occupy a representative monopoly. In a political system with almost no restrictions to access of the decision making process, there are strong incentives for segments of members to deviate from the umbrella organization. The trend of increasing fragmentation of interest representation was amplified by the emergence of new actors such as employer groups specializing in health policy. Since the growing number of actors has also eroded the stability of coalitions, this network characteristic has provided the Reagan administration with new room to maneuver. In Britain, the government-led introduction of general management in the NHS had an even more positive impact on the opportunity structure. The implementation of the internal market concept would have been unthinkable without this new actor whose creation has led to the opportunity of a new coalition formed between center and periphery.

The most sweeping changes in the area of *governance* are again occurring in the US. The already existing dominance of markets as a mode of economic coordination was augmented even further by the transformation of single medical entrepreneurs into large multi-unit enterprises in which profit-orientation governs most service parameters. The opportunity which accrued in the Reagan administration lay in the chance to treat health care similarly to other sectors of the economy. This relieved the Reagan administration from the onerous exercise of having to justify its unabashed preference for markets as an instrument for providing and distributing health services. In this respect, the German and British governments have been in a much more defensive position. But the Thatcher government was able to influence the governance of the NHS to such an extent that efficiency and internal markets became a new operating ideology whereas in the German case, not markets but rather an extension of collective associational bargaining has to be considered as a change of governance. Changes in the network structure in Germany, therefore, have *not* increased the opportunity for a competition strategy but have reinforced the locked-in strategy of collective associational bargaining.

This is also reflected in the *patterns of interaction* which in Germany basically have remained the same. Even in situations in which the Christian-Liberal coalition tried very hard, it was not able to deviate from the established patterns of corporatist decision making. A quite different picture can be observed in Britain, where the inherited consultation principle was increasingly replaced by the hierarchical technique of "non-negotiability". This has enabled the Conservatives to make policy decisions without taking into account the "veto" of organized interests such as the BMA, which has lost its privileged clientelist relationship with the ministry of health. This change in the policy style became possible because the consultation principle has always been a "convention" (Page 1985: 105) without protecting institutional support as is the case in the German health policy network. The major change in the US policy style consists in the "new activism" (Brown 1990) of Congress and the executive. On the one hand, this has contributed to a slightly enlarged governmental enforcement capacity, on the other hand, however, this change was ambiguous in terms of contributing to the implementation of pro-competitive health policy strategy because it also strengthened the capacity of state intervention-oriented policy makers who are gaining ground.

The simple diagnosis that there is no goodness of fit between a network structure and a market-oriented strategy is not sufficient in order to explain the success or failure of neo-conservative governments. Of crucial importance is an assessment of the opportunities to reorganize the network. This twofold opportunity structure is included in the variable *selectivity*. In the German case, there is a well developed preselection against market and competition policies. However, German policy makers are not completely restricted in their choice. Although the health policy network appears to be trapped by "reform blockades" (Rosewitz/ Webber 1990), this observation only describes *one side* of strategic adaptability. The other side consists of a continuous, although incremental, path-dependent development ("Weiterentwicklung") and path dependency is not an equivalent to structural and strategic deadlock but denotes a *selective* exclusion of policy alternatives (Krasner 1988: 83). There is certainly some change in German health policy but it is in the direction of *negotiated* prices and not in the direction of competition. This suggests that one of the fundamental obstacles to a neo-conservative turn-around in Germany can be found in the institutional *lock-in* of a particular strategy.

Exactly the lack of this characteristic has been responsible for the greater strategic discontinuities in the US case. Even before the Reagan administration came into office, there have been two rival health policy strategies: one relying on the forces of the market and a second one oriented towards an interventionist regulation of the health care market. At first this enabled the new administration to catch up to the already practiced market strategy. However, because neither the state interventionist nor the private market alternative tested during the Reagan presidency achieved a firm establishment in the structures of the network, even under Ronald Reagan, health policy fanned out in two different directions. The Thatcher government has been fairly successful because it adopted a strategy according to network selectivity and remained *within* the institutional framework.

These results can be summarized into two general conclusions. The predisposition of policy networks towards strategic changes strongly depends on a) *network stability* defined "as a situation in which relations between organizations within a bounded population remain the same over time" (Aldrich/ Whetten 1981: 391), and b) the *structure of ties* between actors within a network. Both the "loose coupling" of the US health policy network and the vertical and hierarchical network structure in Britain have enabled the governments to implement their strategies to a certain extent. In Germany, on the other hand, the vertical and horizontal interconnecting structures formed a barrier which was extremely difficult to overcome.

References

Ärzte Zeitung, April, 6./7. 1990: In der Industrie wachsen nun die Präferenzen für Preisverhandlungen.

Aldrich, Howard/ David A. Whetten, 1981: Organization-sets, Action-sets and Networks: Making the most of Simplicity. In: Paul C. Nystrom/ William H. Starbuck (eds.), *Handbook of Organizational Design*. Vol. 1. Oxford: Oxford University Press, 385-409.

Alford, Robert R., 1975: *Health Care Politics. Ideological and Interest Group Barriers to Reform*, Chicago: University of Chicago Press.

Altenstetter, Christa, 1985: Hospital Policy and Resource Allocation in the Federal Republic of Germany. In: A.J. Grote/ L. Wade (eds.), *Public Policy Across Nations: Social Welfare in Industrial Settings*, Greenwood: JAI Press, 237-265.

Altman, Stuart H., Harvey M. Sapolsky (eds.), 1981: *Federal Health Programs. Problems and Prospect*. Lexington, MA: Lexington Books.

Arnold, Patricia J., 1986: *The Invisible Hand in Health Care*: The Rise of Markets Within the U.S. Health Care Sector. Manuscript. University of Wisconsin.

Arras, John, 1983: The Neoconservative Health Strategy. In: Ronald Bayer/ Arthur L. Caplan / Norman Daniels (eds.), *In Search of Equity*. New York: Plenum Publishers, 125-159.

Arthur, W. Brian, 1989: Competing Technologies, Increasing Returns, and Lock-In by Historical Events. In: *The Economic Journal* 99, 116-131.

Asher, Kate, 1987: *The Politics of Privatisation*: Contracting Out in the Public Sector. Houndmills: Macmillan.

Bagby, Nancy S./ Sean Sullivan, 1986: *Buying Smart. Business Strategies for Managing Health Care Costs*. Washington, DC: American Enterprise Institute.

Balutis, Alan P., 1984: The Reorganization of the Department of Health Education, and Welfare: What Happened, Why and So What? In: Robert D. Miewald / Michael Steinman (eds.), *Problems in Administrative Reforms*. Chicago: Nelson-Hall, 43-64.

Bell, Clark W., 1987: 1987 Multi-Unit Providers. In: *Modern Healthcare* 17(June 5), 37-58.

Benson, J. Kenneth, 1982: A Framework for Policy Analysis. In: David L. Rogers/ David A. Whetten (eds.), *Interorganizational Coordination: Theory, Research and Implementation*. Ames: Iowa State University Press, 137-376.

Bergtold, Linda A., 1988: Purchasing Power: Business and Health Policy Change in Massachusetts. In: *Journal of Health Policy, Politics and Law* 13, 425-451.

Biedenkopf, Kurt, 1984: Die Zukunft des Sozialstaats. In: *Gewerkschaftliche Monatshefte* 35, 494-500.

Birch, Stephen, 1986: Increasing Patient Charges in the National Health Service: A Method of Privatizing Primary Care. In: *Journal of Social Policy* 15, 163-184.

Blumenthal, David, 1983: Federal Policy toward Health Care Technology: The Case of the National Center. In: *Milbank Memorial Fund Quarterly/Health & Society* 61, 584-613.

BMJFFG, Bundesministerium für Jugend, Familie, Frauen und Gesundheit, 1989: Daten des Gesundheitswesens - Ausgabe 1989. Stuttgart: Kohlhammer.

Bourn, A.M./ M.A. Ezzamel, 1986: Organisational Culture in Hospitals in the National Health Service. In: *Financial Accountability & Management* 2, 203-225.

Bovbjerg, Randall R./ Barbara A. Davis, 1983: State's Responses to Federal Health Care "Block Grants": The First Year. In: *Milbank Memorial Fund Quarterly/Health & Society* 61, 523-560.

Brown, E. Richard, 1988: Principles for a National Health Program: A Framework for Analysis and Development. In: *Milbank Quarterly* 66, 573-617.

Brown, Lawrence D., 1983: *Politics and Health Care Organization. HMOs as Federal Policy.* Washington, DC: Brookings.

Brown, Lawrence D., 1990: *The New Activism: Federal Health Politics Revisited.* In: Bulletin of the New York Academy of Medicine 66, 293-318.

Bruckenberger, Ernst, 1988: Von der parallelen Kompetenz bis zur Letztentscheidung der Krankenkassen bzw. des BMA. In: *Das Krankenhaus* 80, 197-206.

Bruckenberger, Ernst, 1986: Großgeräte-Richtlinien als Stein der Weisen? In: *führen und wirtschaften im Krankenhaus* No. 2, 14-17.

Conservative Party, 1979: *The Conservative Manifesto 1979.* London: Conservative Central Office.

Conservative Party, 1983: *The Conservative Manifesto 1983.* London: Conservative Central Office.

Conservative Party, 1987: *The Conservative Manifesto 1987.* London: Conservative Central Office.

Davies, Celia, 1987: Viewpoint: Things to Come: The NHS in the Next Decade. In: *Sociology of Health & Illness* 9, 302-317.

Demkovich, Linda, 1984: Business Drive to Curb Medical Costs Without Much Health from Government. In: *National Journal* 16, 1508-1512.

DHSS, Department of Health and Social Security, 1983: *NHS Management Inquiry - The Griffiths Report,* London: Her Majesty's Stationary Office.

DHSS, Department of Health and Social Security, 1986: *Primary Health Care: An Agenda for Discussion.* Cmnd 9771. London: Her Majesty's Stationary Office.

DHSS, Department of Health and Social Security, 1987: *Promoting Better Health.* Cmnd 249. London: Her Majesty's Stationary Office.

DHSS, Department of Health and Social Security, 1987a: *Health and Personal Social Services Statistics for England*. 1987 edition. London: Her Majesty's Stationary Office.

DiMaggio, Paul J./ Walter W. Powell, 1983: The Iron Cage Revisited: Institutional Isomorphism and Collective Rationality in Organizational Fields. In: *American Sociological Review* 48, 147-160.

DoH, Department of Health, 1989: *Working for Patients*. Cmnd 555. London: Her Majesty's Stationary Office.

Döhler, Marian, 1990: *Gesundheitspolitik nach der "Wende"*. Policy-Netzwerke und ordnungspolitischer Strategiewechsel in Großbritannien, den USA und der Bundesrepublik Deutschland. Berlin: edition sigma.

Döhler, Marian/ Josef Schmid, 1988: *Wohlfahrtsstaatliche Politik der CDU - Innerparteiliche Strukturen und Politikformulierungsprozesse*. IIM/IP 88-6, Wissenschaftszentrum Berlin.

Eckstein, Harry, 1960: *Pressure Group Politics: the Case of the British Medical Association*. London: Allen & Unwin.

Economist, January 14, 1989: Private Health Care: Beds for Sale, 34-35.

Ellis, Norman, 1985: Family Practitioner Committee Independence: What will it Mean. In: *British Medical Journal* 290, 607-611.

Ellwood, John W., 1985: The Great Exception: The Congressional Budget Process in an Age of Decentralization. In: Lawrence C. Dodd/ Bruce I. Oppenheimer (eds.), *Congress Reconsidered*. Third edition. Washington, DC: Congressional Quarterly Press, 315-342.

Enthoven, Alain, 1980: *Health Plan: The Only Practical Solution to the Soaring Cost of Medical Care*. Reading, MA: Addison-Wesley.

Enthoven, Alain C., 1985: *Reflections on the Management of the National Health Service*. Occasional Papers 5. London: Nuffield Provincial Hospitals Trust.

Feder, Judith et al., 1982: Health. In: John L. Palmer/ Isabel V. Sawhill (eds.), *The Reagan Experiment*. Washington, DC: Urban Center, 271-305.

Feick, Jürgen/ Werner Jann, 1988: "Nations matter" - Vom Eklektizismus zur Integration in der vergleichenden Policy-Forschung? In: Manfred G. Schmidt (ed.), *Staatstätigkeit. International und historisch vergleichende Analysen*. Sonderheft 19, Politische Vierteljahresschrift. Opladen: Westdeutscher Verlag, 196-220.

Feldstein, Paul J., 1977: *Health Associations and the Demand for Legislation*. Cambridge, MA: Ballinger.

Financial Times, September 1, 1989: Why Every Chrysler has a $700 Health Bill.

Financial Times, October 6, 1989a: Medical Benefit Proposals for US Elderly Collapse.

Forsyth, Gordon, 1982: The Semantics of Health Care Policy and the Inevitability of Regulation. In: Gordon McLachlan/ Alan Maynard (eds.), *The Public/ Private Mix for Health*. London: Nuffield Provincial Hospitals Trust, 57-93.

Freeman, Gary P., 1986: National Styles and Policy Sectors: Explaining Structured Variation. In: *Journal of Public Policy* 5, 467-496.

Fuchs, Beth/ John F. Hoadley, 1984: *The Remaking of Medicare: Congressional Policymaking on the fast Track*. Paper presented at the annual meeting of the Southern Political Science Association, Savanah, Georgia, November 3, 1984.

Fuchs, Beth, 1987: Health Policy in a Period of Resource Limits and Conservative Politics. In: Jerold L. Waltman/ Donley T. Studlar (eds.), *Political Economy. Public Policies in the United States and Britain*. Jackson - London: University Press of Mississipi, 207-232.

Ginsberg, Paul B., 1989: Physician Payment Policy in the 101st Congress. In: *Health Affairs*, 8(1), 5-20.

Glaser, William A., 1978: *Health Insurance Bargaining*. Foreign Lessons for Americans. New York: Gardner Press.

Gornick, Marian et al., 1985: Twenty Years of Medicare and Medicaid: Covered Population, Use of Benefits and Program Expenditures. In: *Health Care Financing Review*, Annual Supplement, 13-59.

Grant, Wyn, 1984: The Role and Power of Pressure Groups. In: R.L. Borthwick/ J.E. Spence (eds.), *British Politics in Perspective*. New York: St. Martin's Press, 123-144.

Gray, Bradford H. (ed.), 1986: *For-Profit Enterprise in Health Care*. Washington, DC: National Academy Press.

Hall, Peter, 1986: *Governing the Economy*. The Politics of State Intervention in Britain and France. Cambridge: Polity Press.

Ham, Christopher, 1985: *Health Policy in Britain*: The Politics and Organization of the National Service. Second edition. London: MacMillan.

Hannan, Michael T./ John Freeman, 1978: Structural Inertia and Organizational Change. In: *American Sociological Review* 49, 149-164.

Harrison, Stephen, 1982: Consensus Decision-making in the NHS: A Review. In: *Journal of Management Studies* 19, 377-394.

Harrison, Stephen, 1988: *Managing the National Health Service*. Shifting the Frontier? London: Chapman and Hall.

Harvard, J.D.J., 1989: Advertising by Doctors and the Public Interest. In: *British Medical Journal* 298, 903-904.

Havighurst, Clark C., 1981: Health Planning for Deregulation: Implementing the 1979 Amendments. In: *Law and Contemporary Problems* 44, 33-76.

Hayhurst, J.D./ Peter Wallington, 1988: The Parliamentary Scrutiny of Delegated Legislation. In: *Public Law* 32, 547-576.

Haywood, Stuart/ Andy Alaszewski, 1982: *Crisis in the Health Service*. The Politics of Management. London: Croom Helm.

Haywood, Stuart/ David J. Hunter, 1982: Consultative Processes in Health Policy in the United Kingdom: A View from the Centre. In: *Public Administration* 69, 143-162.

Haywood, Stuart/ Wendy Ranade, 1988: *Privatising from Within: The National Health Service under Thatcher*, Ppaper presented at the XIVth World Congress of the IPSA, August 28th to September 1, Washington, DC.

Heclo, Hugh, 1978: Issue Networks and the Executive Establishment. In: Anthony King (ed.), *The New American Political System*. Washington, DC.: American Enterprise Institute, 87-124.

Henke, Klaus-Dirk, 1988: Funktionsweise und Steuerungswirksamkeit der Konzertierten Aktion im Gesundheitswesen (KAiG). In: Gérard Gäfgen (ed.), *Neokorporatismus im Gesundheitswesen*. Baden-Baden: Nomos 1988, 113-157.

Higgins, Joan, 1988: *The Business of Medicine. Private Health Care in Britain*. Houndmills: MacMillan.

Hoadley, John F., 1986: Easy Riders: Gramm-Rudman-Hollings and the Legislative Fast Track. In: *Political Science* 19, 30-36.

Hogwood, Brian W., 1987: *From Crisis to Complacency? Shaping Public Policy in Britain*. Oxford: Oxford University Press.

Hollingsworth, J. Rogers/ Leon N. Lindberg, 1985: The Governance of the American Economy: the Role of Markets, Clans, Hierarchies and Associative Behavior. In: Wolfgang Streeck/ Philippe C. Schmitter (eds.), *Private Interest Government. Beyond Market and State*. London - Beverly Hills: Sage, 221-252.

Howe, Geoffrey, 1981: Health and the Economy: A British View. In: *Health Affairs* 1, 30-38.

Hunter, David J., 1983: Centre-Periphery Relations in the National Health Service: Facilitators or Inhibitors of Innovation? In: Ken Young (ed.), *National Interests and Local Government* London: Heinemann, 133-167.

Iglehart, John K. 1981: Washington Report: The New Role of the Federal Government. In: *Journal of Health Policy, Policy and Law* 6, 179-183.

Iglehart, John K., 1985: Medicare Turns to HMOs. In: *New England Journal of Medicine* 312, 132-137.

Iglehart, John K., 1987: The Political Contest over Health Care Resumes. In: *New England Journal of Medicine* 316, 639-644.

Iglehart, John K., 1989: Medicare's New Benefits: "Catastrophic" Health Insurance. In: *New England Journal of Medicine* 320, 329-335.

IHA, Independent Hospitals Association, 1988: *Survey of Acute Hospitals in the Independent Sector*. London: IHA.

Immersheim, Allen W./ Philip C. Rond, 1989: Elite Fragmentation in Health Care: Proprietary and Nonpropriatary Hospitals in Florida. In: *Social Science Quarterly* 70, 53-71.

Jacobs, David C., 1987: The UAW and the Committee for National Health Insurance. In: *Advances in Industrial and Labor Relations* 4, 119-140.

Jost, Timothy St., 1989: Administrative Law Issues Involving the Medicare Utilization and Quality Control Peer Review (PRO) Program: Analysis and Recommendation. In: *Ohio State Law Journal* 50, 1-71.

Katzenstein, Peter, 1977: Conclusion: Domestic Structures and Strategies of Foreign Economic Policy. In: *International Organization* 31, 879-920.

Kavanagh, Dennis, 1987: *Thatcherism and British Politics. The End of Consensus?* Oxford: Oxford University Press.

Kelman, Steven, 1981: *Regulating America, Regulating Sweden: A Comparative Study of Occupational Safety and Health Policy*. Cambridge, MA: MIT Press.

Key, Tony, 1988: Contracting Out Ancillary Services. In: Robert Maxwell (ed.), *Reshaping the National Health Service*. Berks: Policy Journals, 65-81.

King, Anthony, 1978: Building Coalitions in the Sand. In: Anthony King (ed.), *The New American Political System*. Washington, DC: American Enterprise Institute, 371-395

Kinzer, David, 1988: The Decline and Fall of Deregulation. In: *New England Journal of Medicine* 318, 112-116.

Kinzer, David M., 1989: Why the Conservatives Gave Us Universal Health Care: A Parable. In: *Hospital and Health Services Administration* 34, 299-310.

Kirchberger, Stefan, 1986: Technischer Fortschritt in der Medizin. In: *Medizin und Technologie*, Argument-Sonderband 141, 7-28.

Klein, Rudolf, 1985: Why Britain's Conservatives Support a Socialist Health Care System. In: *Health Affairs* 3, 41-58.

Klein, Rudolf, 1989: *The Politics of the National Health Service*. Second edition. London: Longman.

Kohl, Helmut, 1984. *Reden 1982 - 1984*. Bonn: Schriftenreihe "Berichte und Dokumentationen" der Bundesregierung.

Kosterlitz, Julie, 1986: Organized Medicine's United Front in Washington is Showing more Cracks. In: *National Journal* 18, 82-86.

Krasner, Stephen D., 1988: Sovereignty. An Institutional Perspective. In: *Comparative Political Studies* 21, 66-94.

Krieger, Joel, 1986: *Reagan, Thatcher, and the Politics of Decline*. Cambridge: Polity Press.

Laumann, Edward O./ David Knoke, 1987: *The Organizational State*. Social Choice in National Policy Domains. Madison: University of Wisconsin Press.

Lehmbruch, Gerhard, 1984: Concertation and the Structure of Corporatist Networks. In: John H. Goldthorpe (ed.), *Order and Conflict in Contemporary Capitalism*. Oxford: Clarendon Press, 60-80.

Lehmbruch, Gerhard, 1990: Wirtschaftspolitischer Strategiewechsel und die institutionelle Verknüpfung von Staat und Gesellschaft. In: Hans-Hermann Hartwich (ed.), *Macht und Ohnmacht politischer Institutionen*. Opladen: Westdeutscher Verlag, 222-235.

Levitt, Ruth/ Andrew Wall, 1984: *The Reorganised National Health Service*. Third edition. London: Croom Helm.

Lowi, Theodore, 1979: *The End of Liberalism*: The Second American Republic. Second edition. New York: Norton.

Manow-Borgwardt, Philip, 1990: *Neokorporatistische Gesundheitspolitik?* Die Festbetragsregelung des Gesundheits-Reformgesetzes. Unpublished M.A. thesis. Free University of Berlin.

March, James/ Johan P. Olson, 1984: The New Institutionalism: Organizational Factors in Political Life. In: *American Political Science Review* 78, 734-749.

Marmor, Theodor R. et al., 1986: A New Look at Nonprofits: Health Care Policy in a Competitive Age. In: *Yale Journal on Regulation* 3, 313-349.

Milward, H. Brinton, 1982: Interorganizational Policy Systems and Research on Public Organizations. In: *Administration & Society* 13, 457-478.

Milward, H. Brinton/ Ronald A. Francesco, 1983: Subsystem Politics and Corporatism in the United States. In: *Policy and Politics* 11, 273-293.

Mohan, John/ Kevin Woods, 1985: Restructuring Health Care: The Social Geography of Public and Private Health Under the British Conservative Government. In: *International Journal of Health Services* 15, 197-215.

Morone, James A./ Andrew B. Dunham, 1985: Slouching Towards National Health Insurance: The New Health Care Politics. In: *Yale Journal on Regulation* 2, 263-291.

Mueller, Keith J., 1988. Federal Programs To Expire: The Case of Health Planning. in: *Public Administration Review* 48, 719-725.

New Statesman, October 15, 1982: The Knives Are Out, 8-10.

New York Times, May 8, 1989: A Health Care Taboo Is Broken.

Olson, Johan P., 1988: *Political Science and Organization Theory*. Parallel Agendas but Mutual Disregard. Paper presented at the International Conference on "Political Institutions and Interest Intermediation" in Honor of the 60th Birthday of Gerhard Lehmbruch, Konstanz, 20-21 April.

Page, Edward C., 1985: *Political Authority and Bureaucratic Power. A Comparative Analysis*. Brighton: Wheatsheaf Books.

Parkin, Alan, 1985: Public Law and the Provision of Health Care. In: *Urban Law and Policy* 7, 101-131.

Perrin, James M., 1988: The Distinctive Roles of Private and Public Sector Planners. In: Frank A. Sloan/ James F. Blumstein/ James M. Perrin (eds.), *Cost, Quality, and Access in Health Care*. San Francisco: Jossey-Bass, 171-190.

Peterson, Paul E./ Barry G. Rabe/ Kenneth K. Wong, 1986: *When Federalism Works*. Washington, DC: Brookings.

Pollitt, Christopher, 1986: Beyond the Managerial Model. In: *Financial Accountabiity & Management* 2, 155-170.

Pollitt, Christopher et al., 1988: The Reluctant Managers: Clinicians and Budgets in the NHS. In: *Financial Accountability & Management* 4, 213-233.

Relman, Arnold, 1980: The New Medical-Industrial Complex, In: *New England Journal of Medicine* 303, 963-969.

Rosenthal, Gerald, 1983: The Federal Health Structure. In: David Mechanic (ed.), *Handbook of Health, Health Care and the Health Professions*. New York: Free Press, 379-393.

Rosewitz, Bernd/ Douglas Webber, 1990: *Reformversuche und Reformblockaden im deutschen Gesundheitswesen*. Frankfurt a.M.: Campus.

Sapolsky, Harvey M. et al., 1981: Corporate Attitudes toward Health Care Costs. In: *Milbank Memorial Fund Quarterly/Health & Society* 59, 561-585.

Scharpf, Fritz W., 1978: Interorganizational Policy Studies: Issues, Concepts and Perspectives. In: Kenneth Hanf/ Fritz W. Scharpf (eds.), *Interorganizational Policy Making*. London - Beverly Hills: Sage, 345-370.

Scharpf, Fritz W., 1987: *Sozialdemokratische Krisenpolitik in Europa*. Frankfurt a.M.: Campus.

Schattschneider, E.E., 1960: *The Semi-Sovereign People*. A Realist's View of Democracy in America. Hinsdale, IL: Dryden Press.

Schmid, Josef, 1984: *Die Entwicklung wohlfahrtstaatlicher Programmatik und Praxis bürgerlicher Parteien am Beispiel der englischen Konservativen und der Deutschen CDU*. Das Vorspiel zur "Wende". M.A. thesis. University of Konstanz.

Schmid, Josef, 1988: *Landesverbände und Bundespartei der CDU*. Organisationsstrukturen, Politiken und Funktionsweisen einer Partei im Föderalismus. Ph.D. thesis. University of Konstanz.

Scott, W. Richard/ John C. Lammers, 1985: Trends in Occupations and Organizations in the Medical and Mental Health Sectors. In: *Medical Care* 42, 37-76.

Sheaff, Mike, 1988: NHS Ancillary Services and Competitive Tendering. In: *Industrial Relations Journal* 19, 93-105.

Sigelman, Daniel W., 1982: Palm-Reading the Invisible Hand: A Critical Examination of Pro-Competitive Reform Proposals. In: *Journal of Health Politics, Policy and Law* 6, 578-620.

Skocpol, Theda, 1985: Bringing the State Back In: Strategies of Analysis in Current Research. In: Peter Evans/ Dietrich Rueschemeyer/ Theda

Skocpol (eds.), *Bringing the State Back In*. Cambridge: Cambridge University Press, 3-37.

Sloan, Frank A./ Michael A. Morrisey/ Joseph Valvona, 1988: Effects of the Medicare Prospective Payment System on Hospital Cost Containment: An Early Appraisal. In: *Milbank Quarterly* 66, 191-220.

Smits, Helen L., 1981: The PSRO in Perspective. In: *New England Journal of Medicine* 305, 253-259.

Social Services Committee, 1986: Session 1985-86, *Public Expenditure on the Social Services*. Vol. II. London: Her Majesty's Stationary Office.

Social Services Committee, 1988: Session 1987-88, *Public Expenditure on the Social Services*. London: Her Majesty's Stationary Office.

Staples, Clifford L., 1989: The Politics of Employment-Based Insurance in the United States. In: *International Journal of Health Services* 19, 415-131.

Starr, Paul, 1982: *The Social Transformation of American Medicine*. New York: Basic Books.

Stevens, Beth, 1988: Blurring the Boundaries: How the Federal Government Has Influenced Welfare Benefits in the Private Sector. In: Margaret Weir/ Ann Shola Orloff/ Theda Skocpol (eds.), *The Politics of Social Policy in the United States*. Princeton, NJ.: Princeton University Press, 123-148.

Stockman, David, 1981: Premises for a Medical Marketplace: A Neoconservative's Vision of How to Transform the Health System. In: *Health Affairs* 1, 5-18.

Thiemeyer, Theo, 1984: Selbstverwaltung im Gesundheitsbereich. In: Helmut Winterstein (ed.), *Selbstverwaltung als ordnungspolitisches Problem des Sozialstaates* II. Berlin: Duncker & Humblot, 63-97.

Tierney, John T., 1987: Organized Interests in Health Politics and Policy-Making. In: *Medical Care Review* 44, 89-118.

Webber, Douglas, 1989: Zur Geschichte der Gesundheitsreformen in Deutschland - II. Teil: Norbert Blüms Gesundheitsreform und die Lobby. In: *Leviathan* 17, 262-300.

Weir, Margret/ Theda Skocpol, 1985: State Structures and the Possibilities for 'Keynesian' Responses to the Great Depression in Sweden, Britain, and the United States. In: Peter Evans/ Dietrich Rueschemeyer/ Theda Skocpol (eds.), *Bringing the State Back In*. Cambridge: Cambridge University Press, 107-163.

West, Peter A., 1986: Sharing the Cost of High Technology Medicine: The Economics of Public and Private Co-operation. In: *Hospital and Health Services Review* 51, 15-17.

Whitney, Ray, 1988: *National Health Crisis. A Modern Solution.* London: Shepheard-Walwyn.

Wilson, Graham K., 1982: Why Is There No Corporatism in the United States? In: Gerhard Lehmbruch/ Philippe Schmitter (eds.), *Patterns of Corporatist Policy-Making*, Beverly Hills: Sage, 219-236.

Wittkämper, Gerhard, 1982: Entwicklung und Kritik der gesundheitspolitischen Programme. In: Harald Bogs et al. (eds.), *Gesundheitspolitik zwischen Staat und Selbstverwaltung*, Köln-Lövenich: Deutscher Ärzte-Verlag, 237-326.

Zysman, John, 1983: *Governments, Markets, and Growth: Financial Systems and the Politics of Industrial Change.* Ithaca, NY: Cornell University Press.

Chapter 9
The Preconditions for Policy Networks: Some Findings from a Three-Country Study on Industrial Restructuring

Patrick Kenis

1 Introduction

Theories on the production and reproduction of social, political and economic orders have been dominated for a long time by the juxtaposition of two polar forms of social organization: market and organization - or hierarchy, bureaucracy, state, etc. (for a good illustration of this argument see Vanberg 1975, 1982). In the last decade, however, a literature has developed which distinguishes many alternative governance arrangements. In this discussion, *networks* as a mode of governance acquired an important status (e.g. Williamson 1975; Hollingsworth et al. n.d.; Hollingsworth 1990; Powell 1990; Marin 1990a; Traxler/ Unger 1990). In chapter 2 of this book, it was shown that such network forms of social organization emerge as well and exist in processes of public policy making - an observation which also was made by a number of American and British scholars (Rainey/ Milward 1983; Wilks/ Wright 1987; Wright 1988; Jordan 1990; Marsh/ Rhodes 1991; Marin 1990b; Laumann/ Knoke 1987). It is also important to notice that next to these *public* policy networks, additional forms of policy networks developed which consist either of private or of a mixture of public and private actors. These *private* networks, too, often play an increasing role in the production and reproduction of social orders. The concept of "private policy network" finds its parallel in the by now well-established *private government* concept. Private-interest governments are "... arrangements under which an attempt is made to make associative, self-interested collective action

I would like to thank Bernd Marin, Renate Mayntz, Volker Schneider and Franz Traxler for helpful comments on earlier drafts of this chapter. For linguistic assistance I am grateful to Suzanne Stephens.

contribute to the achievement of public policy objectives" (Streeck/ Schmitter 1985: 17). There is one basic difference between private interest governance and private policy networks, however: the first directs its attention to single organizations, whereas the second directs its attention to loosely-organized organizational networks.

By now, a whole series of studies exist which illustrate the importance and relevance of private policy networks - without, however, directly referring to the concept.[1] What is still missing, however, is systematic knowledge about the factors which account for the development of policy networks. The answer to this question is equally significant from a policy making point of view, since it appears that those policy fields which are primarily governed by policy networks, produce different - and often more successful - policy outcomes. Traxler and Unger (1990), for example, clearly demonstrated that the metal, automobile and machine tool industry coped much more successfully with challenges of world-wide competition in those countries where these sectors were characterized by network or neo-corporatist governance structures.

This chapter attempts to find some general answers to the question of why and under which circumstances policy networks develop, by offering some empirical insights into policies towards industrial restructuring within a specific sector. The study is based on an empirical analysis of industrial restructuring in West Germany, Britain, and Italy between 1968 and 1985 (as described in detail in Kenis 1991).

---

1   The construction industry (Eccles 1981; Marin 1986), the publishing industry (Coser/ Kadushin/ Powell 1982), the film and recording industry (Hirsch 1972), the diamond trade (Ben-Porath 1980), the aircraft industry (Mowery 1987), the high-tech industry (Mariti/ Smiley 1983), the industrial region of Emilia-Romagna (Sabel 1989), the Japanese textile industry (Dore 1983), the Japanese economy (Wright 1989), the Swedish economy (Pestoff 1990), the food-processing industry (Pestoff 1987), etc. For an overview of some of these studies, see Powell (1990).

2   Policy Networks as a Mode of Governance in Industrial Restructuring

Industrial policy towards industrial restructuring can be accomplished by different governance structures. In addition to the traditional *market/state* dichotomy, *policy networks* were more recently identified as another distinct, significant, and frequent governance mechanism in industrialized countries. In the case of industrial restructuring, governance through policy networks means that an environment exists in which the parties concerned negotiate among themselves either over the need for or, the distribution of, mutual burdens and benefits of industrial restructuring plans. Policy networks constitute observable and relatively stable groups of organizations formed in an alliance or coalition to promote the collective interest of all or part of the industry's members. They do this by negotiating common interests as well as by ranking their collective priorities.

Industrial governance by policy networks differs from state-led industrial policy, in the sense that the principal mode of coordinating is not based on command or direction but rather on negotiation and bargaining. It also differs from market-led industrial restructuring in that every individual firm is not merely pursuing its own private interests. In contrast, policy networks are horizontal systems of coordinating among firms, public administration, and associations. They tend to be more stable than market types of governance, even though this stability is not hierarchically imposed. Instead, shared norms, attitudes of trust, considerable knowledge about and respect for one another, stabilize the relationship among the actors. Normative mechanisms, negotiations, and socialization within the group coordinates relationships and discourages opportunism over relatively long time periods. As such, a governance mode is given in which medium- and long-term policies are formulated and implemented to cope with the structural problems of a specific industry.

Take, for example, the problem of overcapacity in an industry producing basic goods and which is exposed to all the pressures of the world market - as, for example, the chemical fibre or steel industry. These industries are characterized by low technological complexity and mass production. High economies of scale and significant fixed costs also tend to be basic characteristics. In these industries, full-capacity utilization is the major condition for competitiveness. Therefore, when the firms are confronted with high fluctuations in demand - as was most usually the case in the 70s and 80s - they are almost immediately hit with high risks. Much is at stake: many workers stand to lose their job, and investors stand to bear huge losses. As a consequence during a period of recession, market-led industrial policies in such sectors led to closing down plants - eventually leading to the complete disappearance of an industry at the national level. This, in turn, means large-scale capital depletion and massive unemployment - the latter having even broader social implications.

In order to prevent or overcome these negative results of market-led industrial restructuring, an industrial policy led directly by the state might be preferred. In most cases, such a state policy amounts to subsidizing industries in order to save jobs. However, at the same time, such actions often increase the danger of slowing down the long-term structural adaptabilities of that industry.

Alternatively, in order to compensate for the shortcomings and self-destructive elements within the market - and, at the same time, to pre-empt state intervention - firms within an industry can organize themselves and band together to cope with an impending crisis. In such a situation, they agree upon mutual rules of conduct, linking their own individual autonomy to their medium and long-term collective interests. Policy networks put actors in a situation where they are less time-dependent, more flexible, and less constrained by disruptive developments. Therefore, a governance mode is offered through which they can better adapt to changing circumstances. Industrial restructuring through policy networks is based on intensive integration and cooperation between the parties concerned. The actors explicitly negotiate and define rules of conduct, even though they do not necessarily specify them in contracts or other formal agreements. These arrangements enable the design and implementation of medium- or long-term policies for greater competitiveness, as well as facilitating collective decisions on high-risk investment projects of the firms involved. They help to discuss the need for, and distribution of, mutual burdens and benefits of restructuring plans; and they can diffuse know-how among the firms in non-competitive areas.[2]

---

2   In these terms, policy networks may seem similar to cartel-like arrangements. This would indeed apply to industries with limited foreign trade relationships. With such industries, policy networks do not necessarily result in establishing long-term adaptive capacities; they rather maintain and obtain exclusive positions. Cartel-like arrangements on a national level can never be successful in industries with extensive foreign trade relationships - for instance, the chemical fibre industry. However, policy networks can

3   The Case of the Chemical Fibre Industry in West Germany,
     Britain and Italy

The late 1960s and early 1970s were periods of rapid growth in the chemical fibre industry in general, and in Western Europe in particular. Output of both acrylic and polyester fibres in Western Europe more than tripled between 1967 and 1973, while output of nylon virtually doubled. The same period also witnessed the development of an integrated Western European market following the expiration of the major nylon (or polyamide) and polyester patents in the early and mid-1960s. As a consequence, the major European producers penetrated each other's national markets, both through exports and through the setting up of manufacturing subsidiaries.

Whereas other parts of the world continued to display an impressive increase in fibre output during the 1970s, in Western Europe the rapid growth phase came to a halt after 1973. Output of all three fibres declined in 1974 and 1975; and - in spite of recoveries in 1976, 1978 and 1979 - the overall level of output was only three per cent higher in 1979 than it had been in 1973. In 1980, output declined once again to below the 1973 level. Stagnation, even absolute decline (particularly for nylon), replaced rapid growth in output. However, capacity continued to expand until at least the mid-1970s. Expectations of continuing growth, together with competitive aspirations for increasing market shares (which had led to this increase in capacity in the first place), thus exacerbated the deteriorating competitive environment.

A number of factors contributed to these changing conditions. They included factors such as the world recession, sharply increased costs for raw materials, a change in fashion from some synthetic fibres back towards natural fibres, and increasing competition from outside Western Europe. In this changed situation, severe excess capacity emerged; and the Western European chemical fibre industry became highly unprofitable. In the seven years between 1974 and 1980, the average capacity utilization of all chemical fibre plants in Western Europe was only 68 per cent. Losses were huge for all major European producers between 1975 and 1983 - in 1980, for example, this amounted to a sum of DM 1.9 billion. As a result in some European countries, many - and in some cases, all -

---

lead to policies for long-term adaptive strategies within such industries.

firms left the industry. In other countries, the firms became dependent on state subsidies. In other countries, the major form of industrial restructuring was through private policy networks.

On the basis of interviews with representatives from firms, associations, and administrations - as well as through a study of their internal reports and through an extensive study of over 3,000 newspaper and magazine clippings - *collective* industrial restructuring strategies were identified which developed in the chemical fibre sector in West Germany, Britain, and Italy between 1968 and 1985.

In Table 1, the presence of different collective strategies observed among chemical fibre producers is summarized. It is important to notice that the table does not include all possible forms of industrial restructuring. Rather, it refers exclusively to those strategies which are organized *collectively*, which are located on a *sectoral* level, and which were observed empirically in at least one of the countries studied.

Space does not permit a detailed description of the 27 different cells of Table 1. However, a short description of the nature of the different restructuring strategies is helpful before discussing them in a framework of private policy networks.

Vertical integration refers to strategies where chemical fibre producers extend their activities to later production phases (i.e., towards the textile industry) in order to absorb environmental interdependencies. By having stable relationships of sales, as well as price-setting with the textile industry, costs can be reduced without constantly having to deal with the market. Although this strategy is also very often pursued by firms *individually,* several instances could be observed where firms *collectively* regulated their relationship with the textile industry. A good example of this collective action is the way in which chemical fibre firms, through associations or consultant agencies, stimulate the textile industry to develop efficient production units. These consultant services both convince and help their colleagues in textiles to consolidate into larger economic units; they organize export stimulation policies for the textile producers (textile firms exporting to markets with low fibre prices are given discounts relative to the share of chemical fibres contained in the products purchased).

Publicity and trade mark policy can be seen, from the point of view of the producers, as the creation of a more or less stable link between one's product and the clients. Instead of competing only through quality or price, firms can compete on the basis of services linked to brand

Table 1: Collective Restructuring Strategies among Chemical Fibre Producers in West Gernamy, Italy and Britain 1968-1985

COLLECTIVE STRATEGIES	West German Chemical Fibre Industry	Italian Chemical Fibre Industry	British Chemical Fibre Industry
Vertical integration policy	++	++	–
Publicity and trade mark policy	++	– –	–
Lobbying	+	+	+
Participation in concerted action	– – (no direct state policies for the sector)	1968 - 1973: + 1974 - 1980: – 1981 - 1985: ++	–
Reduction of competition within the national sector through division of labor	+	–	–
National cartel	+	–	–
Concerted sector	– –	– (too many producers)	– (too few producers)
Reduction of competition from foreign producers through price policy	+ (through price leadership)	+	–
Policies for labor force reduction in the industry	++	++	– –

++   collective action stable over entire period
+   several instances of collective action over period studied
–   unsuccessful attempts to come to collective actions
–   no collective actions at all

                                                       Source: Kenis (1991)

fibres, thus distinguishing themselves from other producers producing similar products. In the chemical fibre industry especially, this strategy is often pursued by firms individually (examples of brand names of large firms promoted extensively, are Dralon, Courtelle, Terylene, Trevira, etc.). Collective actions among fibre firms on the basis of brand names are, of course, logically impossible. But in the same manner as when a firm promotes its own fibre individually, a sector can promote its products using *generic names*. Here the idea is not so much to be competitive *vis-à-vis* other firms producing the same product, as to compete with other industries producing substitute goods - in the present case, the natural or the cellulose fibre industry. Collective organized actions promoting the total group of chemical fibres are a very common strategy. Cheap imports of substitution products - or in the 70s, the producers' shock at the unexpected but significant consumer trend back to natural fibres - were situations that triggered such collective actions.

Lobbying or pressure politics has been extensively studied and described in political science as a strategy for industry to deal collectively with changing circumstances. In all three countries, instances of collective lobbying could indeed be observed; but they were much less common than many other forms of collective actions. The reason for this may be that the chemical fibre industry, being part of the chemical industry, profits from more favorable state policies than other sectors - and without having to organize for them. There seems to exist something like a *generalized loyalty* of the state towards the chemical sector.

Participation in concerted actions is similar to the previously-mentioned lobbying, in that the relationship between the industry and the state is involved. It is different, however, in that the strategy is not so much based on pressure but on cooperation through comprehensive industrial restructuring schemes.[3] Two important cases of concerted action in which collective sets of chemical fibre producers participated took place at the international level: the Multi-Fibre Agreements and the European restructuring network. But at the national level in Italy, such industry participation in concerted action has been crucial throughout.

Reduction of competition within the national sector through division of labor is made possible since the chemical fibre industry produces three products: nylon, polyester and acrylic. In the beginning of the 70s,

---

3   This point is especially well covered in the literature on neocorporatism (Schmitter/ Lehmbruch 1979; Lehmbruch/ Schmitter 1982).

there was a clear tendency among all the large producers to add all three fibres to their product range. From 1976 onwards, as a result of the crisis in the sector, the firms suddenly favored specialization and proceeded to concentrate on one fibre. It became clear that this decision was not primarily an individual firm policy (i.e., specialization on the firm level) but rather the result of collective negotiations about who is going to produce which fibre in the future (i.e., differentiation at the sectoral level).

As lobbying is for political science the form of collective action *par excellence,* so are *cartels* the form of collective action *par excellence* for economists. And as with lobbying, cartels are less frequent than other forms of collective action in the case studied. They were common at the end of the 60s and the beginning of the 70s. Since then, however, the foreign trade relationships of the chemical fibre industry have grown extensively, making national cartels a difficult strategy for collectively coping with prices and competition.

The concept of the *concerted sector* refers to those forms of cooperation which go in the direction of binding all chemical fibre sector facilities of one country together in a coordinated production unit. The idea is to put the entire chemical fibre industry under one roof for either arriving at a more efficient use of resources - and thus avoiding some disastrous effects of competition - or to better face international competition.

Reduction of foreign competition through price policy is a rather complex undertaking for a collective action, since two conditions must be fulfilled in order for it to be effective. Apart from the fact that prices must be kept high, it should at the same time not lead to imports of cheaper fibres. As far as a collective closing of the sector is concerned, this has occasionally been achieved by a combination of vertical integration, trade mark policies, the giving of discounts for fibres manufactured in those textiles produced for export, international agreements, price cartels, and price leadership. Among these forms of collective action, the latter two - price cartels and price leadership - are both the most vulnerable and the most difficult to implement. Consequently, they are also the least frequent. There is the problem of free-riding, the difficulty of imposing higher prices on buyers (e.g. in Italy), and the fact that sometimes price increases have to be approved (e.g. the Price Commission in Britain).

Policies for the reduction of labor force in the industry refer to a situation where industry decides to lay off labor in order to cope with changing circumstances. Such a decision is very often taken by the firm individually. The study of the chemical fibre case has shown, however, that firms in a sector can also act collectively with respect to laying off the labor force. There may be good reasons for the producers to act collectively rather than individually in this. In some countries (e.g. Italy), it is very difficult to discharge labor. In order to do so, the entire sector must be formally declared as being in a situation of economic crisis. Once applicable, wages are totally or partially paid by state funds (*Cassa Integrazione* in Italy, *Kurzarbeitergeld* in Germany). With this, firms can externalize restructuring costs to the state without simultaneously having to partially or totally leave the sector. Moreover, the firms have less to fear from labor conflicts; and once the recession is over, the firms can regain the same labor force.

When turning to a vertical reading of Table 1, it becomes clear that the *West German* industry is strongly characterized by the presence of collective restructuring strategies. The study also indicated that all different collective strategies result from a stable private policy network which existed over the entire period studied. All collective strategies resulted from an unchanging set of actors who mutually recognize one another, without at the same time being involved in major conflicts among themselves. Here we have a private policy network which can mobilize collective restructuring strategies for the overall sector in periods of difficulties, while keeping the network latent in periods when collective strategies are not needed.

In *Italy*, collective restructuring strategies are also quite common; but in contrast to West Germany, they did not result from one comprehensive policy network. Rather, they resulted from two different and often competing policy networks: a private policy network integrating the private producers and their associations, and a public policy network integrating public firms and other *quasi*-public institutions. Taken separately, both networks - as in the case of West Germany - were also characterized by the remarkable stability of the participating actors. Moreover, when it became clear in 1983 to all the actors in the two different networks that competing for the same resources had to lead to mutual destruction, both networks melted together for a short period of time in a mixed private/public policy network.

Britain lies at the other end of the scale. As one can see from Table 1, many attempts did exist in the British industry to come to collective restructuring strategies. Most of the time, however, they were nothing more than attempts reflecting coalitions of the day rather than resulting from a stable policy network. Such a policy network never existed in Britain during the period studied.

How such differences in the occurrence of policy networks - and consequently, in collective restructuring strategies - can be explained is the topic of the following sections.

4   Preconditions for Policy Networks

There exists a widespread argument in social science nowadays which states that the actors in a policy network come together because they have interests or goals in common - or in other words, because it is the most rational strategy for them. This approach is certainly not wrong; but it neglects the fact that the existence of collective action is also dependent on other factors. To understand collective action, it is *not enough* to understand the motives for doing things together; one has also to understand the conditions which facilitate cooperation. As Crozier and Friedberg put it,

> In asserting ... a system's existence, our underlying assumption is that there must be a *game* which allows the different strategies of the partners in a relationship to be coordinated. In other words, there must be a *containing system* within which this game takes place, and which makes it possible for the necessary conflicts, negotiations, alliances, and interactions to occur (Crozier/ Friedberg 1980: 125).

As became clear in the study of the chemical fibre sector, this containing system is not an abstract, but rather a reality composed of concrete contexts in which the relevant actors are embedded.

Three different kinds of contexts turned out to be significant for the absence or presence of policy networks:

-   The cluster of *general country variables*, such as the traditional political orientation towards the economy, the level of consistency in how industrial adaptation is managed, the degree to which industrial adaptation has become politicized, and the role played by public agencies.
-   The existence of *general sector variables*, such as personal or/and organizational interlocks and integration within an industry.

- *Structural and situational conditions* of the sector or industry in question: intra-industry competition and crisis, existence and activities of trade associations, frequency and extent of state regulation and influence, degree of international regulation, and degree of influence of international organizations.

4.1 General Country Variables Enabling (or Disabling) Policy Networks

As was stated earlier, industrial adaptation in West Germany relies heavily on private policy networks. Italy relies on private networks to a much lesser extent; and Britain does so only in a minimal way. In this section, possible reasons will be formulated in an attempt to explain why these differences occur among the three countries. It will be illustrated that the use of private policy networks in crisis management is conditioned by ideologies and institutions - or, in other words, by national characteristics, much in the same way that public policies towards industrial adaptation are.

Political and social sciences have produced a number of studies that analyze industrial adaptation in a more comprehensive way (Blank 1978; Duchêne/ Shepherd 1987; Dyson/ Wilks 1983; Esser/ Fach/ Dyson 1983; Grant/ Paterson/ Whitston 1988; Hayward 1974; Horn 1987; Katzenstein 1978; Kreile 1978, 1983; Posner 1978; Ranci 1987; Shepherd 1987; Strange/ Tooze 1981; Wilks 1983). All of them have identified a list of national characteristics which influence the particular form which industrial adaptation will take: the general political tradition regarding the economy, the level of consistency in how industrial adaptation is managed, the degree to which industrial adaptation has become politicized, and the role played by public agencies.

The same categories will be used in the following analysis to demonstrate why some countries can constitute a better ground than others for industrial adaptation via policy networks.

Regarding the economy, *West Germany's* political tradition is generally characterized by two seemingly contradictory tendencies. On the one hand, there is a strong tradition of non-interventionism in industry; and on the other, there exists a long tradition of organized capitalism (or *social partnership*).

In Germany, the state is usually absent (or at least in the background) as far as concrete action is concerned. This tendency is coupled with long-standing cooperative relations between the various parties in public policy and industry - both in depth and in width. Such an environment is indeed an ideal ground for the development of policy networks, since the private policy network here is part of a comprehensive public policy.

There are however, also three other factors - namely, the level of consistency in how industrial adaptation is managed, the degree to which industrial adaptation has become politicized, and the role played by public agencies. These constitute additional stimulants to the development of policy networks within German industry.

The consistency of West German industrial policy lies in a widely and deeply held principle: *Strukturpolitik*. This means that government support is given to make adjustments *led by the private sector.* Public agencies do not compete with policy networks, but rather stimulate them. *Strukturpolitik* allows structural intervention only (1) when the difficulties concern *a whole sector*, and (2) when they are based on lasting economic changes. In crisis situations, the government's role is to support measures of self-help. A significant example here is the possibility given to German industry to receive *Kurzarbeitergeld* (short-time allowance). However, such special governmental help or other governmental interventions can be considered only if the sectors are undergoing major changes at a rapid pace - and if the changes would generate undesirable economic and social consequences (see also Esser/ Fach/ Dyson 1983: 125). Defining a problem as structural, depends primarily on a collective strategy by the industry itself. Throughout the entire period of study, temporary labor has been a common practice in West Germany's chemical fibre sector. It is not known precisely how much such a scheme has cost the West German government, but a figure of some hundred million DM has been mentioned for the one-year period of 1975-76 alone.[4]

West Germany is also characterized by a "depoliticized" process of industrial adaptation: this means that it comes closest to a model of *technocratic* management of industrial adaptation (Dyson/ Wilks 1983: 257). This model is at the same time both the outcome and the founda-

---

4   The competitive advantages resulting from this scheme, when compared to other countries, have been described in more detail in Kenis (1990).

tion of policy networks. Historical experiences have shown that cooperate networks were successful and advantageous for all parties concerned, thus contributing to the stability of such arrangements and to their diffusion into other domains. In West Germany, such networks are not only facilitated by but also constitute a genuinely stateless industrial policy. As is illustrated in Figure 1, this phenomenon has also been called "closed private-sector management" (Dyson/ Wilks 1983: 257; Ronge 1980).

Figure 1: Forms of Sectoral Management in the Chemical Fibre Sector

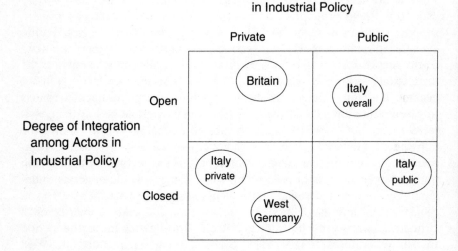

In *Britain,* the situation is quite different from the one in West Germany. In Britain, *closed* sector management has never been an option. Here *openness* prevailed, characterized by an "incremental pattern of decision making" (Lindblom 1977; Richardson and Jordan 1979 for the specific case of Britain). This was portrayed by Hayward (1974) as the "humdrum, unplanned and pluralistic" style.

This style of management most probably finds its roots in Britain's political tradition, where principles of autonomy and *individual* self-government form the basis of institutional life. They materialize in the economy as a moral code for the autonomous, self-reliant firm. Thus, Britain not only lacks a basis for the *development* of policy networks; it also lacks the *environment* in which such networks would make any sense. Utterly absent in Britain is the West German consistency in the management of industrial adaptation. Britain is characterized by great ideological instabilities (Grant 1982). These fluctuating polarities have undoubtedly led to failure on the part of industry along certain lines. British industry has been unable to develop the organizational capacity so necessary for the anticipatory management of industrial adaptation. The politicizing of industrial adaptation, however, has reached high peaks in Britain. Relevant here are both the openness mentioned earlier and the firms' desire to organize their own affairs. Individual firms engage in consultation with their employees in a haphazard and irregular manner. This amounts to oscillation between a hesitant and suspicious approach to industrial change, or else resorting to a dramatic *fait accompli.*

What makes the situation even worse for the entire sector is, that this did not lead to the *purification crisis* so praised (and expected) by conservative economists (i.e., the elimination of less efficient market participants). The deeper the crisis in the British chemical fibre industry became, the worse the chances for crisis management grew; and the more fragmented, unpredictable and uncoordinated the institutional responses were.

Regarding the role of public agencies, Britain is a very interesting case. It is interesting to note that the British "disease" cannot simply be imputed to weak public institutions. Such administrative structures as the Civil Service, the City, the distribution circuits, and - at times - even the National Economic Development Councils, can all certainly be called strong public institutions. Moreover, in the field of economic policy, the British government has been neither weak nor vacillating (Blank 1978: 91). However, two aspects are missing: first, close interorganizational collaboration between firms, enabling both the development of collective learning processes and the effective management of successive crises; and second, a politically secure and equally interlocked environment in which such institutions could have an influence on the outcome of domestic or international economic objectives.

Although the political and social environment in *Italy* is fundamentally more favorable for building up private policy networks, both the growth and existence of such networks were limited. Industrial policy was carried out from the top down and was led almost completely by the state. Additional obstructive factors also emerged, especially during the 70s.

In a country where the price for thousands of goods is strictly regulated but where no anti-trust legislation exists, one should expect a stable basis for networks. Industrial culture in Italy accepts principles both of order and of integration, as well as the importance of common or corporate interests. This type of industrial culture has supported the emergence of highly formalized institutional structures which can be subsumed under the heading of *organized capitalism.*

In the West German case, collective goals have often been pursued under the concept of *social partnership;* but for the Italians, this mission has mainly been pursued by the public enterprise. Ironically enough, the existence of public enterprises - along with the Italian pattern of direct and detailed intervention in industrial affairs - has more often than not had the reverse effect of dividing firms against one another. Many attempts by the state to arrive at a coordinated and integrated chemical fibre sector failed, leading both to redundancies in investments and to spectacular crashes. The Italian government would have liked to see a national network of firms building a holding company through which all Italian production units of chemical fibres would be coordinated. However, the Italian state has never been able to overcome the mixture of intimacy, cooperation, and rivalry between the producers. For example, the massive chemical fibre complex in Sardinia's Val de Tirso area was planned and carried out through a joint venture of Montedison Fibre and ANIC, a joint venture initiated and strongly favored by the state. This cooperation between a private and a public firm was built more on the good intentions of the Italian state than on good understanding between the firms. An overall rivalry always existed between their parent firms (Montedison and ENI) in the chemical fields, and both groups generally do not agree on each other's future plans. From the first day of operation, the joint massive plant in Val de Tirso produced enormous losses and was referred to as "the cathedral in the desert". It can be said that Italy has generally experienced difficulties in arriving at a coherent industrial strategy. Obstacles here are the factionalism and immobility of the ruling Christian Democratic Party, the patronage system, and the directly ensuing administrative inefficiency.

In principle, the management of industrial adaptation in Italy is relatively depoliticized and uncontroversial. Catholic - as well as communist - social ideas, together with a national consensus in favor of regional policies, are all legitimate grounds for intervention - as well as for a general admission of the inadequacy of the market. The Italian version of *organized capitalism* is not organized from the bottom up (as in West Germany) but from the top down. This political reality renders it difficult for firms to find a general basis for cooperation.

The overall Italian chemical fibre industry can be characterized as an open public sector: it does not constitute an integrated set of firms (see Figure 1). Instead, the firms are embedded (all along different lines) not only in a public web of trade unions and economic institutions (i.e., *Cassa Integrazione*, GEPI, CIPI, IMI, CIPE)[5] but also in the political parties, the bureaucracy, central and regional governments, etc. Private firms and public institutions form a large, undifferentiated public sphere. Most of the time, this sphere produces nothing but "ad hoc unsystematic and sometimes inconsistent measures" (Diebold 1980: 6) - and these make for short-term "fix-its" rather than long-term adjustments.

4.2 General Sector Variables Enabling (or Disabling) Policy Networks

Whether a policy network exists or not, however, is not exclusively dependent on country variables. Especially at the sectoral level, complementary factors are decisive if a policy network is to develop. For example, in countries with an overall *positive* climate for policy networks, it is possible for policy communities or networks *not to develop* within certain sectors. For example, it seems obvious that a sector with thousands of geographically dispersed actors will only develop as a policy network under very specific conditions - even in a country with a *positive* climate.

In the case of an industrial sector, the chances for developing a policy network will increase in relation to existing forms of integration and interpenetration among firms. There are different indicators which express this: the degree of concentration according to market shares as well as mutual capital shares; the firm's degree of vertical integration and its degree of differentiation and integration regarding public/private

---

5   CIPE = Comitato interministeriale per la programmazione economica; CIPI = Centro interministeriale di guida delle politica industriale; GEPI = Gestione pubblica industriale; IMI = Istituto mobiliare italiano.

ownership, domestic or foreign origin of producers, production of a single sort of fibre versus different ones, and regional concentration; and lastly, the history of the industry. Along these lines, let me give a short account of the three national sectors under study.

Britain: Firms producing in the chemical fibre industry could rely *in no way* on interlocks and forms of integration within the industry. The sector showed the highest concentration regarding market shares. This was true to such an extent that it proved counterproductive, since it led to continuous quarrels between ICI and Courtaulds.

As regards mutual capital shares, the firms were penetrated only to a limited extent by banks as intermediaries and were coordinated only to a limited extent through joint shareholdings. What did exist in the British case, however, was a rather high level of vertical integration towards textile firms. Such a form of integration, however, counteracted integration among the fibre producers themselves.

In the British case, many additional factors were present to divide firms into different groups. Small firms and large firms acted in totally different spheres; foreign producers were not integrated into the home industry; and finally, the regional concentration of plants in Northern Ireland did not enhance integration of firms producing chemical fibres in Britain.

The one form of company integration which was successful in Britain was the division of labor between different firms with regard to the production of specific fibres. Each major producer concentrated on the production of one specific fibre. In the short run, this can be seen as a mode to avoid future intra-industry competition, as well as a way to solve collective action problems. In the long run, however, it renders even more unlikely any future development of a policy community - and consequently, comprehensive political restructuring of the overall sector through a policy network.

West Germany: Although politicians and producers paid continuous lip service to the idea of a free market, their position compared to Britain was exactly the opposite. The degree of firm integration was very high. Concentration measured by market share was also high, but not so high that it produced conflicts. Even more important for this integration were indirect mutual capital shares - and above all, interlocking directorates (through German banks). These were crucial factors for the formation of an accommodating network in the West German chemical fibre sector.

Vertical integration was almost absent. This certainly helped to reduce particularistic interests, since it facilitated agreement on universalistic strategies for handling demand. All West German producers continuously insisted on not following the trend of vertical integration: a trend which was, at times, very fashionable in Western Europe's chemical fibre industry.

Another factor in West Germany was the way in which different groups of firms worked side by side: small and large firms, foreign and domestic firms, public and private firms. Similar to the other countries, in West Germany small firms were not part of the national policy community. Apart from this division, however, none of the other differentiations among groups had any negative effect on the integration of firms in the West German chemical fibre sector. Historical factors probably played a much greater role in the integration of West German firms. After all, the three major producers of chemical fibres had not so long ago constituted one single firm. Moreover, the tradition of cartels in the chemical industry was a strong promoting factor as well.

Italy: Regarding the degree of company integration, Italy is a less clear-cut case. Company integration may appear high in Italy, but a closer look provides a more complex picture. Concentration according to market share was lowest for the three countries; but there was a great number of direct mutual capital shares. However, these direct mutual capital shares - often politically initiated - produced much more conflict than integration among firms. A high degree of vertical integration also led to particularistic supply politics by the firms. The main difference from the British case, however, is that at times vertical integration became an important part of industrial policies. These policies which tried to bring together private and public firms, were mostly imposed by the state rather than voluntary; and consequently, most of them lasted only a very short time.

The domestic firm/foreign firm division did not play a role, simply because foreign firms were absent. Almost every other imaginable category played a role in dividing the firms among themselves. Policy network development was undermined by the factional politics of clientelism, as different party factions cultivated their relations with industry. Firms could be public or private, large or small, northern or southern, and party or not to any governmental program of sectoral intervention or restructuring.

However, in 1981 under the Presidency of Prime Minister Cossiga an Italian government commission was able to immunize the factionalism all-too-typical in Italy. The large, overall, and - for once - successful sectoral restructuring scheme which resulted from this, can therefore be read as a plan which *organizationally* immunized many of these conflicts. Two years afterwards - and for the first time in a decade - the Italian chemical fibre producers could break even.

In general terms, one can conclude that the trend is the same as with the country variables. The West German sector is structured in such a way that it stimulates the existence of policy networks. In Britain, the policy domain factors are counterproductive to the development of policy networks. Italy lies somewhere in between; here additional situational factors seem to be of particular importance for the existence of policy networks.

4.3 Structural and Situational Factors Shaping Policy Networks

The above factors are necessary but not sufficient conditions leading to the emergence of policy networks. Empirically stated, the following four *structural* and *situational* factors have been found to play an important role in understanding why policy networks come about at certain points in time and not at others:

- the degree of intra-industry competition and crisis,
- the existence of sectoral trade associations,
- the frequency and extent of state regulation and influence, and
- the degree of international regulation and the influence of international organizations.

The Degree of Intra-Industry Competition and Crisis

In almost all instances, forming, elaborating, relying on, or mobilizing policy networks went hand in hand with *increasing intra-industry competition* and crisis. Competition is not simply equated with the working of the *free market* but rather is defined as a situation where different actors compete for the same resources (market shares, for example). This amounts to a zero-sum situation. It can then be said that the individual firms are in a situation of crisis. This situation was already observed by Marx:

So long as everything goes well, competition effects a practical brotherhood of the capitalist class ... so that each shares in the common loot in proportion to the magnitude of his investment ... But as soon as it is no longer a question of sharing profits, but of sharing losses, everyone tries to reduce his own share to the minimum and to shove it upon another ... How much the individual capitalist must bear of the loss, i.e., to what extent he must share in it at all, is decided by power and craftiness, and competition then transforms itself into a fight of hostile brothers (1954-56, Vol. 3: 253).

The pattern found in the case studied, however, shows that the destructive effects of such a competitive situation or "fight of hostile brothers", can be solved by the firms as a collectivity. A typical *policy network's* history will thus look like a succession of periods of sharing benefits from the market - with an absence of policy networks - coupled with periods of sharing losses. In other words, competition is followed by periods of attempts to collectively deal with crisis situations and reinstall the non-competitive order through policy networks.[6] In cases where one cannot rely on a policy network (e.g., the British), the burden of the crisis is borne by the individual firm: it will succumb to the game called *survival of the fittest* where, again according to Marx, "All is decided by power and craftiness."

This succession of phases - from non-competition to competition to trying to act collectively and re-arrange non-competition and so on - could be observed to be the general logic of affairs throughout the period studied. This ranged from trying to collectively avoid imports on a national level, to the European restructuring cartel (see Kenis 1985). In the latter case, the challenges to the national sectors were so massive that no national collective action could have handled them. As a result of overly optimistic investment plans, the European chemical fibre industry in 1976 found itself in a situation where the capacity utilization was only 68 per cent and huge losses were borne by all European chemical fibre producers. Only thanks to CIFRS (Comité International de la Rayonne et des Fibres Synthétiques) and the then-indispensable help of the EC (European Community), could a European policy network be installed. After a second try, this network was able to collectively reinstall a crisis-resistant European order.

---

6   Note that this is different for the labor market. Here *real competition* nearly always existed. Only a limited number of jobs are given, which put labor in the zero-sum situation that characterizes *real competition*. And as we know, labor unions can do almost nothing about it except to try to smooth over the effects.

The process view taken here, restrains us from viewing the economy in either of two ways: as totally controlled by networks of capitalists, or as a system where no competition exists any more - as some theories seem to assume. This latter view may hold true for certain points in time (as, for example, immediately after the European restructuring cartel). But when considering the productive system as a *process,* it becomes clear that firms are continuously confronted with new factors challenging their new-found, collectively-organized system of *non-competition:* imports, changing exchange rates, emerging capacities in newly-developing countries, etc.

This also means that theories are wrong which see the economy as a system in which only the most efficient firms can survive. Just as the state can interfere in the productive process with public policies, capital can implement policies through policy networks - for similar goals. However, this does not imply that capital has the capacity to form stable networks over time. Mancur Olson (1965) has rightly shown the problems inherent in collective action. If stable collective action existed, that would be monopoly capitalism in the sense of Hilferding's *General kartell* of an all-for-one, one-for-all creation of a collective order. Policy networks are certainly challenged, must constantly reproduce orders of non-competition and, in turn, are called upon to reorganize these orders whenever they are destabilized.

Reacting to intra-industry competition and crisis, the study on the restructuring of the chemical fibre sector found that policy networks tend to go in two directions. On the one hand, they will try to achieve non-competitive orders within their policy community: diversification, division of labor, price leadership, etc. On the other hand, they will try to detach their non-competitive order from potential competitive challenges: blocking imports, preventing newcomers, etc.

Existence and Activities of Sectoral Trade Associations

Broadly speaking, trade associations are *formal* organizations through which firms in an industry collectively attempt to promote and protect common interests. This can be done by means of ordering, managing, and stabilizing both the relations within the industry - as well as the relationships between industry members and those whose strategies and activities can decisively affect the industry's future success. (Pfeffer/

Salancik 1978; Schmitter/ Streeck 1981; Staber/ Aldrich 1983; Grant/ Coleman 1987).

In this respect, associations fulfil the same function as private policy networks. This could theoretically mean that a *negative* relationship exists between the efforts of trade associations and the existence of policy networks. Both would constitute *functional equivalents* within the collective management of the chemical fibre industry.

The empirical data, however, lead to two different conclusions. First, there seems to be a *positive* relationship between the existence of policy networks and the efforts of sectoral trade associations. Second, while studying policy networks, it often occurred that trade associations in the chemical fibre sector do not fulfil the functions defined above.

As to the unimportance of trade associations regarding these *traditional* functions and their no-less-significant importance regarding the existence of policy networks, both point to a specific kind of relationship. This interaction appears to be different from functional equivalency.

Sectoral trade associations were, in some instances, an important means for successfully arriving at policy networks. The most striking case here was certainly the European restructuring cartel. Here, CIFRS has been an important actor in many ways: centralizing information, serving as a meeting place for firms, or legitimating forms of action by firms which would otherwise have been defined as a simple cartel.

Another indication for the mutual functionality of sectoral trade associations and policy networks is the fact that the firms making up the respective policy networks are exactly the same as those who are members of the sectoral trade associations (in West Germany, *Industrievereinigung Chemiefaser;* and in Italy, the federation within Aschimica (for private firms) and *Associazione sindicale delle aziende del gruppo ENI* (ASAP, for public firms). This holds true despite the fact that in all countries, the sector contains many more firms; and these associations do not specify rules of exclusion.

All this points to the fact that business associations can play an important role in the existence of policy networks. Whereas business associations of small firms directly promote and protect interests on behalf of their members, business associations of large firms seem to provide crucial organizational and cultural resources for the realization of collective actions - such as policy networks.

Frequency and Extent of State Regulation and State Influence

From the existing literature on collective actions by industry, two factors can be deduced which specify in which way their existence is dependent on the state. First, it is stated that collective actions by industry exist in order to enhance the industry's power within the political arena and thus act as a force counter to the state. Second, the state may favor collective actions by industry by granting them the right to autonomously produce policies (see Hollingsworth et al. n.d.). Interestingly enough, neither factor helps to explain the existence of policy networks as a case of collective action. First, since policy networks are not *organizational* forms of collective action, it is difficult for the state to delegate power to such an ad hoc system of action. Second, although the probability of policy networks stands in positive correlation to the state's regulating influence, the underlying logic of this relationship is different. It does not seem to be the case that business, through policy networks, aims at constituting a force counter to the state.

The opposite rather holds: i.e., the more power the state exerts in the economy, the more policy networks can use the state's influence to arrive at their own goals. This is all the more true in proportion to the diminution of state policies directed specifically towards a given industry. In cases where the government strongly regulates a specific industry, this industry will probably constitute a counter-force through trade associations. This does not, however, contradict a basic rule: i.e., in order to arrive at certain goals, business needs the state as a partner. A good example is the case of increasing imports, where pressure comes from foreign countries, not state regulation. One way of coping with these imports is precisely to ask the state for help.

The state theory implicit in this observation is that business, far from always acting against the state, actually needs it in many instances to arrive at certain policies. The primary rationale is not to exert influence on government, but to secure common benefits for the participating actors - be they government or business (for a similar conclusion, see Cawson/ Holmes/ Stevens 1987:15; and recently, Traxler/ Unger 1990[7]). To illus-

---

7   In a study of the industrial restructuring of the automobile, machine tool, and steel industry in different countries, it is concluded that: "Da der Staat die allgemeinen Rahmenbedingungen wirtschaftlicher Beziehungen setzt, fällt ihm auch die entscheidende Rolle für den Aufbau und den Fortbestand korporatistischer und netzwerkförmiger Steuerungsinstitutionen zu. Für alle drei der hier betrachteten Sektoren gilt, daß in jenen Ländern,

trate this point, let me briefly present the West German case, in which policy networks were a common mode of governance for industrial restructuring of the chemical fibre sector. Accepting that there is a relationship between the existence of policy networks and the presence of the nation-state, how does this relationship function?

What makes West Germany so different from the other cases studied, is that the industrial policies developed by industry itself are congruent with the stance the state takes towards industrial policies. All takes place within the same sectoral circle: early warnings (often by the banks), policy formulation, bargaining, and policy implementation. The private policy network is thus part of an overall public policy: one which allows for minimal transaction costs, avoids politicizing, enables time management of policies, and prompts organizational learning. It manages to avoid a central problem, seen as fundamental to industrial policy: "To analyze industrial policies and performance is one thing: to establish connections between them is quite another. Government, planners and banks cannot run firms themselves. Whatever their formal powers, in the end they have to rely on managers. Their influence is inherently indirect" (Duchêne 1987: 233).

Seen from such a perspective, it is difficult to place the West German state along a traditional weak-state/strong-state axis. The primary role of policy networks is neither to exert influence on government nor *vice-versa*. The strong/weak perspective implies that relationships operate as formal channels of state influence - or of resistance to it. Instead of putting West Germany into the middle ground, as it has been suggested (e.g. Wilks/ Wright 1987: 282), I prefer to put it on the *weak* end as far as direct interventions are concerned. It is, however, *strong* in facilitating a framework for policy networks. In this respect, Katzenstein (1978: 328) is certainly right when he maintains that "... even today ... there are traces in the West German policy network which resemble the Japanese model more than the Anglo-Saxon one". The traditional role of West Germany in international economic policies - which consists in defending the free market - happens to coincide with its own economy and industrial policy: that of relying on organizational nuclei in order

---

in denen solche Steuerungsinstitutionen bestehen, deren Enstehung und Funktionsfähigkeit wesentlich auf staatliche Organisationshilfen zurückzuführen sind. ... Dies bedeutet, daß dem Staat eine Funktion *strukturpolitischer Metasteuerung* zufällt" (Traxler/ Unger 1990: 217-218).

to be able to react effectively to changing circumstances. In general, instances of lobbying and concerted practices were not as much reactions to state interference as they were possibilities to solve problems through the state - problems which otherwise could not have been solved. Individual capitalists tend to be opportunist and pragmatic. While they might have a tendency to prefer the minimal state role prescribed in *laissez-faire* ideology, they certainly have a tendency to adapt to the political realities they face.

Degree of International Regulation and Influence of International Organizations

The above description of the relationship with the nation-state, can be extended to include international regulations and influence. The case of the MFAs (or Multi-Fibre Agreements) probably best illustrates this similarity of functions.

International trade in textiles is partially regulated by the MFAs. These were established under the auspices of the General Agreements on Tariffs and Trade (GATT). The MFAs encompass the majority of the world's most important exporters and dates from 1973, renewable every four years. The policy actor system for the MFAs includes the United States, Japan, the EC, Canada, Austria, Sweden, Finland, Norway, Switzerland, the Eastern European Countries, the newly-industrialized countries, and the developing countries. On the basis of a common commercial policy, the EC acts as a single unit on behalf of its member states. In formulating its policy, the EC therefore has first to reach agreement among member states on a common position in textile trade talks. It is important to notice here that the interest of the chemical fibre producers in the MFAs is only indirect - but nevertheless, very strong. In principle, little possibility is given for the producers to take part as a collectivity in concerted action in this international regime.

Interestingly enough - given the absence of direct representation of producers in GATT, as well as the fact that representation of EC member states is handled through the EC within GATT - *national* policy networks of producers nevertheless involve themselves in the outcome of the MFAs. I have argued elsewhere that the position taken by the EC in the MFA talks is not a *European* one; it is *de facto* a mix of particular national policies of different member states (Kenis and Schneider 1987). Consequently, this power of the nation-state in final decision making, almost always leads to the fact that producers primarily promote their interests through *national* policy networks. It could indeed be observed that organized interests of chemical fibre producers, in concert with organized interests of textile producers, participated in formulating the national stance regarding the MFA talks.

Internationalization certainly means an increase of interdependencies at the international economic level - along with a loss of power for national actors. Nevertheless, the above illustrates that one should not be tempted to conclude that resulting contingencies can only be dealt with on the international level. The contrary is true: in situations of international interdependence, the strength of well-organized sectoral policy networks at the national level becomes especially relevant. To be sure, it is usually much more *efficient* to deal with contingencies at the level where they arise. It is, however, often still more *effective* to deal with them at the level of *national* policy networks. Survival for a sector within the international economy, then, depends more than anything else on the *rule of the best organized* - as the West German case clearly illustrates.

5   Conclusion

The most plausible conclusion from the presented study, is that the development of policy networks depends on several factors. Formulating a theory on the development of policy networks should therefore be handled with caution. If we take a closer look at the relationships between the different factors explaining the emergence of policy networks, it is seen that not all factors have the same weight, that some factors are conditional upon others, and that some of the factors are highly interrelated.

What if we were to select a single factor as being *the* central explanatory one, *the* crucial condition for many other factors? Due to its interrelation with many other factors, it would undoubtedly be the *institutional structure of the nation-state*. Nevertheless, when considering the nation-state and its diverse institutions, we are obviously dealing with quite a complex situation. Rather than one or more clearly deducible independent variables to explain the emergence of policy networks, there is an interrelated set of historical structures. The relationship between governance structures and state structures is so complicated that it is difficult to confine it to a simple causal and/or linear model.

Instead, allow me to draw attention to two more general tendencies which refer to the development of policy networks and in particular, to the relationship between policy networks and the state - at least in the cases studied here:

- First, the development of policy networks seems to be dependent on the state, since it sets the general framework for coordinating the economy. More specifically, though, one can say that it is not so much the structure or activities of the state, nor the structure or activities of policy networks, which are of crucial importance: it is their mutual meeting ground. The strength of the West German case seems to arise from an overall sectoral governance characterized by a functional *mix* of private policy networks and public institutions. From a process perspective, one could expect the role of the state to encourage the existence of policy networks - while existing policy networks encourage the state to rely on them, and so on.
- Second, it is remarkable that in the identified cases of private policy networks, the state is characterized by a *limited* claim - not by the traditionally self-exalted claim of total rationality, total sovereignty, and total steering. Nonetheless, private policy networks prove to be a mode of providing public goods. From an institutional point of view, the state develops here in a *decentralized* and *cooperative* way.

The decentralization of the state is a theme which has recently been discussed with growing frequency. It is argued that the state is not a monolithic whole, but a set of relatively discrete institutional *apparata* that vary across industries, sectors, and societies - as well as over time.

Within governance institutions in which private policy networks play a role, the structure of the state is not only characterized by decentralization but also by *cooperation*. This cooperation results from a social fact: in many policy fields, public goals are increasingly more difficult to obtain without the cooperation of private collectivities (see Schuppert 1989). This might be taken as an indication of a state which is less involved in substantive regulation; but the state we see here nevertheless tries to influence the *premises* of the policies. Importantly too, this state also tries to provide "rules of the game" for societal problem-solving processes (see, for example, the distinction between "procedural" and "substantive" regulation introduced by Mayntz 1983).

Consequently, a "strong" decentralized and cooperative state seems to be fruitful ground for the development of private policy networks. Direct state intervention is absent from the governance structures in which private policy networks exist. Nevertheless, the state does seem to fulfil important functions (called *Meta-Strukturpolitik* in Unger/ Traxler, 1990). This is also important from a policy making point of view. On the one hand, avoiding or being incapable of implementing direct state intervention does not necessarily mean that industrial restructuring has to be left to either individual firm strategies or to the market. After all, the destructive effect of this became clear in the British case. On the other hand, choosing to rely on private policy networks means that the state must consider how those networks can be governed - hopefully, in such a way that clear lines of accountability and consistency in control systems can be ensured. This, however, opens a new research agenda - and one which will need even further research on policy networks.

References

Ben-Porath, Y., 1980: The F-Connection: Families, Friends, and Firms in the Organization of Exchange. In: *Population and Development Review* 6, 1-30.

Blank, S., 1978: Britain: The Politics of Foreign Economic Policy, the Domestic Economy, and the Problem of Pluralistic Stagnation. In: P. J. Katzenstein (ed.), *Between Power and Plenty - Foreign Economic Policies of Advanced Industrial States.* Madison, WI.: University of Wisconsin Press, 89-137.

Cawson, A./ P. Holmes/ A. Stevens, 1987: The Interaction between Firms and the State in France: The Telecommunications and Consumer Electronic Sectors. In: S. Wilks/ M. Wright, *Comparative Government-Industry Relations.* Oxford: Clarendon Press, 10-34.

CIFRS (Comité International de la Rayonne et des Fibres Synthétiques) (Annually): *Information sur les textiles synthétiques et cellulosiques.* Paris: CIFRS.

Coser, L./ C. Kadushin/ W.W. Powell, 1982: *Books: The Culture and Commerce of Publishing*. New York: Basic Books.

Crozier, M./ E. Friedberg, 1980: *Actors and Systems: The Politics of Collective Action*. Chicago: University of Chicago Press.

Diebold, W., 1980: *Industrial Policy as an Industrial Issue*. New York: McGraw-Hill.

Dore, R., 1983: Goodwill and the Spirit of Market Capitalism. In: *British Journal of Sociology* 34(4): 459-482.

Duchêne, F., 1987: Policies for a Wider World. In: F. Duchêne/ G. Shepherd (eds.), *Managing Industrial Change in Western Europe*. London/ New York: Francis Pinter, 210-239.

Duchêne, F./ G. Shepherd (eds.), 1987: *Managing Industrial Change in Western Europe*. London/ New York: Francis Pinter.

Dyson, K./ S. Wilks (eds.), 1983: *Industrial Crisis - A Comparative Study of the State and Industry*. Oxford: Martin Robertson.

Eccles, R., 1981: The Quasifirm in the Construction Industry. In: *Journal of Economic Behavior and Organization* 2, 335-357.

Esser, J./ W. Fach/ K. Dyson, 1983: Social Market and Modernization Policy: West Germany. In: K. Dyson/ S. Wilks (eds.), *Industrial Crisis: A Comparative Study of the State and Industry*. Oxford: Martin Robertson, 102-127.

Grant, W., 1982: *The Political Economy of Industrial Policy*. London: Butterworth.

Grant, W./ W. Coleman, 1987: Conclusions. In: W. Grant (ed.), *Business Interests, Organizational Development and Private Interest Government: An International Comparative Study of the Food-Processing Industry*. Berlin: Walter de Gruyter, 208-227.

Grant, W./ W. Pattersen/ C. Whitston, 1988: *Government and the Chemical Industry - A Comparative Study of Britain and West Germany*. Oxford: Clarendon Press.

Hayward, J., 1974: National Attitudes for Planning in Britain, France and Italy. In: *Government and Opposition* 9(4), 397-411.

Hirsch, P. M., 1972: Processing Fads and Fashions: An Organization-set Analysis of Cultural Industry Systems. In: *American Journal of Sociology* 77(4), 639-659.

Hollingsworth, J. R./ P. C. Schmitter/ W. Streeck (n.d.): *Comparing Capitalist Economies: Variation in the Governance of Sectors*. Proposal for a Research Development Project to the Joint Committee on Western Europe. University of Wisconsin, Madison, WI.

Hollingsworth, J. R., 1990: *The Governance of American Manufacturing Sectors: The Logic of Coordination and Control.* MPIFG Discussion Paper 90/4. Köln: Max-Planck-Institut für Gesellschaftsforschung.

Horn, E.-J., 1987: West Germany: A Market-led Process. In: F. Duchêne/ G. Sheperd (eds.), *Managing Industrial Change in Western Europe.* London/ New York: Francis Pinter, 41-75.

Jordan, G., 1990: Sub-governments, Policy Communities and Networks: Refilling the Old Bottles. In: *Journal of Theoretical Politics* 2(3), 319-338.

Katzenstein, P. J. (ed.), 1978: *Between Power and Plenty - Foreign Economic Policies of Advanced Industrial States.* Madison, WI.: University of Wisconsin Press.

Kenis, P., 1985: Industrial Restructuring: *The Case of the Chemical Fibre Industry in Europe.* EUI Working Paper No. 85/191 (reprint 86/191). Florence: European University Institute.

Kenis, P., 1990: Le due logiche della flessabilità: alcune "lezione" dal settore delle fibre chimiche. In: M. La Rosa/ L. Benedetti, *Flessibilità, lavoro, impresa - Modeli normativi, strategie di mercato e qualità del lavoro.* Milan: Franco Angelli, 298-303.

Kenis, P., 1991: *The Social Construction of an Industry - A World of Chemical Fibres.* Frankfurt a.M./ Boulder, CO.: Campus/ Westview.

Kenis, P./ V. Schneider, 1987: The EC as an International Corporate Actor: Two Case Studies in Economic Diplomacy. In: *European Journal of Political Research* 15, 437-457.

Kreile, M., 1978: West Germany: The Dynamics of Expansion. In: P. J. Katzenstein (ed.), *Between Power and Plenty - Foreign Economic Policies of Advanced Industrial States.* Madison, WI.: University of Wisconsin Press, 191-224.

Laumann, E. O./ D. Knoke, 1987: Policy Networks of the Organizational State: Collective Action in the National Energy and Health Domains. In: R. Perrucci/ R. Potter (eds.), *Networks of Power: Organizational Actors at the National, Corporate, and Community Levels.* New York: Aldine, 17-55.

Laumann, E. O./ D. Knoke, 1987: *The Organizational State. Social Choice in National Policy Domains.* Madison, WI.: University of Wisconsin Press.

Lehmbruch, G./ P. C. Schmitter (eds.), 1982: *Patterns of Corporatist Policy-Making.* London: Sage.

Lindblom, C. E., 1977: *Politics and Markets: The World's Political-Economic Systems.* New York: Basic Books.

Marin, B., 1986: *Unternehmerorganisationen im Verbändestaat - Politik der Bauwirtschaft in Österreich.* Vienna: Internationale Publikationen.

Marin, B. (ed.), 1990a: *Generalized Political Exchange. Antagonistic Cooperation and Integrated Policy Circuits.* Frankfurt a.M./ Boulder, CO.: Campus/ Westview.

Marin, B. (ed.), 1990b: *Governance and Generalized Exchange. Self-Organizing Policy Networks in Action.* Frankfurt a.M./ Boulder, CO.: Campus/ Westview.

Mariti, P./ V. Smiley, 1983: Cooperative Agreements and the Organization of Industry. In: *Journal of Industrial Economics* 31(4), 437-451.

Marsh, D./ R. Rhodes, 1991: *Policy Networks in British Government.* Oxford: OUP.

Marx, K., 1954-56: *Capital - A Critique of Political Economy.* Third edition. London: Lawrence and Wishart.

Mayntz, R., 1983: The Conditions of Effective Public Policy: A New Challenge for Policy Analysis. In: *Policy and Politics* 11, 123-143.

Mowery, D. C., 1987: *Alliance Politics and Economics.* Cambridge, MA.: Ballinger.

Olson, M., 1965: *The Logic of Collective Action.* Cambridge, MA.: Harvard University Press.

Pestoff, V. A., 1987: The Effects of State Institutions on Associative Action in the Food-Processing Industry. In: W. Grant (ed.), *Business Interests, Organizational Development and Private Interest Government: An International Comparative Study of the Food-Processing Industry.* Berlin/ New York: de Gruyter, 93-116.

Pestoff, V. A., 1990: Joint Regulation, Meso-Games and Political Exchange: The Role of Organized Capital and Labour in Swedish Industrial Relations and Socio-Economic Bargaining. In: B. Marin (ed.), *Governance and Generalized Exchange: Self-Organizing Policy Networks in Action.* Frankfurt a.M./ Boulder, CO.: Campus/ Westview, 315-346.

Pfeffer, J./ G. R. Salancik, 1978: *The External Control of Organizations - A Resource Dependence Perspective.* New York: Harper & Row.

Posner, A. R., 1978: Italy: Dependence and Political Fragmentation. In: P. J. Katzenstein (ed.), *Between Power and Plenty - Foreign Economic Policies of Advanced Industrial States.* Madison, WI.: University of Wisconsin Press, 225-254.

Powell, W. W., 1990: Neither Market nor Hierarchy: Network Forms of Organization. In: *Research in Organizational Behavior* 12, 295-336.

Rainey, G. H./ H. B. Milward, 1983: Public Organizations: Policy Networks and Environment. In: R. H. Hall/ R. E. Quinn (eds.), *Organizational Theory and Public Policy.* London/ Beverly Hills: Sage, 133-146.

Ranci, P., 1987: Italy: The Weak State. In: F. Duchêne/ G. Sheperd (eds.), *Managing Industrial Change in Western Europe.* London/ New York: Francis Pinter, 111-144.

Richardson, J. J./ Jordan, A. G., 1979: *Governing under Pressure: The Policy Process in a Post-Parliamentary Democracy.* Oxford: Robertson.

Ronge, V. (ed.), 1980: *Am Staat vorbei. Politik der Selbstregulierung von Kapital und Arbeit.* Frankfurt a.M.: Campus.

Sabel, C. F., 1989: Flexible Specialization and the Re-emergence of Regional Economics. In: P. Hirst/ J. Zeitlin (eds.), Reversing Industrial Decline? Oxford: Berg, 17-70.

Schmitter, P. C./ G. Lehmbruch (eds.), 1979: *Trends Towards Corporatist Intermediation.* Beverly Hills: Sage.

Schmitter, P. C./ W. Streeck, 1981: *The Organization of Business Interests: A Research Design to Study the Associative Action of Business in the Advanced Industriel Societies of Western Europe.* Berlin: International Institute of Management, Discussion Paper IIM/LMP 81-113.

Schuppert, G., 1989: Zur Neubelebung der Staatsdiskussion: Entzauberung des Staates oder "Bringing the State Back In?" In: *Der Staat* 28(1), 91-104.

Staber, V./ H. Aldrich, 1983: Trade Associations Stability and Public Policy. In: R. H. Hall/ R. E. Quinn (eds), *Organizational Theory and Public Policy.* London: Sage, 163-178.

Strange, S./ R. Tooze (eds.), 1981: *The International Politics of Surplus Capacity - Competition for Market Shares in the World Recession.* London: Allen and Unwin.

Streeck, W./ P. C. Schmitter (eds.), 1985: *Private Interest Government: Beyond Market and State.* Beverly Hills/ London: Sage.

Traxler, F./ B. Unger, 1990: Institutionelle Erfolgsbedingungen wirtschaftlichen Strukturwandels - Zum Verhältnis von Effizienz und Regulierung aus theoretischer und empirischer Sicht. In: *Wirstchaft und Gesellschaft* 16(2), 189-223.

Vanberg, V., 1975: *Die zwei Soziologien.* Tübingen: Mohr.

Vanberg, V., 1982: *Markt und Organisation.* Tübingen: Mohr & Siebeck.

Wilks, S., 1983: Liberal State and Party Competition: Britain. In: K. Dyson/ S. Wilks (eds.), *Industrial Crisis - A Comparative Study of the State and Industry.* Oxford: Martin Robertson, 128-160.

Wilks, S./ M. Wright, 1987: *Comparative Government-Industry Relations - Western Europe, the United States, and Japan.* Oxford: Clarendon Press.

Williamson, O. E., 1975: *Markets and Hierarchies.* New York: Free Press.

Wright, M., 1988: Policy Community, Policy Network and Comparative Industrial Policies. In: *Political Studies* 36, 593-612.

Wright, M., 1989: *Contextualizing Policy Networks in the Comparative Analysis of Industrial Policy.* Paper presented at the Conference on "Policy Networks: Structural Analysis of Policy-Making", Cologne, 4-5 December 1989.

Contributors

Professor *William D. Coleman,* McMaster University, Hamilton, Ontario

Dr. *Marian Döhler,* Max-Planck-Institut für Gesellschaftsforschung, Cologne

Professor *John P. Heinz,* Northwestern University, Chicago

Dr. *Dorothea Jansen,* Ruhr-Universität Bochum

Dr. *Patrick Kenis,* European Centre, Vienna

Professor *David Knoke,* University of Minnesota, Minneapolis

Professor *Edward O. Laumann,* University of Chicago, Chicago

Professor Dr. *Bernd Marin,* European Centre, Vienna

Professor Dr. *Renate Mayntz,* Max-Planck-Institut für Gesellschafts-forschung, Cologne

Associate Professor *Robert Nelson,* Northwestern University, Evanston, Illinois

Professor Dr. *Franz Urban Pappi,* Universität Mannheim

Professor *Robert Salisbury,* Washington University, St. Louis

Dr. *Volker Schneider,* Max-Planck-Institut für Gesellschaftsforschung, Cologne

Dr. *Raymund Werle,* Max-Planck-Institut für Gesellschaftsforschung, Cologne

Publication Series of the Max-Planck-Institut
für Gesellschaftsforschung Köln

Volume 1

Renate Mayntz, Bernd Rosewitz, Uwe Schimank, Rudolf Stichweh
Differenzierung und Verselbständigung
Zur Entwicklung gesellschaftlicher Teilsysteme
1988 332 pp.

Volume 2

Renate Mayntz, Thomas P. Hughes (Editors)
The Development of Large Technical Systems
1988 304 pp. (copublished with Westview Press)

Volume 3

Clemens Schumacher-Wolf
Informationstechnik, Innovation und Verwaltung
Soziale Bedingungen der Einführung moderner Informationstechniken
1988 342 pp.

Volume 4

Volker Schneider
Technikentwicklung zwischen Politik und Markt
Der Fall Bildschirmtext
1989 298 pp.

Campus Verlag · Frankfurt am Main

Publication Series of the Max-Planck-Institut
für Gesellschaftsforschung Köln

Volume 5

Bernd Rosewitz, Douglas Webber
**Reformversuche und Reformblockaden im deutschen
Gesundheitswesen**
1990 354 pp.

Volume 6

Raymund Werle
Telekommunikation in der Bundesrepublik
Expansion, Differenzierung, Transformation
1990 414 pp.

Volume 7

Hans-Willy Hohn, Uwe Schimank
Konflikte und Gleichgewichte im Forschungssystem
Akteurkonstellationen und Entwicklungspfade in der staatlich finanzierten
außeruniversitären Forschung
1990 450 pp.

Volume 8

Jens Alber, Brigitte Bernardi-Schenkluhn
Westeuropäische Gesundheitssysteme im Vergleich
Bundesrepublik Deutschland, Frankreich, Großbritannien, Italien, Schweiz
1991 ca. 700 pp.

Campus Verlag · Frankfurt am Main

Public Policy and Social Welfare
A Series Edited by the European Centre - Vienna

Campus Verlag / Frankfurt a.M. · Westview Press / Boulder, CO

Public Policy and Social Welfare
A Series Edited by the European Centre - Vienna

Volume 5

B. Marin (Editor)
Governance and Generalized Exchange
Self-Organizing Policy Networks in Action
1990   386 pp.

Volume 6

R. Kraan et al.
Care for the Elderly
Significant Innovations in Three European Countries
1991   248 pp.

Volume 7

V. Pestoff
Between Markets and Politics
Co-operatives in Sweden
1991   246 pp.

Volume 8

P. Kenis
The Social Contruction of an Industry
A World of Chemical Fibres
1991   220 pp.

Campus Verlag / Frankfurt a.M. · Westview Press / Boulder, CO